WHISKEY BOTTLES AND BRAND-NEW CARS

THE FAST LIFE AND SUDDEN DEATH OF LYNYRD SKYNYRD

MARK RIBOWSKY

CHICAGO REVIEW PRESS
An A Cappella Book

First edition
Published by Chicago Review Press, Incorporated
814 North Franklin Street
Chicago, Illinois 60610

ISBN 978-1-56976-146-5

Interior design: Jonathan Hahn
Cover design: Marc Whitaker / MTWdesign.net

Library of Congress Cataloging-in-Publication Data
Ribowsky, Mark.
Whiskey bottles and brand-new cars : the fast life and sudden death of Lynyrd Skynyrd / by Mark Ribowsky. — First edition.
pages cm
Includes bibliographical references and index.
ISBN 978-1-56976-146-5 (cloth)
1. Lynyrd Skynyrd (Musical group) 2. Rock musicians—United States—Biography. I. Title.

ML421.L96R43 2015
782.42166092'2—dc23
[B]

2014037743

Printed in the United States of America
5 4 3 2 1

FOR MY SON JAKE,
WHO THINKS "FREE BIRD" IS TOO SHORT

CONTENTS

★ ★ ★ ★ ★ ★ ★ ★ ★ ★ ★ ★ ★ ★

ACKNOWLEDGMENTS

★ ★ ★ ★ ★ ★ ★ ★ ★ ★ ★ ★ ★ ★

Readers of this book will be able to play a participation game—trying to figure out who and what the man who almost singularly made Lynyrd Skynyrd was. Ronnie Van Zant, who dominates these pages, was both a redneck and an anti-redneck, which makes every effort to define him a very complicated thing. How complicated was he? There may not even be a definitive answer to the question. The fun and the challenge will be watching him grow and mature into a man who, no doubt, would have grown only larger in dimension but for an inept flight crew on an old, troublesome airplane.

Not much that has been written before about Van Zant puts flesh on his bones. An alarming amount of the Skynyrd literature, such as it is, falls under the category not of history but hagiography, lore, legend, and—let's face it—bullshit. What's more, his family and his band are either dead or have vigorously pledged not to be helpful to any outsider seeking the truth rather than a fable—unless there is something in it for them to pocket; this reality today serves as "that smell," not the scent of drug addiction and self-destruction Van Zant sang about in the famous song with that title. The mercenary profit motive of the extant Skynyrd is also well documented here, as part of the band's tragic epilogue.

For all these reasons, the copious research that formed the book made me feel more like a miner, not necessarily for a heart of gold but for observations with the satisfying ring of truth. There was indeed gold in them thar hills of books, newspaper articles, magazine pieces, and Internet postings, though mainly that turned up fool's gold. Thus I am indebted to several souls who were there in real time and knew Van Zant like few others—not dilettantes who pretend they did—and whose recollections were invaluable to history's ultimate place for Lynyrd Skynyrd. My thanks to two original Skynyrd members who played with the band as it rode to eminence, Bob Burns and Ed King, and two former managers of the group, Alan Walden and Charlie Brusco—all of whom still bear the scars of that ride, none having been able to stay on the horse without being thrown from it painfully.

My thanks also go to Alex Hodges, one of the most respected men in the entertainment industry, who learned the lessons of his trade booking gigs for Skynyrd as part of the management agency that put them on the map. Alex had never before spoken of being on the inside of the Skynyrd operation, and his name had never been mentioned in that respect. His "coming out" to me was of inestimable value to the story. The same could be said of the studio wizards who helped turn screaming guitars and backwoods pride into nuanced music of technical perfection, Barry Rudolph and Muscle Shoals legend Jimmy Johnson. My deep appreciation also goes to Jennie Thomas, head archivist at the Rock and Roll Hall of Fame, and Paul Friedman of the New York Public Library's peerless Music Division and Library for the Performing Arts; and to Vanessa Kromer, Alex Hodges's personal assistant, who patiently arranged interviews with him and made sure they went off like clockwork.

Finally, this book is as much to the credit of my agent Jim Fitzgerald of the James Fitzgerald Agency and Chicago Review Press editor Yuval Taylor, both of whom saw the need for a definitive Skynyrd biography after all these years and wanted it to be more than a timeline and playlist but instead a story that breathes life into the southern culture that bred it and then was gone with the same wind that took Van Zant to his demise. Kudos to them for that insight and perspective.

INTRODUCTION

★ ★ ★ ★ ★ ★ ★ ★ ★ ★ ★ ★ ★ ★ ★ ★ ★ ★

A Sunday night in Boca Raton, Florida, January 2014

The gray-haired man in his sixties wears a T-shirt with LYNYRD SKYNYRD printed across the chest. He orders some food at a fast-food counter and walks toward the door.

"Hey, Skynyrd!" comes a call of the wild from a slightly older man with thinner, grayer hair, the back tied up in a ponytail. The voice has long been scabrous, obviously from way too many unfiltered cigarettes and whiskey shots, and the southern accent has gotten only thicker. A T-shirt from an auto body shop hangs loose over an ample belly. After asking the man in the Skynyrd shirt, "Ever see 'em?" he wanders down a memory trail, eyes focused on days long ago.

"I saw 'em," he says. "Saw 'em in '74, in Nashville. Helluva show. My wife here, she saw 'em too."

The woman next to him, still pretty after all these years, has a smile on her face. "Saw 'em?" she says. "Hey, I'm from Georgia—Doraville," which happens to be the home of the studio where Lynyrd Skynyrd recorded their most enduring songs. "Those guys were around there all the time. They were like all of us—they sat and talked with you. They were like part of a big family in town. The Atlanta Rhythm Section were there too. I remember one time, I was in this big old car, with the drummer—oh, what was his name . . . ?"

"Nix. Robert Nix," the stranger says.

"Yeah, he was driving me all over town. They just liked being with the folks in town. That's how it was then. Skynyrd, Atlanta Rhythm Section, Joe South—they were all southern boys doin' what they loved doin'. Wasn't about fame or money. They had somethin' to say in their songs."

The husband wears a plaintive look. "Those were the days," he says. "The boys like that, they meant a lot to guys like me. We were young, teenagers, early twenties. We looked up to 'em. We *listened* to 'em. Went where they were playin' to see 'em. We'd ride the train, the box cars, just like what they sang about, to get there."

He has a question. "Where you from?" he wonders.

"New York."

He shakes his head, laughs easily. "I never thought anyone from the North even knew about Skynyrd," he says. "But here you are in Florida. You came to the South, and maybe music like that had something to do with it. All I know is, I go around the country, and I hear that music to this day, and I see that it got in their blood, all that southern way of life, and it felt good."

The man in the Skynyrd shirt, who was in the midst of writing this book when this interlude happened, shook hands with the husband and wife, said he'd meet them right back here at some time in the future to continue the conversation, and left the fast-food place, another lesson learned. He had heard more than once the exclamation of "Skynyrd—'75!" or "'Free Bird'—*yeahhh*!" while wearing that shirt. It happened everywhere, but with the most feeling in the South, and each time it became more obvious that it was more than a recognition of a band. It was a recognition of themselves, how they once were, how the South once was, when the whole world sat up and took notice.

But it was also a recognition that those days ain't never comin' back.

* * *

In the late 1960s, the Old South—the courtly, cotillion-celebrating, civilized South that lived high, large, and mighty in all matters save the degradation and exclusion of an entire race of dark-skinned riders in steerage—had been deconstructed and demythologized, its sacred land paved over for highways, strip malls, and sewage treatment plants. And then, out of the most prosaic of outposts in the Old South, Jacksonville, Florida, came a vehicle of redemption, rebirth, and renaissance—albeit a fleeting, teasing one. It rose high into skies so blue, until one day, a day that the riders on the storm seemed to know was coming, they rose too high and were smacked down, their ill-equipped Convair CV-300 falling to earth, its twisted metal becoming the tomb of a rock-and-roll fable and a pungent era.

In that tragic fall Lynyrd Skynyrd's lead singer Ronnie Van Zant; guitarist Steven Gaines; his sister, backup singer Cassie Gaines; and assistant road manager Dean Kilpatrick died on impact, and everyone else on the flight was left with broken bones, mangled limbs, and punctured organs. That day—October 20, 1977—can be more accurately called the "day the music died" than the occasion of the first of too many such famous crashes, the one that killed one of the first southern-based crossover rock-and-roll stars, Buddy Holly, along with Ritchie Valens and J.P. Richardson. For rock and the South could ill afford the death of a band that brought a new and much-needed transitional link to a cultural and geographical landscape.

While they soared above the musical and cultural clouds, Lynyrd Skynyrd chartered a journey in time when the South indeed rose again—a matter of great curiosity to those for whom the region was the land of the damned, the butt of jokes about backwoods inbreeding. When Skynyrd arrived, a constantly changing unit fronted by a clear-throated, sallow, blond-maned, blue-eyed, porkpie-hat-wearing, hungry pile of smugness and snark named Ronnie Van Zant, they had no intention of bending over for anyone or anything. Their vital core was always the same: Van Zant's fisty and feisty vocals, fronting three lead guitarists, the constants being original members Gary Rossington and Allen Collins, two spindly cobras, coiled and cocked, locked and loaded. When they went off on extended solos, they didn't compete for the best riffs so much as challenge each other to find some cosmic source of truth and possibility. They had groove. They had meaning. They had a rhythm that darted from pure rock thunder, pouring from the electric guitars and Leon Wilkeson's bass, to jazzy swirls on pianist Billy Powell's keyboard. The almost visually scenic resonance of their work became the brand of a South that had never before existed—an updated South prideful for the right reasons, ones that had little to nothing to do with race and everything to do with the habitat that spawned them, the soul of desperado itchiness and dare, wanderlust, cheap thrills, and the battle within to keep faith with God. It was, without trying to be, the soundtrack of a new southern sensibility, yet in its fealty to in some cases wretched convention one as old as the region itself.

On stage Skynyrd emblazoned the walls with a skull-and-crossbones logo and flew the Confederate flag in a new-wave rebel yell that came directly from the South's long-rooted psyche. Their rallying cry was new wave because the yell wasn't about race—how could it be when so much of it embraced the seminal blues music of the great black Deep South?

It was more of a yelp, actually, a release of long-pent-up emotion, the Southern Man's whoop in finding a way to cherish tradition while facing down the guilts left by the past, all without wiping them away or pretending they weren't there. It was about venerating the land they had a yen to traverse by getting out on the road again and again, on interstate highways and backwoods dirt roads. Skynyrd looked less like music royalty than sharecroppers out on a bender on a Saturday night. There were no sequins and rhinestones, no slicked-back pompadours. They piled almost satiric cowboy Stetsons on their heads but draped themselves in plaid flannel, T-shirts, leather vests, torn jeans, and scuffed boots. They looked the part of contemporary, urban country cowboys, but their sound wasn't country at all. There were no yodels, fiddles, or Buddy Holly–style hiccups. Like the Allman Brothers Band before them, who also dressed down and played not country but the blues, Skynyrd played unapologetic rock and roll, not loud but *loud*, without any of them fiddles or weepy steel guitar licks. The country part came in with their piquant nativist themes, an edgy, don't-fuck-with-me pose and attitude, a gnawing male chauvinism undercut by sentimentality for women, kin, and the Lord.

Only a few years removed from high school in Jacksonville, a group with a name that was a goof on an old gym coach who had ridiculed them for wearing long hair detonated a new *thing* in rock, though it stemmed from pathology built over a century when the kingdom of kingdoms was dashed into dust by the Civil War, forcing Southern Men to approach life as Common Men, driven by pride and conceit. Skynyrd's first major hit, "Sweet Home Alabama" (1974), branded them as soldiers eager to take up arms, figuratively this time, in defense of the homeland; this was despite having no connection to Alabama beyond being at the receiving end of the metaphoric slur to all Dixie dwellers hurled by Neil Young—ironically a strong country music ally—in his twin imprecations, "Alabama" and "Southern Man," in which he excoriated such men for brandishing Bibles but forgetting to "do what your Good Book says" in matters of racial comity. Ronnie's poison-pen response took aim at a man whose work he admired, letting "ol' Neil" have it between the eyes. Trouble was, in rhapsodizing about a place where "the skies are so blue," he referenced the segregationist governor George Corley Wallace, seemingly not with reproof but as a man beloved by the neo-Confederate brigades of Birmingham, a crucible of degenerate racism. That clipped lyric still sparks scholarly (and comically absurd) debate about one of the most misunderstood songs in rock history, in which a fleeting chant of "*Boo! Boo! Boo!*" was Skynyrd's own diss of southern men who *did* sully the region—and it remains a jab at those who, decades later, would embrace the song as a right-wing battle hymn. Conservatives constantly appropriate songs they want to believe mean what they don't, but no one ever went so far into dementia as John J. Miller of the *National Review Online* when he dreamt that "Sweet Home Alabama" is one of "the 50 greatest conservative rock songs" and "a tribute to the region of America that liberals love to loathe," notwithstanding Van Zant's own long-on-the-record explanation of his intent.

Some never did get, or refused to get, the impish, against-the-grain subtleties of a group seemingly as subtle as a kick in the groin. The acid-penned, ill-fated blade runner of the rock press Lester Bangs, son of a Texas truck driver himself, was so taken aback by what he perceived as dusty, slobbering goobers screeching about southern manhood while waving the Stars and Bars that he filed them away as "crude thunder-stomper hillbillies." Here, too, the underlying reality—it was Skynyrd's record company, Van Zant once said, that had them use the Confederate flag as a gimmick, contradicting the band's wishes—played second fiddle to first appearance. Still, the dichotomy of Skynyrd seemed clear to some in the rock intelligentsia. The haughty music critic Robert Christgau sniffed that Skynyrd "makes music so unpretentious it tempts me to give up subordinate clauses," yet he had to admit that he "loved" them, realizing that a Yankee had to put aside regional prejudices to be able to appreciate what the hell they were doing.

Whether a guilty pleasure or not, Skynyrd just could not be ignored, not by the intelligentsia and certainly not by the bourgeois proletariat. Any qualm or quibble about Skynyrd was swallowed up in the overall slam-bang impact they made. A case in point is their most persevering echo, "Free Bird," the dizzying, eight-minute sorcerer's journey through take-me-or-leave-me defiance—with Van Zant asking, while not really caring about the answer, "If I leave here tomorrow, would you still remember me?" While not released as a single, the song immediately began to dominate FM radio, demanding to be performed live in arenas and stadiums, where arms stuck in the air clutching lit cigarette lighters would languidly sway back and forth to the indelible slide guitar opening, birthing a new rock concert tradition (one that, lamentably, evolved from lighters to backlit cell phones). "Free Bird" was only possible because Skynyrd, by eschewing the power centers of the music industry, believed they could ignore the rules about such things as song length, and held firm that their eight-minute magnum opus was not to be cut by even a second on the album. Rather than the band giving in to the establishment, it gave in to *them*. They played gambles like that—and won. Only after "Free Bird" had won its spurs in long form was it allowed to be truncated in half for AM play, and it hardly fazed the band that it became a hit on the Top 40 stations. Another winning gamble was their refusal to remove the Stars and Bars from their stage shows, always a matter of concern to promoters and critics. To them, it wasn't a symbol of slavery, the whipping post, and the hanging tree, and damn if they were gonna cede it to those who *did* see it as such. If the message seemed mixed to some, to Skynyrd it was a nonissue, a convenient position given the ruckus they stirred up. And still do. In 2008, "Sweet Home Alabama"—a tune that has been downloaded as a cell phone ringtone over two million times—became the official motto in that state, embedded on its license plates, replacing the discarded "Stars Fell on Alabama." It seemed innocuous enough—but that old line about how up in Birmingham they love "the Gov'nor" is still worn as a badge on the lapels of unreconstructed racists. If you cannot put the Stars and Bars on a license plate in Dixie, might the next best thing be the song with a wink and nod to the Old South of Jeff Davis? If so, this would surely disturb Ronnie Van Zant. As inscrutable as he was, there can be no doubt that his vision of the Old Confederacy was very different than, say, that of Ted Cruz.

* * *

The truth that many never have grasped about Skynyrd is that their oeuvre is chock-full of surprisingly antistereotypical themes that are still quite relevant. Times indeed haven't changed much, given that Van Zant sang forty years ago about the easy availability of cheap handguns ("Saturday Night Special"), which he warned were good only for "putting a man six feet in a hole." Laughing about the far-out nature of such a tune for a southern redneck band, Ed King, who with Van Zant wrote that song and other aces such as "Poison Whiskey" and "Swamp Music" while serving as one of the band's three lead guitarists until 1975, asks the perfectly obvious question: "What kind of redneck writes an anti-gun song?" Not that Van Zant shied from guns—although, contrary to assumption, he did *not* express gun-love in the follow-up "Gimme Back My Bullets," the ammo in question here being those figurative bullets appended to songs that ran the quickest up the charts. A rational man—except when he was drunk or high, times in which he was a vile and violent, not endearing, redneck—Van Zant reasonably cared not to be on the wrong end of a gun while facing a redneck with a grudge, a situation he was not unfamiliar with.

Still, if the staunch southern men of Skynyrd were macho to the core, reckless to the bone, and self-destructive to a fault, songs like the ostensibly innocuous "What's Your Name" reveal a certain moral conundrum about the too-easy availability of something else out there on the long road, especially for a married man like Van Zant, who loved his wife but also loved many others—well and often. There is, too, not defiance but desperation in "That Smell," a harrowing vérité piece written after Rossington, tanked on booze and cocaine, nearly killed himself in a car wreck, prompting the immortal opening line about whiskey bottles and brand-new cars and the oak tree that got in the way because there was "too much coke and too much smoke." Van Zant may have been waving a finger at Rossington when he warned, "Look what's going on inside you," but in truth he was also singing into a mirror, metaphorically the same one on which he laid out his own lines of cocaine, to be followed by Quaaludes, which he popped into his mouth like jelly beans. When Van Zant sang that "the smell of death surrounds you," he knew that no one in Skynyrd could say, "Not me, pal." Once, it had seemed like great, baroque fun to live the lifestyle of rock-and-roll outlaws, to tear out hotel walls and let the accountants pay for it all. But "That Smell" was hard, cold reality setting in. Its message: something had to give.

This sort of material was a sharp scalpel cutting into the group's pathology, allowing the world in on the little secret that a Southern Man can and does admit to weakness. And that kind of departure was a perfect counterweight to comfort food for the masses, the songs about brawling and drinking and fooling around with other men's women. These also were based on truth—"Gimme Three Steps," for example, was the result of an interlude in a Jacksonville bar when just such a betrayed man stuck a gun in Ronnie's face. Another tune, "Don't Ask Me No Questions," ripped record-company executives who had avoided signing the band, while "Double Trouble," Ronnie's description of himself when drunk and stoned, spelled out the feel-good joys of bad intentions. One of their best blues riffs was a rough-cut B side called "Mr. Banker," an indictment of a moneylender who refuses funds for a poor man to bury his father—a thinly veiled roman à clef born of Ronnie's range of emotions about the father he felt he could never please. Just about every Skynyrd song had this sort of magnification of a dream, a failing, or the betrayal of a broken social contract, and even the few covers they did connected to these conditions. Consider, for example, their cover of early country legend Jimmie Rodgers's "T for Texas," the lyrics of which perfectly channeled their pugnacious insistence on being taken seriously on their turf or any other. To wit: "I'd rather drink your muddy water, sleep down in a hollow log / Than to be in Atlanta, Georgia, treated like a dirty dog."

* * *

One suspects that Skynyrd all the while knew they were just that, dirty dogs, albeit ones with enormous skill and singularity. Their range was many miles wide; yet whatever the subject, they never seemed to miss their target, and they struck right to the bone. They funneled to the world the sights, sounds, and even the smells of a not-yet-forsaken, riven but belatedly risen South. Indeed, unwittingly but inexorably, they found a place among the artistic giants of the American South, their thematic content deceptively simple but as soul deep as any Faulkner novel or Tennessee Williams play. Like the best southern writers and musicians, Skynyrd provided a set of new definitions about the region. To the amazement of critics and other students of musical history, vocal and visual echoes of Old Confederacy white-glove society mixed and mingled in a New South assimilation with flower-power fashion, the expansion of booze consumption, and pills and powder going up the nose. All in all, by the mid-1970s, southern fried was the way rock was being served. Damn, no one expected that. Call it redneck chic, in all its honest, shit-faced glory. Or, in the coda of another Skynyrd song title, "Whiskey Rock-a-Roller."

Before Skynyrd, the preposterous assertion that country rock was based out of L.A. had somehow been deemed logical. Not that the Byrds, Poco, and the Flying Burrito Brothers didn't perform in that role with conviction and skill, not to mention credibility, as they went about giving the new idiom an old-fashioned, romanticized face, a fact that can be gleaned from the title of the wonderful Byrds album *Sweetheart of the Rodeo*. But Skynyrd had no intention of following the Allman Brothers' road to the left coast; when Van Zant, proud to be a homegrown boy, sang in "When You Got Good Friends" that L.A. "never cared for me," the line was a proud declaration of independence from the capital of soft country rock, whose in crowd liked to slag them as hicks. In turn, he and his mates fully intended to dirty up the face of country rock but good. The Southland rose around this payback, and with it came a cool regression of hip culture, back to what rock's original soiled face had been before it was annexed by corporate overlords. And the cool kids, the smug critics, the Yankee Ivy League college boys, the foreign audiences, who only knew the American South as a swamp-soaked monument to churlishness, jumped aboard the bandwagon. Christ, the band may even have helped elect a peanut-farming Southern Man to the presidency of the United States in 1976—a Democrat, at that—a decade after the last southern president, Lyndon B. Johnson, had passed the Civil Rights Act. Johnson himself predicted that his party would "lose the South for a generation," and with the exception of 1976, 1992, and 1996, he was right. In the Skynyrd South, however, such easy inductions and punishments were inoperative; in general, nativism trumped politics.

★ ★ ★

Skynyrd was a product of many factors, some running deep, including the cultural transitions of the 1950s and 1960s, which splintered Southern notions of patrician morality and brought its underbelly of woe, booze, brawls, and life on the road into the rock-and-roll arc. As such, they fed off the region's Gothic literature and music, becoming a part of that tradition themselves. The South harbors the most pungent and tragic undercarriage in the American experience; thus it stands to reason that the most pungent and tragic rock band sprung from its fertile and foreboding soil, a group of riders who were perfectly timed and placed for a musical epiphany.

Alas, like so many other children of the South who created a southern identity in their artistry, Lynyrd Skynyrd was not built for a long run but rather a breathless sprint for the finish line before the tab came due. Suspecting this themselves, none of them took a thing for granted and often dreaded the dawning of another day ahead, though no one was prepared for that cursed flight on October 20, 1977, when the devil claimed his bounty. To be sure, back during the shank of the Skynyrd phenomenon, neither they nor their fans would have shied from the directive they are often credited with coining: "Live fast. Die young. Leave a pretty corpse." They moved forward, chary but hopeful that success might be the antidote to a cruel fate. But that was not to be, and the pain would never subside. The survivors of the crash were never whole again, most doomed to die young. Indeed, the flames that engulfed all of them—eerily presaged by the album cover of what would be the original band's final work—were metaphorically perfect: the rebirth of the Old Confederacy died as had the first, when the skies over the South were not so much blue but burnt orange from the fires below. Margaret Mitchell wrote of those flames in *Gone with the Wind*, a phrase that had deep meaning for Van Zant, whose paean to movin' on, "Tuesday's Gone," contained the lyric "Tuesday's gone with the wind." Neither Mitchell nor Van Zant knew that Southern tradition would for the second time, literally in this case, be gone with the wind, the one that dropped a plane from the sky.

* * *

For purists of the now-fabled era shaped and molded by Lynyrd Skynyrd, there is little to correlate between the band then and the touring attraction by that name today, fronted since 1987 by Johnny Van Zant, Ronnie's kid brother, a remarkably talented singer himself and a ghoulishly familiar-looking doppelganger recycling his brother's songs in a similar gruff and growling country-boy burr. Gary Rossington, one of only two survivors of the crash to make it this far, gets himself up on stage with his guitar, his rumpled presence bearing witness to unimaginable glory and unspeakable tragedy, bearing the scars of his own too-close call with mortality. To be certain, Collins, Wilkeson, and Powell hastened their premature demises by drinking themselves into the grave. Ed King is hanging on, having suffered congestive heart failure in the 1990s and undergoing a heart transplant in 2012. Since two latter-day group members have also caught the last train for the coast during their tenures in the band, one can plausibly believe that the old devil is still looking to claim his bounty. The other survivors lived long enough to take a final bow at the 2006 induction of the band into the Rock and Roll Hall of Fame. The honor was thin soup, and in itself a reminder that anti-South prejudice still lives on in the industry's northern, corporate-based elitism so perfectly embodied by the most effete rock power broker of all, *Rolling Stone* founder Jann Wenner, who with his staff of high-minded nabobs had kept Skynyrd out of the Hall the first six years the band was eligible.

Not that it mattered much to a southern band that had never needed benedictions from the suits, just some bread and the suits keeping out of the way. Hell, the Hall had stiffed Johnny Cash for years too. And Wenner and his cronies—per the wishes of Van Zant's widow, Judy, in her muddy power struggle with Gary Rossington in all band matters—also limited to nine the number of Skynyrd members who would receive a statuette. Just those who had played in the band between its debut album and the plane crash got to take a bow. This was an arbitrary slap in the face to the others who had labored to keep the band alive—Rickey Medlocke, for example, who had been an early member and returned to keep its memories animate through several incarnations. To the industry suits, the members of Skynyrd were always tramps, boxcar stowaways on rock's grand journey. Even so, the majestic, inexplicable, confounding breadth of rock could be gleaned on that night, when the inductees included the Sex Pistols, Blondie, Black Sabbath, Miles Davis, and the prodigal sons of Jacksonville.

* * *

Skynyrd's only real relevant body of work, the five albums of the Van Zant era, all monster hits in their day, are now among the highest-selling albums in history, pushed into the stratosphere in the era of CDs and mp3s. Three—the debut, titled *(pronounced 'lĕh-'nérd 'skin-'nérd)*; *Second Helping*; and the finale, *Street Survivors*—have gone double platinum. *Nuthin' Fancy* is platinum and *Gimme Back My Bullets* is gold. A live album from 1976, *One More from the Road*, is *triple* platinum. The post–Van Zant incarnations have released nine studio and five live albums, the last two of which, *God & Guns* and *Last of a Dyin' Breed*, landed in the Top 20. Perhaps the most salient barometer of the enduring popularity of the old brand is that there have been no less than twenty-one compilations of the old stuff, eight of which have gone platinum, one triple platinum, and one—1989's *Skynyrd's Innyrds*—quintuple platinum. What was intended as a one-shot reunion of the surviving band in 1987 has become an enormous commercial concern. Skynyrd tours are chronic sellouts, and the hawking of licensed merchandise is a million-dollar enterprise by itself. Ronnie Van Zant's widow, Judy Van Zant Jenness, operates a Lynyrd Skynyrd tribute website and the successful Freebird Live music club on North First Street on Jacksonville Beach, the strip where the nascent Skynyrd cut their teeth.

The business of Skynyrd nowadays is business, the conversion of the Skynyrd name into leisure-class gold, a boardwalk attraction. In Choctaw, Mississippi, a marquis card reads: LYNYRD SKYNYRD BRINGS SOUTHERN ROCK TO PEARL RIVER RESORT. In an eon of sapless, soulless music built on marketing plans rather than anyone's creative suffering, nostalgia can find a new audience of free spenders every generation. Thus, MCA, the corporate behemoth that took a chance and put out those first five albums in real time—though at the start any liability was shouldered by the band's producer, Al Kooper, not the company—has sold more than 30 million Skynyrd albums, making them the company's top-selling artist ever, outselling even the Who. According to BMI records, "Free Bird" has been played on the radio more than two million times, which may not be on "Hey Jude" or "You've Lost That Lovin' Feelin'" terrain but is rather astonishing given that it's usually played at its full, elongated length, meaning only on the niche format of classic rock. Consider this: two million plays is the equivalent of approximately one hundred thousand broadcast hours—or more than eleven years of continuous airplay—and still counting.

* * *

The Atlanta-born author of *The Prince of Tides*, Pat Conroy, said, "My mother, Southern to the bone, once told me, 'All Southern literature can be summed up in these words: On the night the hogs ate Willie, Mama died when she heard what Daddy did to sister.'" Southern to the bone as they were, Skynyrd added a few more components to the equation, all without ever once trying to *sound* like a southern stereotype. That was tricky—and ballsy—but it worked. And in so doing, they did what few great artists can ever claim: they were actually *underrated* for what they meant to the frames moving all about them. Their legacy was so rich and resonant that it suggests southern tradition in various, evolving stages, darting by turns from imagery that could be found between the covers of works by W. Somerset Maugham, Graham Greene, and Kinky Friedman. The rebirth of the Old South invoked by Skynyrd had nothing to do with race yet was a secession nonetheless, a willful and wistful flight of fancy, swagger, and defiance—in the end, a flight doomed by its refusal to cooperate with the logical order of the universe. Maybe that's why the band moved fast, recklessly, at one speed—jacked up.

When the devil came to collect and they fell from the sky to the muddy woods below, the soul of southern culture crashed to the ground with them. This time, for good, except for the steeped, misty echoes of what once was and what will never be again.

1

★ ★ ★ ★ ★

LORDS AND MASTERS

Most men are a little better than their circumstances give them a chance to be. And I've known some that even circumstances couldn't stop.

—William Faulkner, *Go Down, Moses*

During the nascence of Lynyrd Skynyrd, the nuts, bolts, and guts of which were assembled at a typical sort of titular hallmark of the Old South—Robert E. Lee High School, a squat building still standing on McDuff Avenue in southwest Jacksonville, Florida, seven blocks from the Saint Johns River—Ronnie Van Zant was already a compelling fellow, if not always for the right reasons. In 1965 at the age of seventeen and soon to be a dropout, he stood five foot seven and 160 pounds, built like a fireplug, his face round as the moon, his wavy blond hair streaked almost platinum by the hot sun, and his handsome features usually bloated from the steady stream of beer and junk food he shoved into his mouth or from a fat lip he proudly displayed.

Because of his unrelenting confrontational attitude—his own mother called him the meanest kid in the neighborhood, a good thing to be on the hard-scrabble streets of Shantytown, as it was called—he was in scrapes all the time. He was also a crafty, advanced sort of redneck. For one thing, he was sharp—smart and calculating. When he wasn't bored with school, he made the honor roll. But he was bored and could regularly be found in dive bars, hanging with the real rednecks, sneaking beers, and looking for a fight.

When he got one, picked over some imagined slight or challenge, he would sometimes deck the other guy with his bare knuckles. Other times, having been taught to use his dukes by his father, he'd arrange a bout on some dirt road somewhere. He'd go home, get two pairs of boxing gloves, his and his old man's, and then give his father's gloves to his opponent to use. In these matches, with no referee, Ronnie almost always won, pounding away until the other guy cried uncle. Afterward, they would both return to the bar, the loser buying drinks.

As Van Zant described his home turf, "it was rough . . . like the ghetto, black and white, and there was a lot of street fighting, a lot of adventure. . . . Lynyrd Skynyrd are nothin' but street people, right straight off the streets, skid row. It's very easy for us to relate to that. We can relate to that much more than anything else." The way he said it, he was the "Street Fighting Man" that Mick Jagger had sung about in his famous detour from "palace revolution" to "compromise solution." For Van Zant, there was no such thing as compromise solution.

★ ★ ★

To his classmates, Ronnie was a short stack of mercurial impulses and moods, with ambitions that seemed to change by the day. It wasn't that he had a thing for violence or wanted to hurt people; it was just his way of blowing off steam and winning a personal challenge, something he seemed to need to allay his own insecurity and to constantly prove to himself that his father would admire him if he were the toughest kid in town. As a result, even his friends knew they had to be aware that Ronnie might be apt to come up to them willy-nilly and pop them one upside the head.

That was, however, just one side of him—one of many. The last thing he wanted was to end up a thug or be seen as an ignorant redneck with shit for brains. Rough-hewn traits aside, he was a peripatetic figure around Shantytown. He was a marvelous athlete who seriously went after a career as a professional baseball player. He worked at an auto body shop where the foreman recalled that the kid had a photographic memory for the minutiae of car parts.

He was whip smart and cocksure; he could express himself and could sing on key and with feeling, which he did in the mid-sixties with a band he got together at Lee High. He called the group Us, which he thought sounded hip, similar to the folk-rock group the We Five, who had a hit called "You Were on My Mind." Us was just one of numerous ragtag bands who used the gym to practice. Another was an instrumental group in the mold of the Ventures called You, Me and Him; it was led by Gary Rossington, a skinny kid with Botticellian curls, who was two years younger than Ronnie and, frankly, scared to death of him, a common reaction around town. "Everyone knew Ronnie in Jacksonville because he was Mr. Badass," Rossington said. "He would just stand on street corners flipping people off."

Months later Van Zant's band had trailed away, and he and Rossington crossed paths after a Babe Ruth League game they played in down at the sandlot. Ronnie only knew Gary in passing, but he knew enough: Gary could play a mean electric guitar, and a couple of other guys in his band, called You, Me, and Him, drummer Bob Burns and bass player Larry Junstrom, who also played in that Babe Ruth game, could keep a tight backbeat. With no warning, Van Zant had some startling news for the younger teen. Commencing that day, he informed Gary, "I'm gonna be your singer."

As was usually the case with Van Zant, there was no discussion. What he said went. He was so adamant about it, in fact, that the four of them went right over to Burns's house and, without changing out of their dirty uniforms, began jamming. Ronnie pronounced quick judgment. "When we started playing," he would recall years later, "we were just terrible."

It didn't take long before the band was in his control, reliant solely on his full-throated baritone voice, which seemed to seamlessly shift from mellow to bellow but could tire easily and start to crack. Accordingly, he kept it in a tightly controlled range, never launching into a falsetto flutter or twang. Like Gregg Allman's vocals on the big Allman Brothers hits to come, there was no obvious connection of voice to region beyond that flat northern Florida drawl. He wasn't Elvis or Conway Twitty. This wasn't Nashville; it was Jacksonville.

Ronnie knew exactly what direction he wanted for the band, which would go through a half dozen names before finding the right one. That direction was rock and roll, not country—and no one would argue the point with him. Clearly the future of the group, which added one more guitar player, Allen Çollins, was going to be determined by one factor: Ronnie Van Zant. He had the attitude and presence of a good lead singer. Knowing he had two left feet, he didn't try to prance around like Mick Jagger. He would stand there, erect, foursquare, under his Stetson, pouring out the words he composed. His aura projected an animal magnetism, his guise as a prowling lion enhanced by the sincerity of his voice, the cock of his head, the wink of his eye. He bit off the words of a song in earnest and sometimes in anger. He was, well, *different*.

He was, wrote one chronicler of southern culture, Mark Kemp, "at once honest and wily, good-hearted and mean as a rattlesnake, sometimes innately progressive, other times as reactionary as George Wallace." Undeniably, there was *something* about him, something that pulled people into his world without giving them the feeling that they'd been dragged in. And, by instinct, he was prepared to go to the mat, down and dirty, to make this project a success. He would fight with his voice and, if necessary, with his fists to convince people. To be sure, one could call Ronnie Van Zant many things; but "harmless" would not be one of them. Thank God, too, because all that was dangerous and excessively redneck about him was the propulsion that sent Skynyrd skyward and kept them flying higher and higher for as long as the devil allowed.

⋆ ⋆ ⋆

At seventeen, Ronnie Van Zant was a young man on the make, with a battle plan in his head. He also was a young man with a range of feelings and loads to say. For more reasons than he understood, he had a hard side and a soft one, the latter rising up when a girl he was sweet on, Nadine Incoe, a classmate at Lee High, entered his life. Actually, no one girl at a time was enough for him. Always on the prowl, he also took up with another girl at the school, a redhead named Marie Darsey. How he was able to pull *that* off no one knows, but each of the girls believed she was the only one. Both saw the charmer in him, probably because they received the same love letters, with only the names changed. One that Darsey has kept to this day reads, "I would really love to have a date with you. I think you are very, very cute. I really crave red hair." Perhaps leaving himself some wiggle room, he added that, most of the time, "I just want to be alone."

When Ronnie and one of the girls were together, it was usually in the front of his '65 Mustang or in the dark of the neighborhood movie theater. It mattered little what film was playing; tough guy that he was,

Ronnie didn't mind if it was Doris Day up on the screen being virginal. Darsey laughs, "He even took me to see *Mary Poppins*." All that mattered was that he could let his hands roam without interference. For the record, Darsey reports, he was "a good kisser" and "a sweet, caring person."

Coincidentally, most every girl or woman he made time for gave the same kind of verdict. He was that good at playing the game, though it bit him when he knocked up Nadine and, in the noble tradition of courtly southern manhood, married her—at least until they inevitably divorced soon after. But his talent for heartfelt poetry and not a little bullshit became transmuted from love letters to song lyrics, much of which would be inscrutable but irresistible.

As he moved forward, the fighter moved with him. Charlie Brusco, who managed the first Skynyrd reunion band in 1987 and ensuing editions until 1999, was absolutely riveted and sometimes repelled by him. "There was a lot to Ronnie, which was the reason he could write so many songs with different emotions and topics," says Brusco. "He was both the sweetest guy in the world and the biggest prick in the world. He would tell you how much he loved you, then take a swing at you for no apparent reason other than he just had to. But he kept that band focused all the time, man. And he was absolutely magnetic, a fascinating guy. A very odd character and a very complicated person, sometimes a very confused and angry person, and I don't think anyone ever figured him out, and I don't know if he ever figured himself out. But this was something that doesn't come around often, a meteor, an unexplainable force field that needed to be around longer than he was. A lot longer."

* * *

No richer trough of Gothic culture, whether in the written or sung word, has ever existed than the American South. Indeed, though many have tried to alter its fundamental genetic underpinnings, no one ever has. The cultural ingredients of the continental shelf that sits below the Mason-Dixon Line down through the sleepy, dusty Delta, the contours of the Gulf, the jagged Florida panhandle and peninsula, and the massive sweep of high plains and low swamps that is Texas have not only been ingrained in the region but have seeped, in the blood of the spoken and sung word, into every other region across the continent. Not by accident did a man like Levon Helm, the heart, soul, and comforting beat of the Band, a man from Turkey Scratch, Arkansas, a man for whom every minute of his seventy-nine years on earth was a revelation and a life lesson, make his mark in music in Woodstock, New York, collaborating with men bred in the Great White North of Canada.

In the Great White South of America, such expatriate reverse flow was common. Many artistically bent southern men took to the road, dating back to the Delta bluesmen who migrated to Chicago in the 1920s, and their work bled from border to border, enriching the cultural stock that congealed in ensuing decades, giving identity to genres not homegrown. In fact the exile of nativist southern music is almost alarming in retrospect, seeming to foretell of a southern civilization shorn of its glory and its honor. Even with the shield of Jim Crow to deflect the sting of Reconstruction, the Confederacy was dead, and rather than a grand society and an American Rome, there were white hoods, colored-only fountains, and bumper stickers crowing that THE SOUTH SHALL RISE AGAIN!—none of which could alter the basic geometry, the fatalism that declared that the glory of the South was never to be again.

In the absence of revival and with the gradual eroding of the topology and psychology of the South came imagination and longing. Through this looking glass, like the lost souls of Faulkner and Tennessee Williams, southern men were no longer plantation swells but weary, guilt-scarred, middle-class survivors dealing with morals and conundrums. This was the South from which the new generation of artists and musicians would come in the 1960s. Through heredity, they would carry the glory of the Old South within them, as well as the innate fear that stoked almost parodic hubris. As weathered and withered as they were, Southern Men—that is, southern *white* men—were, as regional historians Anne Goodwyn Jones and Susan V. Donaldson write, "still 'lords and masters' at home in the South, regardless of class," even if only in their minds.

One heady example of the cultural clash and angst-ridden pride within the New South was a rock band from the prosaic streets of Jacksonville, who would flourish as the vanguard of southern pride and rebirth by recasting the ethos of the Southern Man in all his glory and anguish. It was quite a ride they got themselves on. But, inevitably, it was an illusion, a devil's bargain, for them and the new Confederacy.

* * *

Far from Jacksonville's booming downtown corridor of corporate skyscrapers, waterfront hotels, the University of Florida campus, and the NFL Jaguars' home turf at EverBank Field, the old Van Zant homestead still stands today as it did half a century ago, buried deep "across the tracks" on the city's west side. They don't call the neighborhood Shantytown these days; it just doesn't sound appropriate anymore—though, given this conscience qualm, it is ironic that one *can* find the name Shantytown, as if given éclat by the band that hailed from these streets, far from its original latitude, on a bar in the chichi Springfield downtown section. Fans of the contemporary music culture of the city also know Shantytown as one of the scene's clique of native rock bands.

Back where time has stood still, however, in an area no one would ever call an American Rome, the Van Zant place is, as it was back then, a one-story white, wood-frame house set back behind shrubbery at 1285 Mull Street near the junction of Woodcrest Road. The place has been remodeled a few times, but one can easily imagine the Van Zants' quotidian activities here. In the backyard, wash hangs on a line. Bikes and toys are strewn on uncut grass. Old mattresses are stacked high outside a shed in the corner of the yard. A pickup truck is parked in the driveway. A ROOM FOR RENT sign sticks out of the ground. Dogs bark. The sky is bright blue; the sun shines. Faint music streams from a radio somewhere inside the house.

In the rootstock of mid-twentieth-century civilization, this milieu and not anything close to a manor house *was* the South and, thus, the only life that Ronnie Van Zant knew and could write songs about living in and getting away from. As Ed King, an early, vital member of Lynyrd Skynyrd who added the signature third lead guitar to their congealing sound, recalls the band's sine qua non: "When you get right down to it, Ronnie was a country singer fronting a rock band. He was writing country songs, because that's what he knew. His musical roots were very southern."

This was something Ronnie had no compunction about owning up to. His music may not have been in the mold of George Jones or Lefty Frizzell, but his blood ran with the same genetic code. When he sang openly of this in the self-explanatory "I'm a Country Boy" on *Nuthin' Fancy*, he did so with a defiant chauvinism:

> I don't like smoke chokin' up my air
> And some of those city folks well they don't care
> I don't like cars buzzing around
> I don't even want a piece of concrete in my town.

Van Zant's world was one in which he didn't feel concrete under his feet when he trod his streets, headed somewhere through abandoned properties and weed-strewn lots or, later, down the roads in his red Mustang, usually way too fast. The west side of Jacksonville, which can't really be called poverty stricken, is typical of much of the bowels of Florida: hard-working, lower-middle-class men and women happy to be given a mortgage and to have enough to put on the table for their families. For them, as for Ronnie's father, who spent twenty years providing for his wife and six children by driving a truck through the snakelike interstate highways of the South, having an old pickup on a dirt driveway is the definition of contentment.

Lacy Van Zant certainly was content right where he was—even when his boy was a millionaire, living in splendor several miles away, with a pool in the shape of a guitar, Lacy would refuse to budge the family from the house he considered his homestead. But that was not the life that Ronnie dreamed of, and he was determined that it would not claim him as it had Lacy.

★ ★ ★

A hard-livin' good ol' boy with a head of high, prematurely graying hair, Lacy Van Zant—one of eleven children fathered by a rugged logger named George Van Zant—was born in 1915 in Evergreen, a sparsely populated woodland northwest of Jacksonville. It seems George must have had a wry or twisted sense of humor, as the name Lacy derived from his own father's not-so-kind pet name for him: Lazy Boy.

It was a description no one could accurately use for the adult Lacy, who was doing odd jobs at twelve and would work almost every day of his life. When the Japanese bombed Pearl Harbor, he was one of the first in line at the navy recruiting station, and he went on to serve four years on a battleship in the Pacific. During a furlough in Jacksonville, he met and romanced a pretty fifteen-year-old girl, Marion Hicks, who was called "Sister" or "Sis," a nickname given her by her grandfather. Worn down by his proposals, she married him in 1947, by which time he had a job as a trucker and she already had a child, a daughter named Betty Jo Ann, from a failed marriage. Lacy adopted the girl, and the family bounced around trailers and shotgun shacks in Shantytown until they had their first child together, a son born on January 15, 1948, in Saint Vincent's Hospital.

They called him Ronald Wayne Van Zant, a fairly high-falutin' name for the son of a truck-drivin' man. He was a big, robust, loud baby and as a toddler was apt to wander off on his own, impatient for something challenging to do, climb, or hit. Tales are told about a young Ronnie going after a teenage gang that had stolen his bicycle, and leaving a few bloody noses in his wake while getting it back. He also liked to sing, and when he did, it was not "The Wheels on the Bus" or "I'm a Little Teapot." Aping what he had heard Lacy croon at home or behind the wheel of his rig, Ronnie got up in front of his first-grade class at Ramona Boulevard Elementary School and trilled "Beer Drinking Daddy" and "Ricochet Romance." Sis Van Zant got a kick out of telling people how she was called to the school to rebuke Ronnie for his precocious behavior. But even then, nothing could have made him change his ways.

Many families in postwar Jacksonville were headed by former or current employees of the naval yards over at the port area on the ocean. In this amorphous, blue-collar town, postwar optimism ran high, but uncertain days lay ahead. As anyone within these borders could tell you, nothing was ever taken for granted in Jacksonville. Moreover, the city was something of a poor stepchild with a hazy identity when compared with other booming Florida cities like Tampa, Fort Lauderdale, and Miami. For one thing, people had less to live on here. For another, the state as a whole had developed as almost two separate states with discrete identities. The old saying was that in Florida the North is in the south, and the South is in the north; the more north you go, the more southern it got.

This contradiction was due to the original settlement of the northern part of the state by predominantly German and Dutch immigrants, creating a dialect flatter and blunter than the twangy, melodic

Anglo-American accent prevailing in the rest of the state and region. However, while the panhandle identity is in some ways less southern than in the phallic peninsula, pride in being a Southerner has been, and is, feverishly high. Nowhere is the heritage mantra of the Confederate flag issue heard more often or louder than in these parts, where it is still a matter of great pride that Florida was the third state (after South Carolina and Mississippi) to secede from the Union—and that Tallahassee was the only Confederate capital never captured by Abe Lincoln's generals.

In Jacksonville, a port city located on the eastern coast, there were fewer ties to southern traditionalism than the more obvious southern culture of other Florida cities to the south. A curious anomaly is that, despite being just over the border from Georgia and within tobacco-spitting distance of Alabama, the twangy accent is largely absent, largely due to the constant coming and going of transient populations.

Lacy wanted to live in a certain style, but the postwar flood of returning soldiers looking for work created an instant middle class, all competing for jobs and living space. With limited resources, Shantytown was his only option for a home, and driving a truck his only choice for a job. Lacy, a descendant of that wave of Dutch immigration—his surname a derivative of Van Zandt, Old World Dutch for "from the sand" or "from Zante," an island in the Mediterranean—never complained about the hand dealt him. He was a proud man with rock-ribbed, conservative southern values, who would work like a maniac to provide for his family. He may not have kept all his teeth by the 1960s, but he kept his wife and would continue to do so for just short of half a century, until her death in 2000, preceding his by four years.

Sis Van Zant, like most wives of the era, stood respectfully in the shadow of her husband, but in the privacy of the home, she had the dominant hand, a necessity with her husband on the road so often. Because Lacy wanted a big family, she obliged him, giving birth to a parade of children—six in all, including Betty Jo, with a rhythmic progression of names: Ronnie, Donnie, Marlene, Darlene, and Johnny. Yet Sis somehow found the time to work nights in a doughnut shop to add extra cash to the family pot. When Ronnie was two, she had to be the one to go down to the bank and persuade a loan officer to give the Van Zants a loan to mortgage the house on Woodcrest where Lacy would live, happily if not always easily, until the day he died in 2004.

* * *

Lacy could never quite understand his boy, in particular the unfocused sense of boiling anger inside him. Ronnie, he once said, "had a temper and a 'don't mess with me' attitude, which he would need growing up." With pride and a little bit of a wince, he recalled that when his boy was all of two, "he had miniature gloves that I bought for him and he gave me a black eye." He paused for a beat and then added, "He's been giving me black eyes ever since," though he meant this only in the figurative sense. His conclusion was that Ronnie "was well thought of, very popular—because he fought for his rights."

Lacy indeed could be proud that the boy, for all his rough-and-tumble traits, had a good side. He was quick-witted and completely charming; he could sing and express himself, and he excelled on the football and baseball fields. The football dream ended only when he broke his ankle during a game, leaving him with a faint limp, but the individualism of baseball was more his thing anyway. As a fleet centerfielder with a big, lusty cut at the plate and a Ty Cobb–like zeal to slide into bases with his spikes up (aimed right at someone's head), he led his American Legion team one year with a simple batting philosophy: "I just swung for the fences," he once said. "That was my whole philosophy in life."

As it happened, of course, he and Gary Rossington had met on a ball field, the Hyde Park Elementary School field on Park Street, where all the sandlot teams played. In 1965, Ronnie, a junior at Robert E. Lee, was playing for the Green Pigs, sponsored by a restaurant of that name. Rossington, not yet fifteen, was on the Lakeshore Rebels, his junior high team. That gap in age and experience should have made him a blip on Ronnie's screen, except for the fact that Ronnie always seemed to know who the talented kids were, as if he had filed away such data for future reference. Besides, Us, the band Ronnie had formed when he was attending Lakeshore, had become an afterthought; no one in it could play a guitar as well as Gary.

Ronnie also had a good deal of sympathy for the younger teen, who had lost his father when he was ten; for Ronnie this harsh fact redefined the itchy relationship he had with Lacy, giving him a cold chill at the thought that his old man might not always be around to give him hell. Death indeed was a matter that unsettled Ronnie and gave him much food for introspection. His later work would occasionally feature death as a theme, most prominently on "Free Bird," a song he kept in his head for years before setting it down on vinyl, with its metaphoric yearning for eternally open skies, a sadly ironic consequence.

This might seem to conflict with his tough-guy ways, but anyone who knew him understood that Van Zant was not out to hurt a guy he egged on to fight him; rather, the fine distinction was that he was laying down who was boss of Shantytown. Indeed, when the prospect that he might in fact have done serious damage to someone arose, which happened at least twice, the kid who was always in control of his emotions nearly came unglued. One time he and a buddy drove to the woods to hunt squirrels. Wielding a .22-caliber shotgun, he fired at one but missed; a woman standing nearby, whom he hadn't seen, collapsed to the ground. As it turned out, she was an elderly woman who lived in the woods and drank heavily; coincidentally, she had passed out just as the shot was fired.

Ronnie came running over, almost in tears. "You all right?" he kept asking the fallen woman, who finally stirred, looked up, and made a request.

"Give me my bottle," she said.

Per Skynyrd legend, a remarkably similar incident supposedly occurred out on the ball field. During one at bat, Ronnie hit a blistering foul line drive down the third-base line. At the time, Rossington was standing in foul ground with Bob Burns, the friend from Forrest High School who also played drums in You, Me and Him. They ducked, but the ball glanced off Burns's head. More stunned than hurt, he went down to the ground. Aghast that he might have killed the kid, Ronnie dropped his bat and tore down the third-base line.

"You killed him, you bastard!" Rossington growled at him—taking his own life in his hands.

Burns, who lives in Seminole, Florida, and still plays in local bands, remembers it differently. "It looked like an aspirin comin' at me, and I turned around to run, and it caught me right between the shoulder blades. It hit me hard, knocked the breath out of me. And I'm layin' on the ground, and the coaches are pullin' my belt up, saying, 'Breathe, son, breathe.' I finally came around, and I looked up, and Ronnie was staring down at me. He went, 'Sorry, kid,' and he walked off."

After a few minutes Burns rose, and all was well. Greatly relieved, Ronnie went back to bat. Then, after the final out, he sought out the two younger kids and pulled some beers out of his duffle bag, and they got to talking about music in one of the dugouts. It was during that colloquy that Ronnie decided he was going to annex their band and become the singer they didn't have, whereupon they repaired to Burns's basement and, still wearing their sweaty uniforms, informally jammed—badly.

The problem was that Gary had the right equipment but couldn't play it to maximum effect. He owned a Silvertone electric guitar, an inexpensive in-house brand sold at Sears, which for years had a record label by that name. Those Silvertone models would be discontinued in the early 1970s, later making them rare and enormously popular among musicians such as Bob Dylan, John Fogerty, Jerry Garcia, and Chet Atkins. A Canadian band that began in the 1960s as the Silvertones, in homage to the guitar, became the Guess Who.

But Gary was *not* getting out of his Silvertone the commonly played rock riffs of the day, not yet having mastered bar chords, which are played with multiple fingers or even a whole hand pressing down strings on the fingerboard. Indeed, country music had made liberal use of bar chords, with guitar players sliding their entire hands up and down the fingerboard, yielding a twangy, wailing sound. Not incidentally, Ronnie had been to a Rolling Stones concert at the Jacksonville Coliseum in May 1965, observing at close range Keith Richards's work on the fingerboard of his guitar. While it said something about the town that the arena was only half filled that night, the show no doubt produced for Ronnie more than one epiphany.

Agreeing with Ronnie's assessment that a second guitarist was needed, Gary brought up the name of a classmate, Allen Collins, who could play those pleasing bar chords on his own Silvertone, bought for him by his mother Eva, after whom he named the instrument, etching it in the body just like the LUCILLE inscribed on B.B. King's guitar. Collins, originally taught to play by his grandmother, Leila Collins, a low-level country singer, was a serious music student, and he had a band called the Mods. That was all Ronnie needed to hear. He decided, before even meeting him, that Collins, a frizzy-haired string bean of a kid with jack-o-lantern facial features, was going to be the second guitar player in the still-unnamed band.

Ronnie, Gary, and Bob jumped into Ronnie's Mustang and drove over to Collins's house in Cedar Hills, to the east across I-295. When they got there, Allen was riding his bike in the street in front of his house. Seeing Van Zant eyeing him, he became uncomfortable, a not-uncommon reaction when Van Zant stared at someone. Collins pedaled hard, tearing down the street, the Mustang on his tail. In a panic, he jumped off the bike and ran through some woods. The trio in the car got out and followed him on foot, with Gary shouting, "Allen, man, we ain't gonna hurt you—we just wanna play!"

Collins finally stopped running, and listened, at a distance. Then he said, "Gee, guys, I'd like to play with y'all, but I'm afraid the Mods would beat me up." Those, of course, were fightin' words for Ronnie. The target: not Collins but his band.

"Everybody get in the car," he ordered, and the whole bunch of them motored to a place where the Mods hung out. He jumped from the car, ambled into the yard where they were, and ripped off his shirt.

"We're here to take Allen—anybody got a problem with that?" he asked.

In Burns's recollection of the possibly slightly overbaked story, "they said, 'Nope, we've got no problem with that. In fact, we'll help you load all of his equipment—and good luck to y'all!'"

★ ★ ★

With the first lineup of the band now complete, they turned their attention to finding a name for it. They had no good choices and settled on the Noble Five. Like many American kid bands at the time, they chose the name because it sounded faintly British, something that had worked out pretty well for a Brooklyn band named the Left Banke, which scored a number-one hit, "Walk Away Renée," causing people to proclaim them the newest British band. If a group from Brooklyn could pull off a con like that, why not a bunch of streetwise guys from Jacksonville?

As the band progressed, however, it was apt to look a bit different from gig to gig, as one or another of them would be unable to make it, either buried by homework or chafing under an early curfew dictated by parents. One observer of their earliest sets, Gene Odom, a pal of Van Zant's, recalls that the first song the group ever sang, from the back of a pickup truck in a church parking lot, was a cover of a cover: the Byrds' version of a song Jimi Hendrix would also cover, a brutal tale of the consequences of infidelity, "Hey Joe." The bass player that night was not Junstrom but a local kid named Billy Skaggs; another stand-in, Jimmy Parker, a former cohort of Ronnie's in his defunct band Us and a future solo country star, joined in on guitar.

The amorphous nature of the band that would alter the topology and geography of rock was to continue. Yet that was a trivial issue to Ronnie Van Zant. What really mattered was that he was the nucleus of the band. He expected he would move heaven and earth—all by himself if he had to.

2

★ ★ ★ ★ ★

A DIFFERENT LIGHT

In later years, speaking of the germination of Skynyrd, Ronnie Van Zant would navigate around reality, saying, "I handpicked all these boys to play for me." But then, in his worldview, he *had* handpicked them to be included in his orbit. He may not have played any instrument, never having had the patience to learn how, but as a teen his musical palette was extensive. He had heard classic country songs on the radio since he was a tot. Lacy always had his radio tuned to the music of his roots, and when he sometimes took his son on truck routes, the kid heard nothing but that for days on end. As he matured, he became a fan of Merle Haggard—who wasn't?—the Nashville "outlaws" Willie Nelson and Waylon Jennings, and the prototypical Man in Black, Johnny Cash, who indeed "walked the line" between yearning survival and reckless self-destruction. But Ronnie had become far more influenced by non-southern rock stars of the era, the Beatles and the Stones, as well as the soulful dance grooves of Sam and Dave. Within a few years, his favorite sound would be the guitar-driven blues-rock and breathy vocals of Paul Rodgers of Free, whose Top 5 hit "Alright Now" would become a virtual template for Skynyrd.

"I managed Paul Rodgers at one time, and when I arranged for Ronnie to meet Paul, it was the biggest thrill Ronnie ever had, bar none," says Charlie Brusco. For Ronnie, people like Mick Jagger and John Lennon paled by comparison to the swarthy, bushy-browed Brit, who may own the only voice in rock more accommodatingly serrating and melodious than Van Zant's.

Even so, as Ed King attests, the road that led to the phenomenon that was Lynyrd Skynyrd ran not through England but straight through the musical and cultural history of the South, dating back half a century to those Delta blues and folk infusions that gave country music its amenability to new forms. By then a new generation of musicians born and nurtured in the south was forming. The first, of course, had been Tupelo, Mississippi-born Elvis Presley, who spent his teenage years in Memphis. A fortuitous coincidence when he auditioned for Sam Phillips' small country label, Sun Record Company, in 1953 landed him in what would soon be a Hall of Fame stable with Johnny Cash, Jerry Lee Lewis, and Carl Perkins. All of them broke away, signed by big labels, into the rock orbit, but with a rockabilly flavor heavily influenced by black R&B. Another, Buddy Holly, whose hiccup cadence and throaty twang were more organically country than Elvis's style, proved he too could fit perfectly into electric guitar–driven rock. His premature death in 1959 in the first plane crash that demoralized rock came as the rock charts were dotted with hits by southern boys like the Everly Brothers, Conway Twitty, and Roy Orbison, all of whom helped define a new Nashville sound with songs of heartache and unrelenting loneliness.

The old-guard music men of the South tried to provide a buffer to the British Invasion that remodeled the sixties. Merle Haggard's proud identity as an "Okie from Muskogee," where, he crooned, they don't smoke marijuana but get drunk as a skunk, was funny enough to make it plausible that the song was a send-up of the old guard. Indeed, an increasing number of grizzled country veterans were becoming eager to wear the "outlaws" label that was claimed by the older and wiser country rebels, who paved the way for a younger generation of similarly free-thinking, against-the-grain redneck antiheroes. That movement was on the horizon everywhere, nowhere stronger than in north Florida.

* * *

Van Zant, Rossington, Collins, Burns, and Junstrom were fortunate to have grown up with a wide variety of influences, not the least of which were southern soul singers who had cut their teeth in the meridians of Georgia, Alabama, and Florida. Ronnie would tune the radio in his old pickup truck to the stations at the far end of the dial, unleashing the country-blues soul of Otis Redding, Eddie Floyd, and "Wicked"

Wilson Pickett. Like Lacy, Ronnie had no demons about race, no imaginary boogeymen to hate on—the boogie men he knew were the ones who could play the hillbilly blues rendition of "Guitar Boogie" made famous in 1945 by Arthur Smith's Rambler Trio or, more likely, Chuck Berry's clanging rock-and-roll version. This broad musical view wasn't so unusual among his generation, but Ronnie's blindness to color could be incongruent in his hometown.

Ronnie could often be seen at Speedway Park, a half-mile-long brickyard a few blocks from his house, at one of the stock car or NASCAR race events that were held there from 1947 to 1963. (Its grounds are a housing complex today.) A number of race car drivers lived in Jacksonville, but LeeRoy Yarbrough was the best. LeeRoy, who won fourteen NASCAR races and earned over $1 million in 1969 alone, lived on the west side near the track and was a favorite of the Shantytown boys—who had no idea how troubled he was until he was committed in 1980 after trying to strangle his mother. But at the November 1963 Grand National race at the oval a black driver, Wendell Scott, beat LeeRoy and everyone else, breezing to his only career win, still the only Grand National event won by a black driver. However, Scott had to endure a charade when local NASCAR officials, apparently loath to the reaction of handing the trophy to a black man in the Deep South—"[They] didn't want me out there kissing any beauty queens," Scott said—declared the second-place driver the winner, even though he had finished two laps behind.

If most of the crowd was content with this theft, Ronnie, who was there with a buddy, Gene Odom, was not. "LeeRoy don't mind racing with him," he told Odom, "and if he can beat LeeRoy, he deserves to win."

While no one would have called Ronnie Van Zant a flaming liberal, neither would anyone ever see a trace of knee-jerk southern prejudice. And matter-of-fact logic, which always cut through bullshit with him, left an impression on Odom, who years later said, "I thought a little differently about black people after that, and I began to realize that Ronnie saw things in a different light than most of the rest of us."

In Jacksonville—where it took until 2014 to change the name of Nathan B. Forrest High School, so christened in 1959 for a Confederate general and the first grand wizard of the Ku Klux Klan—that was not an easy light to see. NASCAR would eventually award Scott the win—*two years* later—but it was not until 2010, twenty years after Scott had died, that the association sent his family the winner's trophy for that landmark victory. Those were the kinds of southern traditions that Ronnie Van Zant could do without.

⋆ ⋆ ⋆

Ronnie's hubris could only get him so far. In fact, with the future looking so uncertain, his overconfidence seemed almost comical. Even he knew he was walking a fine line and that, if he fell off it, he would wind up in a place familiar to some other Shantytown tough guys: a jail cell. He used to say, only half in jest, that only two people from Jacksonville ever became famous: LeeRoy Yarbrough and a career criminal named Eston Bullard Jr. The latter was in and out of jail until he was sentenced to life in the 1980s for murdering a man; he committed suicide in his cell. According to Ronnie, he would be more famous than either LeeRoy or Bullard; he just didn't know which.

(Surprisingly, he omitted two far more pertinent hometown talents who had made some amazing music history—original Oklahoma natives Mae Boren Axton and her son, Hoyt. Mae, an English teacher at Dupont High, had been the one to introduce Elvis Presley to "Colonel" Tom Parker after Elvis performed in Jacksonville in the mid-fifties. After the Colonel signed him to the legendary personal services contract, Mae promoted him to RCA's Nashville office, leading to his long tenure with the label. She then cowrote "Heartbreak Hotel," his first number-one hit. Later, writing for country singers like Willie Nelson and Mel Tillis, she earned the nickname "the Queen Mother of Nashville." Hoyt, a 1960 Lee High graduate, became a folk and country singer, actor, and writer of 1960s and 1970s hits such as "Joy to the World," and others for Elvis as well.)

To be sure, as Ronnie cruised through his teen years, he became familiar with the inside of jailhouses, and by the time he dropped out of school already had a prison record of petty crimes. One of his plethora of brawls, this on Hendricks Avenue, landed him in the pokey at age nineteen, charged with "disorderly conduct, fighting." Cops took his fingerprints and then called Lacy, who sighed and came down to the station to bail him out for fifty dollars. The court assessed a fine of the same amount and dismissed the case. But there would be others. According to

Gary Rossington, a few years later, Ronnie was busted again, and when Gary was bailing him out, he told Ronnie, "Man, you're double trouble." The phrase stuck in Ronnie's head until he pulled it out in 1975 to write a song with that title and with lyrics that fell in the truer-words-were-never-spoken category. He sang: "Double Trouble, is what my friends all call me."

★ ★ ★

To keep his first-born son on the right track, or try to, Lacy worked hard to indulge him by reaching into his own pocket. As soon as Ronnie obtained his driver's license in 1964, Lacy bought him a used Chevy Corvair, the compact car that, according to Ralph Nader, was a death-trap, its steering wheel apt to impale the driver in a collision. Ronnie, for whom collisions were a regular occurrence, didn't have the car long enough to test its safety. Lacy, seeing how his boy salivated when the Ford Mustang hit the market in '65, sprung for one in fire-engine red, which Ronnie spent his nights drag racing up and down the wide lanes of Plymouth Street and Lenox Avenue. A human crash-test dummy, he wound up in the hospital once with injured ribs and then in a ditch in '66, totaling the car. Either a miracle or the hand of fate spared him.

Lacy would vow never again to waste his paychecks on a car for a boy with so little sense or caution. The boy, he would tell Sis, was never going to live long enough to see his thirtieth birthday. Yet Lacy would eventually give in and buy him another car. Ronnie was working at the auto parts store at that time and more than once bought himself some piece of crap—as he did when he came home with a one-seat dirt-racing car that looked like it could be blown over by a good wind. If, as it seemed, Lacy was trying to buy the kid's love, he expected something in return. His son would try to win his love through empty symbolism—such as the tattoo of his father's name he got at seventeen. But neither cars nor tribute tattoos were ever satisfactory substitutes for expressions of mutual love.

Their relationship was palpably, hopelessly conflicted. On the one hand, as Charlie Brusco recalls: "It was a typical southern family, a great family, a very close family. Ronnie loved Lacy, Sister, all his kid brothers. In fact, Ronnie, even though he was twelve years older than Johnny, would always tell people that Johnny had the best voice in the family."

One might indeed make that case based on Johnny Van Zant's vocal range, which can be heard in his work in the late 1970s with the Johnny Van Zant Band, which was more blues and pop than country, far from his later attempt to channel Ronnie. Then there's Donnie, still the lead singer of .38 Special, whose country-pop 1980s hits "Hold on Loosely" and "Caught Up in You" proved he had one smooth set of pipes too. Each brother, but primarily Johnny, is in every way an eerie doppelganger.

To be sure the Van Zants were an amazingly talented family. But for all their closeness—Ronnie loved taking his little brothers down to the river for a day of fishing and, most likely, a few beers slipped to them if they promised not to tell Lacy—it wasn't the kind of love that was either verbally expressed or shown in the form of hugs and kisses. This was a reflection of Lacy, a haughty sort of patriarch. If Ronnie seemed to need positive reinforcement more than his siblings, Lacy could only offer it in his way, without any mushiness and usually in a stream of consciousness that wandered far off the original point.

"Let me tell you about Lacy Van Zant," Ed King begins. "He was the kind of man who would tell you these long, rambling stories that would go on and on—he'd start at one place and go off on these wild tangents, then maybe two hours later he'd wind up right back where he started. He would take you on these fascinating, fantastic journeys. He was the quintessential southern man. And that's what Ronnie's songs were like. Ronnie was the spitting image of his dad."

This obvious reality was something that both pleased and bedeviled father and son, the dividing line being when Ronnie, like any other teenager in the 1960s, needed ballast in a storm of alienation. One suspects a few words of heartfelt love from his father might have prevented a good many of the scraps he got into when he just felt like lashing out for no good reason—a character trait handed down by Lacy. What he needed most, he figured, was to strike out on his own, and that put him into further conflict with Lacy, flaring up the archetypical love-hate thing between them. Lacy would hear about the drugs, the drinking, the recreational sex—and the rock and roll.

Lacy worked hard, believing a man's first responsibility was to support his family, not to go off and sing. "I don't know if they ever sat down and aired it out, you know, Lacy saying he understood what Ronnie wanted and that he was proud of him," Brusco says. And as much as

Lacy would later get on board the strange trip his son was on—and even take to calling himself the "Father of Southern Rock" and writing liner notes on a Skynyrd album—Ronnie still courted that stamp of approval. He would die without ever believing he had gotten it.

⋆ ⋆ ⋆

Going off on his own two weeks before his eighteenth birthday, Ronnie made a major decision, or so he thought, when he popped the question to Nadine Incoe. Doing the "right thing" after impregnating her, the old-world side of Ronnie's sensibility led him to figure he had no choice but to drop out of Lee High so he could go to work to support his wife and child. As Bob Burns recalls, this was hard to figure—at least to anyone but Van Zant, who, when he made his mind up about something, could not be deterred.

"Ronnie," he says, "had one half of an English course to graduate, and he was a straight-A student at every subject—gym, geometry, history . . . straight As."

Even so, his mind made up, he went to work. Nadine's brother owned that auto parts store, and he commenced living with his nose to the grindstone. They moved into a cramped trailer park, and when their daughter Tammy Michelle was born on July 30, 1967, he was eking out an existence as a young newlywed dad, hating it more every minute. Still—indicative of his morbid fascination with death—Ronnie had a gravestone erected for her at the Riverside Memorial Park cemetery, where relatives in the Van Zant family were buried. The stone had her name and birth date and read: THE LORD IS MY SHEPHERD. It still sits there today, waiting, almost forebodingly.

Marriage and fatherhood were pivotal moments in the relationship between Lacy and Ronnie. Lacy firmly believed his boy erred in both decisions—leaving school and marrying Nadine; he was ready for neither life without a diploma nor marriage and fatherhood at his age. Indeed, as time went on, Ronnie himself came to regret his impetuous, reckless actions. He would call dropping out of school the biggest mistake he ever made—which, considering the millionaire status he later achieved, could only have been because of the corrosive effect it had on his relationship with Lacy—though knocking up a girl and finding himself the father of a child he loved but felt strangely unattached to was far worse. And the tension all these bad decisions caused between Lacy and him only worsened Ronnie's feeling that he had let his old man down.

Unable to pull off the charade of a young American married couple, Ronnie and Nadine quickly began bickering, and Ronnie took it out on her with verbal abuse, telling her that he had put what he really wanted to do—sing in a rock band—in moth balls. The union lasted only a few months before Ronnie came back home. He was forced to deal with Lacy's smug, I-told-you-so attitude, but at least he now had the freedom to pursue his teenage dreams. He continued working at the auto shop, giving most of his paycheck to Nadine, who without disputation from Ronnie was given sole custody of Tammy and moved back in with her parents. Through the coming years, Ronnie would all but forget about his daughter as anything but a financial responsibility, which for him was something of a self-serving salve for the blunder he had made; by putting her out of his mind, he apparently hoped to reset the clock and start over again.

Getting back to the rock-and-roll dream was a key part of that aim. While Lacy reckoned that the rock-and-roll thing was an affront to him, Ronnie sincerely believed it offered the best shot to make a real success of himself rather than fall into the dead-end street that was life in Shantytown. Singing might have been the only unbroken thread in his life since his infancy, possibly the only thing that could tame the savage beast in him. While he never took a singing lesson or had a stated desire to sing for a living, he did have talent and an ego—*that* was for sure.

* * *

Ronnie believed the Noble Five, which he never quit, were jelling. Moreover, Allen Collins was honing himself into perhaps the best guitarist on the west side, so advanced that his mother, for whom guitars served the same purpose as cars did for Lacy, sprung for another one for her son, a Les Paul model that cost her $500. In a couple of years, when Allen watched the British blues-rock band Cream perform on the *Ed Sullivan Show*, he was smitten with Eric Clapton's guitar, which he immediately identified as a Gibson Firebird. And so Eva Collins again put her pennies together and bought one for him. With their long hair and gleaming guitars, at least the Noble Five had the *look* of a real band—several bands, actually, as Ronnie decreed they change their name to the Wildcats, the Sons of Satan, Conqueror Worm, the Pretty Ones, My Backyard, and then, in a nod to the oft-seen Hell's Angels' tattoo that references the percentage of the population bikers estimate themselves to be, the One Percent. With this last moniker, the band hoped to immunize themselves from being harassed by motorcycle gangs when they played gigs on the back of a flatbed truck in church parking lots. Sometimes it worked; sometimes it didn't. Says Rossington, "When we started out, people would mess with us 'cause we had long hair. And we'd just say, 'Fuck you' and fight."

On a regular basis shiners and bloody, swollen lips marked their faces, giving them the tough-guy redneck look they didn't mind a bit. Image, after all, was important, even at gigs at church socials and school gyms. And in 1968, they were really starting to rock out, with tight, interwoven guitar licks. Collins and Rossington had come to the decision that there would be no lead guitar and no rhythm guitar; the two of them would either alternate leads or double them, an uncommon approach. Burns's drumming and Junstrom's bass were tight—"in the pocket," in musicianspeak—never allowing the beat to stray or become muddled.

The gigs they played were varied. "We used to play one joint until midnight for kids," Van Zant once said, "then they turned it into a bottle club, and we'd go until 6 a.m." Given the many dive bars and hippie hangouts around town where a different band would play every night, there was no paucity of gigs. As if on a carousel, they went round and round, from one joint to another and back again, stopping at the Forest Inn, Comic Book Club, Sugar Bowl, the Still, Skateland, West Tavern, and Little Brown Jug. Though alcohol was prohibited at some of them, the cops would look the other way when a bottle, or case, of Jack or Johnnie was smuggled in. The owners often also owned strip clubs, offering up side benefits for the bands that were worth more than the few bucks they cleared from a set, most of it from passing the hat.

But the chance to compete with other bands was also worth a lot more. With the competition so fierce, some thievery was inevitable, and the boys of the One Percent were hardly above it. One example marks what is apparently the first-known intersection of the early incarnations of Skynyrd and the Allman Brothers Band. In 1967 at the Comic Book the One Percent opened for Hour Glass, a unit formed in L.A. by Duane and Gregg Allman from the remnants of their first group, the Allman Joys, and the Nitty Gritty Dirt Band. Hour Glass was short-lived, the last false step before the formation of the Allman Brothers Band, but they did cut two albums for Liberty Records at FAME Studios in Muscle Shoals, Alabama, the first of which (*Hour Glass*) had been released by the time they came through Jacksonville on tour.

Looking for any clues that might get them the same success, the One Percent went beyond mere study; while Van Zant's band was on stage, they thought nothing of performing all the songs on *Hour Glass*. What was more shocking than the bald theft was that, according to the Hour Glass's keyboard player Paul Hornsby—who later was in Grinderswitch and produced top-selling albums by the Charlie Daniels Band, the Marshall Tucker Band, and Wet Willie—"They played it as good or better than we played it." What's more, with his typical honey-coated bullshit, Van Zant smoothed it over with sweet talk.

"Man, I gotta tell you," he said to Hornsby, "we *worship* you guys!"

Nor did the Allman boys press the point, possibly because they too knew of Ronnie's reputation. As Hornsby remembers it, Duane and Gregg told Van Zant his band was too good to do cover tunes; they had to get crackin' writing their own stuff. Indeed, rival bands would probably not have hesitated to pilfer songs from the One Percent, if only they had some. At the time, they had none that they felt confident enough to play live yet. Jim Daniel, a local booker, had been loosely representing the band for a few years and pleaded with them for original material. One of the earliest attempts, "Chair with a Broken Leg," apparently was the first song ever recorded by the band soon to be known as Lynyrd Skynyrd, who were still the Noble Five at the time, around mid-1967.

"Chair," copies of which do not exist, was some sort of pseudofolk protest rock that few could make sense of. Daniel got it on a reel-to-reel tape, not in a studio but in Ronnie's aunt's house, intending to use it as a demo, but he thought better of it and never did. As the band were reluctant to play any new songs on stage, "Chair with a Broken Leg" went into the dust bin of history. Mainly, they went with covers of distinctly nonsouthern bands—the Stones, the Yardbirds, the Who, Cream. Allen Collins in particular loved to do riffs on Pete Townsend's guitar-playing moves, such as the famous windmilling of his arm. They began to carve out a niche for themselves—rock and roll, hard and intense, stir-fried with a Merle Haggard–type haughtiness, a tang, and an implied twang, with Allen injecting some bottleneck-blues effects by sliding his palm up and down the neck of his guitar and making redneck banter with the audiences, mainly invitations to hecklers to step outside when the songs were over.

There was no distinctive sound to it yet, but the seeds for a mutual accommodation of backwoods southern blues and contemporary British rock were there. They began looking ever more grizzled, the vestiges of county-fair-appropriate dress, with no jeans and high school haircut codes giving way to musty, faded jeans, sweat-stained T-shirts, dangling locks, and bristly whiskers. The search to find the right alchemy, an emblem that was workable and believable in both tonality and look, was in its infant stages in other dive bars within smelling distance of the One Percent's gigs, undertaken by similar bands also on the make. And in the end, it was more the attitude, the smug, put-up-your-dukes component of Ronnie's vocals, not to mention his sinister Elvis-like sneer—and the quick, ingratiating grin signaling that much (but not all) of his tough-guy posing was a put-on—that seemed to stick in minds and ears, propelling the band forward.

Sensing they were in need of original material that would fortify and ideally define them, Ronnie began to collaborate with Gary and Allen, taking the lyricist role he felt comfortable with and leaving the melody to be knitted onto his words by the two guitarists. Naturally, he was a tough taskmaster, a perfectionist even then, sparking prickly arguments about song topics and direction, which would always be the case. However, they reached a critical watermark late in 1968 when yet another name for the band came into being, one that would last into eternity.

3

★ ★ ★ ★ ★

NEED ALL MY FRIENDS

In 1969, Forby Leonard Skinner, a gruff, crew cut–sporting, thirty-five-year-old Army veteran, was the gym teacher at his alma mater, Robert E. Lee High. Nothing about him would have ever portended fame or even a minute of notoriety had he not been placed in history as a foil for two students, members of a still obscure band. Having taken on the sartorial and tonsorial identities of rock-and-roll musicians put Gary Rossington on a collision course with Skinner, who like any other high school gym coach was the enforcer of the lingering dress codes that existed in every high school in America.

A big man at six foot two and two hundred pounds, Skinner was a real ballbuster, taking satisfaction in ragging young men who dared creep up on the line between respectability and hippiehood. Given authority to rag, keep after school, or suspend any kid who violated the dress code, he cut a menacing, foreboding figure when he padded down the hallways. Worse were his excursions through the shower room, where, if he wanted to humiliate a naked, pubescent boy, he could leave a mental scar a mile long.

When Ronnie was a senior at Lee in 1966, Skinner's first year there, Ronnie had run-ins with the coach and was intimidated enough to keep his hair respectably short; with his blond hair cropped above the ears and swept across his forehead, he looked very much like a California surfer boy. That look, of course, had passed as daring in an era dominated by the Beach Boys' candy-striped collared shirts and white chinos, but in '69, it was cause to be labeled a nerd.

Gary, whose curly locks grew like wild shrubbery, overrunning the lawful two-inches-below-the-ears limit, was an immediate target for the coach. Skinner always carried around a ruler to measure, including into the shower room, and he had little sympathy for the young man's defense that being in a working rock band required, as the biggest musical on Broadway noted, "long, beautiful hair . . . down to there." Once, Gary even brought in solid citizen Lacy Van Zant to help make his case. Skinner wasn't totally deaf to the plea; he suggested that the band members wear wigs for their rock-and-roll engagements. They did but quickly grew their long tresses back. For a time, they thought they could con Skinner by wearing *short-haired* wigs to school, tightly fitted over their taped-down long hair, but Skinner wasn't that easy to fool.

Unable to put up with the static, Rossington would drop out in '68 (as had Ronnie before him) as soon as he was sixteen and thus legally able to. Just before that, Rossington, having been suspended yet again, bravely—maybe insanely—looked Skinner in the eye and told him, "Fuck you." Gary's dropping out killed his parents, just as Ronnie's decision had killed Lacy and Sis, but Gary and Bob needed Leonard Skinner like, well, a haircut. Indeed, dealing with him had become so unbearable that they regularly made up obscene limericks and song lyrics about him. It seemed like a gift that Allan Sherman's 1964 novelty song "Hello Muddah, Hello Fadduh!" included the line "You remember Leonard Skinner," prompting them to sing the song when Skinner strolled by. An even better inside joke was calling the band "Leonard Skinner" in jest when they took the stage. The joke always got a hoot because so many in the audience had gone to Lee High and had their own Skinner tales.

Then one night at the Forest Inn it occurred to Ronnie that the sobriquet actually worked as an identifier on several levels. Because of who Skinner was, the name fit their image as redneck dropouts with an authority problem, and in the mold of perfectly inscrutable rock-and-roll patois used as group names, "Leonard Skinner" added some beguiling mystery. *Skinner*, rolling off the southern tongue, sounded something like a sneer, their predominate stage affectation, or in redneckspeak, something like "I just skinnered that there mule." As the band mounted the stage at the Forest Inn, Ronnie did the joke intro and then on a whim asked the audience, "Hey, how many y'all want us to change our name to 'Leonard Skinner'?" The room cheered its approval, and the deed was done. It did occur to them that Mr. Skinner, not having been asked permission to appropriate his identity for a rock-and-roll band—the idea was just too delicious for them to risk asking and being shot down—might take umbrage and lawyer up to stop it. So, rather than ask, they tried different spellings of the name, going for the time being with "Lynard Skynard" on the blackboards of the local pubs billing their gigs.

It was a turnabout of roles, them mocking *him* now, and proof that they had only the most snarky of intentions. Of only secondary consideration was whether it would ever be commercially useful or if Skinner might still press the issue, it being obvious who "Lynard Skynard" was. For now, however, they knew just a little bit more what they were about. And Lord knows, they wouldn't ever change.

★ ★ ★

Armed with a new name and a good reputation in the local rock scene, the band took the next logical step up the ladder, a recording session. In May 1969, David Griffin, the manager of a Jacksonville record emporium called Marvin Kay's MusiCenter, arranged with a local record company, Shade Tree Records, to finance a session for them and another band called Black Bear Angel at a studio owned by Norm Vincent, a former top-rated disc jockey at radio station WMBR. Shade Tree was operated by producers Tom Markham and Jim Sutton, who, after seeing the band with the revolving-door names at the Comic Book, gave them a five-year contract, for a generous advance of . . . nothing.

Two songs cowritten by Ronnie and Allen were cut in mono on an eight-track recorder in about an hour. Ronnie had written the first song, "Michelle," about his daughter Tammy Michelle. It was produced as a sassy blues riff with Ronnie trying hard to sound like Gregg Allman, singing in a raspy voice, "Michelle, little girl, I need you baby more than the air I breathe," as Collins fired up his Les Paul on a long break and a punchy fadeout. The other cut, "Need All My Friends," was an augury of "Free Bird": "Woman, I have to leave you / I can't stay where there is no pay / And I really don't care where I'm going to." Here, Collins's mellow guitar accents swathed Van Zant's plaint about the call and loneliness of the long road and the comforts of playing music and doing "the things I love." The mellowness was cleaved by spikes of hard rock, backed by fiddles and violins. It's an amazing song to behold, the guitars tightly meshed even then and the strings a real curio, never again to be heard on a Skynyrd recording. The songs ran over five minutes, long by contemporary standards but not deemed finished until Ronnie said so.

Markham and Sutton thought they might be onto something, so they pressed three hundred copies of the two-sided 45-rpm disc by "Lynyard Skynard" and flooded radio stations with them. The publisher of the songs was listed as Double "T" Music—so named by Ronnie, reaching back to the "double trouble" appellation hung on him by Gary in jail—although the group would never see a penny of any publishing royalties. Markham and Sutton contractually owned those rights, a common meed taken by record company honchos in exchange for recording unknowns. Berry Gordy, for example, was notorious for doing this to members of Motown groups who wrote their own material, averse to allowing anyone but his stable of writers (including himself) to profit from the publishing.

Like all unknown bands, Skynyrd signed their rights away for a chance to hit it big. But after they'd heard their first record a few times on the radio, it fell off the radar screen, selling something like a hundred copies. (After the Skynyrd plane crash, Shade Tree would sell the masters to a small local label, Atina Records, which would issue them in 1978 on a 45-rpm disc inside a jacket that read SKYNYRD'S FIRST. In 2000, MCA would issue them again, included as "Shade Tree demos" on the *Skynyrd Collectybles* album of odds, ends, and rarities.) As well crafted as the songs were, the main problem wasn't the music: there just seemed to be no definitive format where it could be played regularly. It was similar to the old conundrum of 1950s R&B crossover records judged too black for white stations, too white for black ones. With country rock still not a format, the question was, where are these records supposed to go? It was a roadblock faced by the Allman Brothers as well, one they would do the most to tear down. Of course, in this case, it could have also been that the songs just weren't good enough.

Still, Markham and Sutton held to their hunch. Early in 1970, they would cut another session with the band, producing two ballads, "No One Can Take Your Place" and "If I'm Wrong," both cowritten by Van Zant, Collins, and Rossington. As with "Need All My Friends," there is some real history to these obscure songs. The former is so anti-Skynyrd, so effusively old-school country, that one would never guess it was them. To the accompaniment of Allen's weeping slide guitar, Ronnie, heartbreak dripping from every syllable about love gone bad, sounds more like Cowboy Copas than Paul Rodgers, his nasal twang almost at parody level—another idiom never again to be heard from him.

"If I'm Wrong" did reflect a rock sensibility, its spare instrumentation pairing a splendid B.B. King–like blues guitar line with a rhythmic acoustic guitar beat. Ronnie, back in his comfy lower register, seemed to rescind the cloying sentiments of "Need All My Friends":

> Don't need no friends, I don't play no games
> I need lots of room to roam before I go home. . . .
> If I fail no one can ever tell
> And if I'm wrong I'll soon be gone.

This theme of breaking free from even those who loved him was clearly much on Ronnie's mind. With time left in the session, the group cut a third song, though without nearly as much attention to detail.

Ronnie and Allen had been honing the composition for a couple of years, expressing a similar worldview in the opening line—"If I leave here tomorrow, would you still remember me?"—an actual question that Allen's girlfriend Kathy Johns had once asked him. The lyrics spoke of the flight of a "free bird" that "you cannot change." Compared with the later, immortal version, the song sounds much like a demo, stripped of its many layers and shadings. An almost identical slide guitar jag by Collins opens the song, and the two guitars fire the same chords but are more clanging and nowhere as nuanced or explosive. Ronnie's vocal is as convincing but a bit thin, leading Markham and Sutton to buff it with a thick echo that nearly swallows it up at times, with an odd "whoa whoa whoa" prelude to the line preceding the long guitar break, which never really takes off, sonically or technically. At seven and a half minutes, it was long, all right, if short by the standard of the later version, but never particularly grabbing.

Shade Tree might have had a tiger by the tail had it released the song, as radical as it was and suited to FM rock play. Instead the record company sat on this tape too. (All three songs would go on *Collectybles.*) But "Free Bird," in more complete form, would soon have a new life, a life without end.

★ ★ ★

Even with scant radio play, the band now had a catalog of original songs, something promoters had been waiting for before booking them. According to some sources, "Free Bird" was played for the first time live in May 1970 at a wedding of a friend of the band's. Moreover, along the underground country rock circuit, a surprising number of people in the clubs knew the songs and could even sing along to them. Now out-of-town gigs came their way: one each in Savannah and Macon, Georgia, and two in Saint Louis. Late in 1970, they were invited to open for Eric Burdon and War at a club in downtown Jacksonville. Things were clearly happening now.

Not that Lacy was convinced it was worth it for his son to wear the stigma of a dropout. He was still after Ronnie to return to school and get a diploma, considering the very real prospect that the rock thing would fizzle. Ronnie, in fact, still worked part time at the auto parts store since the money from the band gigs was hardly sufficient to pay child support to Nadine for the daughter he rarely saw. Band doings aside, everything Lacy had predicted would happen otherwise had already materialized—the failed marriage, the child who now needed to be fed and clothed—and through it all Lacy had less hope that his son knew, or would ever know, how to be a man. To a degree, nearly all the members of Skynyrd had daddy issues of some kind, none as serious as Gary losing his early in life, but a matter of gritted teeth nonetheless. Allen, for example, harbored a deep grudge against his father, Larkin Collins, who split from his mother after much acrimony when he was a small child; the guitar thereafter became a sanctuary in a hardscrabble life.

Possibly as a result of being rudderless and having no paternal influence—which to an unruly kid in the South meant the possibility of a big, wide belt being removed and used to lay down the law at home—Collins began careening easily and a little too fast into the rock netherworld of chemical experimentation. Most of the Skynyrd boys were pot smokers, sharing what was a common enough predilection for those of their generation. In fact, when they went on the road early on, they would brandish their emerging "redneck rebel" credentials with absurd tales about getting their stash from some unusual sources. One time they insisted they had just played in Alaska and had brought back with them "Alaskan Thunder Fuck" ganja—which was really just Jacksonville

Gold; then they passed their joints around to watch the psychosomatic overreaction of the guys who tried it.

But Collins's behavior, even before junior high school, had hinted that he was willing to cross more perilous borders. Gene Odom related that Collins had once told him, probably not completely joking, that he had taken wood shop back then "so he could sniff wood glue every day." One day he blacked out after inhaling toluene, a glue solvent and paint thinner, and fell in a heap against the classroom door. The shop teacher, this apparently not being the first time it had happened, opened the door so that Allen could lie flat until he came to. If these stories are indeed true, then it was just a fact of life that Allen Collins had few limits on self-destructive behavior. Ronnie treated these sorts of incidents somewhat as a joke, not really in a position himself to lecture anyone about the evils of drugs or firewater, having been a hooch drinker since, well, who even knew? Besides, how would a former jailbird even try to play Mr. Clean? For both him and Allen, and for everyone else who would come through the band, the hard lessons about going down the road to addiction and dissipation would only be gleaned after too much time and too much consumption.

As for Ronnie's complicated relationship with his father, all the younger man could do was hope Lacy would one day come around. Lacy would never ridicule his boy about the rock and roll, which he viewed as just a diversion. In fact, always trying to do what he could to get deeper into Ronnie's world, he even helped the band out; after receiving a few thousand dollars in insurance money after a traffic accident, he purchased a drum kit for Bob Burns and a trailer, and then a Chevy station wagon, to help lug their equipment around from gig to gig. But telling his boy he was proud of his excursion into music was a more delicate, complicated affair; that was one thing he felt he could not do. Ronnie took it personally, saying years later that the rift was never healed because Lacy would hold over his head the fact that he had been able to decorate his walls with his son's gold records—"but never a diploma."

* * *

Country rock came through the 1960s with a growing sense of swagger and comfort, perfectly matching the mind-set of a nation that had survived a near meltdown, battered daily by headlines about setbacks in Vietnam and assassinations of men of vision. With Dante's inferno burning out of control, it was a symbolic exclamation point that the last rock-and-roll convocation of the '60s, held at a raceway in Altamont, California, turned barbaric and deadly, causing America to pine for what the Rolling Stones had sung on stage that dark day—"Gimme Shelter." So sick and fearful of turmoil and tumult were Americans that they had actually turned to the mortuarial Richard Milhous Nixon, one of politics' biggest demons, who gained election to the White House by running on a "southern strategy." Nixon, by appealing to their lingering prejudices, won over enough Dixiecrat votes to net five states of the Old Confederacy, while also benefiting from third-party candidate George Wallace's own race-baiting campaign, which grabbed the rest, save Texas.

Down in Jacksonville, with its myriad military installations, and in the home of Army veteran Lacy Van Zant, Nixon carried the vote handily, but as with most national issues, the war and the racial struggle seemed remote. Jacksonville had rarely been the site of any controversy. Martin Luther King had come close in 1964 when he was arrested in Saint Augustine at a sit-in at a segregated lunch counter. That was the same year the Florida Supreme Court ordered Jacksonville to desegregate its schools. The mayor, W. Haydon Burns, resisted the order. During Burns's term, racial violence became common. A 1960 protest to integrate downtown lunch counters in the Hemming Park shopping area was ended by segregationists wielding ax handles.

The grisly death toll of Vietnam hit home hard in Jacksonville—202 of its citizens were killed in combat, more than any other Florida city, and it seemed everyone had a friend or relative who didn't make it home. Not incidentally, Ronnie's old football injury had gotten him 4-F status when in accordance of the law he registered for the draft in 1966 at age eighteen. The others drew high numbers in the draft lotteries from 1969 through 1973. The Shantytown boys talked casually about the war, quietly expressing their opposition to it among themselves if not to their parents. Ronnie's attempt at a protest song was painfully inept, and never again would he try his hand at such a theme, ceding that turf to established rockers like the Doors, who were recording masterpieces like "The Unknown Soldier." Skynyrd would stick to what they knew best, the jagged turf of their homeland, the soil and the state of mind, and resolved that they would not encroach on political issues in the songs they sung. That was wise, given the terrain. Their purview, they decided, would be universal topics of young men.

As they cut their teeth in the clubs around Jacksonville, Daytona, and Sebring, the band's original songs about love and the road to somewhere peaceful and productive were sprinkled into their swaggering sets of Stones and Free cover tunes—the latter's "Walk in My Shadow" was a constant. Somewhere along this locus of touring they also made another modification to their name, settling now on a version that magnified the sneering tone of the surname and made any speaker of the phrase sound like a good old boy. They heard it being pronounced like that anyway, so, tongue twisting and confusing as it was, they went with the new spelling—"Lynyrd Skynyrd."

* * *

By the end of the decade, their upward progression was still slow but more sure. In late 1970 they won a local "battle of the bands" contest at the Regency Square shopping mall in downtown Jacksonville; appeared on a local TV station dance party show where they fake-played and Ronnie lip-synched "Need All My Friends"; and then played at the opening of the Jacksonville Art Museum. The gigs weren't so small anymore, nor were they confined to smoky clubs. Indeed, all this dues paying allowed Skynyrd to open several shows for the L.A.-based psychedelic rock band the Strawberry Alarm Clock, who were still extant three years after recording one of the most gloriously unlikely hits of all time, "Incense and Peppermints." This song, one of the first psychedelic rock works, wrote the Magna Carta of alienation for the baby boom era with the line "Who cares what games we choose / Little to win but nothing to lose." The song went all the way to number one in the summer of 1967, but now, painfully passé and running on fumes, the band was to Ronnie a reminder of how sudden the arrival—and devolution—of fame could be. Seeing them as a soon-to-be corpse, he picked their bones by hastening the departure of their guitarist, Ed King.

The New Jersey–born King, who had composed the sapid guitar solo in "Incense and Peppermints"—a sound that became the stamp of psychedelic rock songs—had been steaming since '67 that the band's producer had deprived him of a writing credit for the song. He also had a desire to relocate to the South. Working him, Ronnie would hang out with the burly, round-faced guitarist between shows, coyly planting in his mind the seed that he would be welcome in another band poised for major stardom, or so Ronnie promised. King might have laughed at such an entreaty from a relative unknown, but he was taken with the young redneck, both as a tintype of the South and as a singer. A few years earlier, the Hour Glass had opened for the Strawberry Alarm Clock for a show in L.A., and King had been blown away by Gregg Allman's soulful blues voice. Now, he was hearing a similarly impressive voice in Ronnie. As a whole, he recalled, Skynyrd "were just borderline. They only had a few original tunes, one of which was 'Free Bird.' But Ronnie was already amazing. I'd never seen anybody with so much charisma. I made up my mind right then that I'd do anything to play music with this guy."

King and his Clock returned to Los Angeles, with a special sort of road map of the back roads from Ronnie, which told them where the cops lurked in the shadows eager to bust guys with long hair. Those cops, Ronnie said, "will pull you over and they will throw you in jail and you'll be there for a while." And of course he knew what he was talking about. King got himself an education about the South during that tour. At one gig in Alabama, when the club owner ordered the Clock to sweep the floor and they refused, "he ran us out at gunpoint." After the group hired a black driver for their van, they felt especially ostracized, to the point of fear. But the driver had an instinctive way of avoiding trouble, another sign of life in the new South. "It was so bizarre," King said. "But it was very interesting." King did subsequently quit and move to the South, to Greenville, North Carolina. He played in a bar band for a couple of years, biding time before he got the call from Skynyrd, something he would learn fell under the category of "be careful what you wish for."

* * *

As Skynyrd gained maturity, record-company bird dogs began coming to see them perform. But clearly they were in the same beaker as other groups of Southern rockers. There was the Toy Factory, a South Carolina quintet with four Vietnam veterans, so named because of front man Toy Caldwell, who had been wounded in 'Nam. Like the Allman Brothers, the band had two brothers, Toy and his brother Tommy, the latter of whom would die in 1980 in a manner eerily similar to the way

Duane Allman would, on a motorcycle. Their easygoing southern-fried style seemed to have gotten the jump on the rest of the talent pool and signaled that competition in the top tier of southern rock was going to be stiff.

A good number of country-rock veterans look back fondly on those early days of the genre, recalling a kind of collegial, even familial, bonding between bands. Charlie Daniels, who was older than the young rednecks but also looking for a big break for his eponymous, fiddle-fueled rockabilly band, attributes this bond to most of them sharing similar Tobacco Road socioeconomic deprivations in their youth. In solidarity, he says, bands would go out of their way to help other bands, offering suggestions, lending out players, getting drunk and stoned with them, and touting them to industry bird dogs.

However, at the very top even friendly rivals were regarded as the enemy. Gregg Allman, for one, seemed to have little use for friendships along the circuit that he and his brother fully intended to own, thus they avoided bending elbows with the competition. Having already seen the lengths to which one particular band would go to steal a good song, the Allmans respected the hell out of Ronnie Van Zant and did indeed bend elbows with him after shows on which they and Skynyrd played. But less and less would Gregg and Duane carry any water for them. That being the case, Lynyrd Skynyrd having a born fighter as a front man, a guy who seemed to know everyone in his orbit but wanted to kick all of their asses, was surely going to be an advantage.

* * *

Indeed, Ronnie was not going to let Skynyrd bask in small-time success. Rehearsing in their living rooms and basements would not cut it anymore, and when complaints by neighbors chased them from house to house, Ronnie and Gary went out scouting locations where they could make their noise in splendid isolation. Splendid or not, what they decided on was a dilapidated wooden cabin with an overhanging tin roof located deep in a wooded field on a farm out in Green Cove Springs in the town of Russell near Black Creek. They rented it for sixty-five bucks a month and made it their center of operations. Soon they had their own phrase for the godforsaken shack with no air conditioning where they sweltered in sauna-like conditions while writing their first two albums—Hell House, they called it. The house became another salient marker of the band's legacy, and it would be preserved as such for years before eventually being torn down to make way for the inevitable interstate highway.

Not surprisingly, Ronnie's rules applied. There would be a band rehearsal and a writing session almost every morning at 10 AM. The atmosphere inside Hell House was brutal. Because there was no insulation in the walls, an air conditioner could not be made to work, rendering the name of the place all too literal on humid summer days. They would stock a fridge with beer and sandwiches and get at the music. At the beginning they'd turn out the lights after a session and go home, barely bothering to lock the door. But that changed when some guitars left in the shack were stolen. Now, by rotation, one of them would stay behind and sleep there, with one eye open, and armed with a shotgun. In an early photo taken of the band at Hell House, a pistol is tucked into Ronnie's waistband. He and Lacy were accomplished marksmen, often spending time at a shooting range or hours in a duck blind. But never had Ronnie thought he might have to use a piece on a human until those expensive instruments became an inviting target for thieves. Fortunately, with the lights on all night, no one tried to pilfer anything; if they had, whoever that night's sentry was would have shot to kill.

But defending their fortress and their instruments was worth the time, trouble, sweat, stench of backed-up toilets, and lack of creature comforts. Indeed, in their Bohemian visions, living in these conditions and extracting down-home music from their collective soul was not unlike what the great old Delta blues men had done. They might have finished the day drunk to the gills or strung out on reefer, but their only true comfort was the music. Their alchemy produced a gusher of song ideas, fragments, and riffs and lent a sweaty, gritty genuineness to whatever they played.

Leon Wilkeson was another piece of the puzzle, though so far his presence in the band had been on-again, off-again; he filled in for Larry Junstrom when the latter had better things to do than play a gig. Nothing was being left to chance, and the work ethic bred inside the log walls of Hell House left the sprite-like Wilkeson, who weighed maybe 120 pounds, bathed in sweat and wrung out like a drained sponge. Wilkeson once said, "Ronnie dropped me and Bob Burns off there one day and told us that we were going to stay there till we could make the bass and drums blend into one sound, so we wouldn't detract from the guitars. He said, 'If you can't do it, you're fired.'" Still, Leon felt swept up in the swelling sense of confidence and swagger. A man of few words, he would later say that Ronnie Van Zant ran Skynyrd like Stalin did Russia, "but without his cracking whip, it would have all been for naught." At Hell House, Wilkeson said, "We worked our asses off . . . and it paid off."

4

★ ★ ★ ★ ★

"THEY SOUND TOO MUCH LIKE THE ALLMAN BROTHERS"

The formula that had eventually adopted the evolving Lynyrd Skynyrd was an almost perfect flip of Graham Nash's "Teach Your Children," which captured the smooth grooves of L.A.-based country rock as it gained traction in the early 1970s. The kick-ass authenticity of the down-home Skynyrd model conjured up visions not of languid days in the canyons of the San Fernando Valley but long days pumping gas at the filling station. But all forms of country rock were joined in a real sense by the history of the form itself and its long trail of bleeding across musical borders. An important transition had come back in the late 1950s and early 1960s, when L.A. producer Snuff Garrett, a good old boy from Dallas, applied a country flavor to white pop singers such as Bobby Vee on songs like "Take Good Care of My Baby." Garrett also cut rockabilly pioneer Johnny Burnette on crossover country tunes like "Settin' the Woods on Fire," continuing the trend of native southern singers migrating westward. And country merged with surf-rock guitars in the Fendermen's 1962 cover of the country classic "Mule Skinner Blues."

Later in the '60s came a belated appreciation for the roots of rock and roll. Bob Dylan's 1965 album *Highway 61 Revisited* paid homage in its very title to the highway Dylan fled on from Minnesota to the picket fences of southern cities en route to the Mississippi Delta. Dylan's *Blonde on Blonde*, the first American double album, was backed on most tracks by Nashville's elite studio musicians and was derivative in part of New Orleans R&B (such as on the 1966 "Rainy Day Women #12 & 35"); and his stripped-down, outright country/folk-rock offering *John Wesley Harding* further soldered the south to the broadening schema of pop music.

The genesis of what can be branded West Coast or L.A. country rock filtered through the Byrds, Buffalo Springfield, and the eventual conglomeration of the remnants of those two bands into the supergroup of Crosby, Stills and Nash (and sometimes Young). Of all the players in these groups, only one, Stephen Stills, hailed from the south, from the same northern Florida incubator as Skynyrd and the Allman Brothers. Tellingly, it was Nash, the Brit expatriate, who wrote "Teach Your Children," a song driven by a ringing pedal steel guitar line—turned in by the pride of Haight-Ashbury, the Grateful Dead's Jerry Garcia. A similar country-by-proxy example was the Band, in which Levon Helm was conjoined with four Canadians; recording in Woodstock, New York, of all places, they indelibly stamped the country-rock idiom, first by backing up rockabilly singer Ronnie Hawkins, then Bob Dylan, before making their own mark by fusing bluegrass into rock with parables of Jesus in Nazareth and a tableau of "the night they drove old Dixie down."

The first avowedly country-rock work—in the spangled, Nashville sense of the term—occurred when Gram Parsons, who was born in the backwoods of Florida, grew up in Waycross, Georgia, and went to Harvard, recorded *Safe at Home* with his International Submarine Band. A few months later, when the album came out, he was already with the Byrds recording their brilliant 1968 album *Sweetheart of the Rodeo*, though most of his lead vocals were later scrubbed. That album landed them a gig at the Grand Ole Opry, a first for a rock band. Parsons then led the first self-identified country-rock group, the Flying Burrito Brothers, who clad themselves in spangled, Nashville-style Nudie suits. But for all their genuineness, these Brothers were an L.A. band. Meanwhile, the soul and rock songs recorded at the Muscle Shoals studios (FAME and Muscle Shoals Sound) by artists ranging from Wilson Pickett to Donny Osmond and the Rolling Stones brought the music back to its roots in the Deep South.

Those roots had already opened the way for an ambitious, lantern-jawed parvenu, Phil Walden, who had actualized the most unlikely of cockeyed dreams. Starting out as a student at Mercer University in Macon, Georgia, having been proselytized by the rhythm and blues of the first-generation rock-and-roll incarnation, and living in a town that seeded Little Richard, James Brown, and Otis Redding, he began booking soul singers—Redding was one of his first clients—into frat houses and dive bars. When Redding was given a contract by Memphis's fledgling Stax Records label in 1962, giving it bite and soul-deep emotion, mighty joy, and quivering vulnerability, the South had its answer to the question of how to compete with Berry Gordy's rising kingdom of distilled black music sifted and aimed at a white market. Whereas Motown called itself Hitsville, Stax was Soulsville, a critical difference—with the added irony that the company was owned by white siblings, Jim Stewart and Estelle Stewart Axton. Walden was practically the conduit of talent for Stax, his client list long and noble—besides Redding, he had under contract Sam and Dave, Percy Sledge, Al Green, and some forty others, all of whom he was the personal manager for.

Walden became a millionaire through his eye for talent and his keen intuition. And he was not caught flat-footed when two events changed the future rock landscape. The first was when Redding, at twenty-six, died in one of the many rock-and-roll death rides in the sky, his private plane crashing into a Wisconsin lake in December 1967, three days after he recorded "(Sittin' On) The Dock of the Bay." The other was when Atlantic Records, the New York–based titan of soul music labels that had cannily distributed Stax Records' products, creating inroads into the South similar to when RCA Records had signed Elvis Presley, broke with Stax and, having maneuvered to control that priceless music catalog, looted Jim Stewart of nearly all the songs that dominated soul in the mid to late 1960s. Soulsville never recovered, and neither did the idiom of southern soul, with the exception of those God-blessed studios in the backwoods of Alabama, FAME and Muscle Shoals Sounds, where Atlantic sent Wilson Pickett and Aretha Franklin to record after Stewart refused to allow any non-Stax artists to use his Memphis digs.

By then Phil Walden had a thriving agency, Phil Walden and Associates, and a separate booking firm called the Paragon Agency and had groomed as an associate his three-years-younger brother, Alan, who had little of Phil's savvy but was an energetic, aggressive, and sometimes abrasive presence in the business. Phil had trusted Alan enough to allow him and Redding to form a music publishing company, Redwal Music, which owned not only Redding's songs but other standards like "When a Man Loves a Woman" and "Soul Man." Alan also had a hand in Premier Talent, which operated independently from Phil Walden and Associates, affording Alan a chance to scout and sign talent and then book it, solely on his own. True to the southern way of keeping things in a tight family circle, Paragon's officers were the Walden brothers; their father C. B. Walden, an ex-newspaperman; and their mother, Carolyn. The only outsider was something like a brother, Alex Hodges, a fast-talking former Mercer classmate of Phil's whom he had hired in the early '70s only because no one else knew how to type and Phil's business relied on a constant churn of press releases. Back then, the business was run out of Phil's garage apartment beside his parents' house; now it was quartered in a fancy office in the Robert E. Lee Building in downtown Macon.

Phil had bigger things in mind than merely managing talent. Sick with grief, the fulcrum of his soul empire gone, he entered into a deal with Atlantic Records in 1969 to fund a new label, Capricorn Records, located in Macon. He aimed to harvest southern country-rock acts, a species yet to be fully formed or discovered. Capricorn's first score would earn back every penny and more. He signed the then-green Allman Brothers, who had won some notice as a curio, a Deep South band that had little use for country music other than the blues aspects of it, a kind of Yardbirds grilled in smokehouse sauce. While it would take a few years for the Allmans to break out, the formation of native southern industry norms and stars would be of immense help to the still-forming genre of music they played.

Phil cut Alan in on Capricorn, but the label was really his baby, and he would run it as a monarch, with no use for the advice or help of others. Nor did he see any kind of conflict of interest in managing the talent he would, by rock-and-roll rote, be seeking to pay only as much as he had to. In this he was not alone: Berry Gordy had the same system in Motown, and as much as groups like the Temptations groused about being underpaid, they had no recourse and no outside manager to take up their case; indeed, they didn't even see the tax returns that were prepared for them by Motown's accountants. Walden, to his credit, paid his talent more than the usual three and a half cents per record sold but made no apologies for hoarding a fortune for himself.

As Capricorn laid down roots, mainstream rock and even soul continued to dip into country—John Fogerty with "Lookin' Out My Back Door" and "Born on the Bayou"; Canned Heat's jug-band boogie; Bobbie Gentry's enigmatic "Ode to Billie Joe"; and soul genius Ray Charles's warbling of "Born to Lose" and "I Can't Stop Loving You." But an open question for music honchos in the South was whether there really were homegrown acts that could break just as big across the mainstream. Fortuitously, one, a band of brothers (at least two of them), was rolling down Highway 41. And another was tuning up, approaching the on ramp.

★ ★ ★

In 1969, Ronnie Van Zant, a man who clearly could not handle the notion of abandonment and being alone, found the woman with whom he would spend the rest of his life. While the band played a gig at the Comic Book Club, Gary introduced him to a pretty, shy, and very hip regular patron of the club, twenty-one-year-old Judy Seymour, who with her friends Mary Hayworth and Dean Kilpatrick—the latter a lanky, shag-haired starving artist who wore long capes and seemed the paragon of cool—shared a house in the Riverside section down the block from the Green House, where several members of the Allman Brothers Band lived. As a goof, the trio called theirs the Gray House.

What made Judy so endearing to Ronnie was that she had little awe for the most popular rockers in town, all of whom she seemed to know by their first names. She certainly didn't throw herself at him groupie-style—not that Lynyrd Skynyrd, or whatever they were calling themselves on any given day, had risen into the category of groupie "gets." But in Ronnie she perceived a conflicted man suffering under the weight of torturous moral dilemmas and unresolved issues every way he turned, including issues of the flesh and with Lacy. Unlike most young rockers, he didn't seem to live for the fringe benefits of his trade and actually had a rather bluenosed opinion abut the parade of young women who would willingly become notches on rockers' bedposts.

The conflict here was that not even he could resist a pretty, willing thing for very long. Indeed, few women were ever turned away from a hotel room by the God-fearin' but self-destructive men of Lynyrd Skynyrd. As if creating a guilt-relieving outlet for themselves, they sang of the Lord, and nearly all would find women they felt compelled to marry in the early years of the band, not that any of these women had any delusions about their monogamy. Such double standards were baked into the loam of rock and roll, not to mention the ethos of Southern Men, etched as it was with misogyny. Judy Seymour certainly understood the rules but could rationalize that Ronnie really did need her to make his life complete. That he had a hard time verbalizing concepts like love seemed to be an indicator of the vulnerable hole in his soul. Thus, when they began dating—and in no time they were inseparable—she accepted that he could himself make the same case that Gregg Allman did in song: "I'm no angel." Ronnie's own songs testified to that, and if Judy had to live with that, so be it.

They soon were shacking up at the Cedar Shores Apartments on Blanding Boulevard near the Ortega Farms section of the west side. The familial nature of the extended, growing Skynyrd brood was such that Dean Kilpatrick now was acting as the band's roadie, lugging instruments and amps onto rented pickup trucks. Soon Dean and his girlfriend Bonnie moved in too. Implicitly, it was understood that Ronnie and Judy would marry, but his haste with Nadine led him to take the necessary precautions to avoid another accidental child and to put off any nuptials until he had the bread to properly take care of a family, while still providing for his first child. Maybe Lacy *could* be proud of him after all. Maybe he *had* learned how to be a man.

* * *

Gene Odom's recollection that the first time Lynyrd Skynyrd performed "Free Bird" in a public setting was the May 9, 1970, reception following the wedding of Allen Collins and Kathy Johns is incorrect; the wedding was actually on October 10, apparently another shotgun wedding, as Kathy had become pregnant with the first of their two daughters, Amie and Allison. According to Skynyrd lore, much of which is urban myth, Kathy's parents didn't like men with long hair, so to placate them the band wore short-haired wigs of the kind they had worn for Leonard Skinner back in high school. If this almost certainly apocryphal story is anywhere near true, it would have meant that Allen Collins's parents-in-law had never seen him and didn't know what he did for a living.

But had Skynyrd actually gotten up after the nuptials and played "Free Bird" for the first of around ten thousand times in comical wigs, the improbable scenario would have made for some sight indeed—though, granted, they were just warped enough to have gotten a kick out of doing something like that. Since the song grew from the now famous question Kathy asked Allen, which became the song's opening line, it was logical to play the song, and they did so with relish. It was also a marker indented in time: when Ronnie Van Zant sang "Lord help me, I can't change. . . . Won't you fly, free bird" that day, he was putting rock on notice about his defiant determination to shape southern rock in a way no one would be able to change.

As if on cue, the band got a break shortly thereafter. David Griffin had taken over Skynyrd's bookings around the Southeast, and he put on a "battle of the bands" show at the Jacksonville Beach Coliseum. This was only a year after Phil Walden had created Capricorn Records as a gold mine for southern rock and hit the mother lode by signing the Allman Brothers. The Allmans, who dressed like cattle rustlers but played the blues like nobody else in rock, had already built a cult following through their sold-out shows at the Fillmore East in Greenwich Village. The cream was their albums, from which came amazing songs like "Whipping Post," "Dreams," and "Midnight Rider," mating Duane Allman's slide guitar and Gregg Allman's growling, soulful keyboard blues licks with blaring horns, vibraphone riffs, and a rumbling rhythm bottom.

Now, the rush was on to get in the door at Phil Walden's Capricorn Records; in an astonishing turn, Macon, the town that had spawned so many soul legends, was becoming the emerging capital of a new generation of white southern music. In 1971 Walden signed a lucrative distribution deal with Warner Brothers, which became the Allman Brothers' ticket to ride all around the rock map. When the show in Jacksonville came around, one of the attendees was there at the behest of Alan Walden, who had left Capricorn in 1970 in an attempt to ape his brother's success, starting a publishing and management firm of his own, unfortunately named Hustlers Inc. Seeking acts outside his brother's long shadow, he scoured shows like these for redneck rockers, and his liege, a guy named Pat Armstrong, invited three acts—Skynyrd, Black Bear Angel, and Mynd Garden—to audition. Armstrong sent word to Walden that Skynyrd was the real item. He had heard, he said, 187 bands, and they were the first he thought had Allman-like potential.

Alan invited them to play for him next and wasted no time in signing on to manage them and book them through Premier.

"I heard them play 'Free Bird,' and I knew from that one song that they were on to something," Walden said, in retrospect an understatement of prodigious dimensions.

Believing he had seen and heard the future of rock, Alan Walden signed them to a contract that gave him 30 percent of all earnings they would make if signed by a record company—double the normal manager's fee (not counting Tom Parker's notorious 50 percent cut of Elvis's income). Walden also would own every cent of publishing royalties, under the name of Duchess Music, the same headlock that had applied to the band at Shade Tree. To Skynyrd, it was nothing that seemed very important. A photo of the band signing the contract shows them with Walden; his partners, Armstrong and Gary Donehoo; and the great Stax soul singer Eddie Floyd of "Knock On Wood" renown, who was also managed by Walden. The smiles were broad. To accomplish this, Walden had to convince Tom Markham and Jim Sutton to release them from their contract, which had two years left to run. The two men, who had all but given up on Skynyrd, had no objections to letting them out, though Shade Tree would still own the publishing rights on any royalties that technically belonged to Double "T," which would one day ring up more than a few shekels for them. Now, clearing their shelves of Skynyrd product, they put out a last two-sided single, "I've Been Your Fool"/"Gotta Go," a combination of titles that seemed a fair summation of both sides' feelings at that moment.

Given how much Alan Walden, if not the band, stood to make—and the fact that, on his own, Walden himself was now about broke—his first order of business was to get them recorded, properly. Wasting no time doing so, he used his connections and a fat wad of cash to schedule a session for Skynyrd, not at the renowned FAME studio in the otherwise obscure northwest Alabama town of Muscle Shoals but rather at the newer jewel of Southern studios, Muscle Shoals Sound Studios, which had been created in 1969 by the rhythm section of the illustrious house band at FAME that Leon Russell had dubbed the Swampers—guitarist Jimmy Johnson, bassist David Hood, keyboardist Barry Beckett, and drummer Roger Hawkins.

The new place was not actually in Muscle Shoals but two miles to the north, on Jackson Avenue in Sheffield (and would be relocated a decade later to larger digs on Alabama Avenue), but no one at FAME begrudged the quartet the use of the brand name they had helped establish. The session, scheduled for early 1970, would be produced by Johnson, who was sent a demo tape of Skynyrd songs and was intrigued by them. It would be his job, he understood, to make the band sound so good that Walden could use the tapes to land a big-time deal from a record company far more important than even his brother's.

Ronnie and his men had no regrets. They anticipated that the Muscle Shoals sessions would surely be a windfall. After all, it wasn't every day, or just any old band, that could walk in the footsteps of the first clients at the new studio: Cher, Boz Scaggs, Herbie Mann, and the Rolling Stones, who in December 1969 cut "Brown Sugar" and "Wild Horses" in the space about to be occupied by the boys of Shantytown. To be able to rig this, they figured, Alan Walden was more than a manager; he was a freakin' titan.

* * *

Alex Hodges, today one of the most powerful men in the entertainment business as CEO of Nederlander Concerts, a massive, worldwide chain of theaters and music venues, and a Georgia Rock and Roll Hall of Famer, has a lot less hair—actually, he has not one follicle of it—and a lot more girth than he did back then when, at not yet thirty, he was assisting both Walden brothers at the Paragon Agency. He has rarely been interviewed, by his own choice, but even through the passage of time and out of all the rock royalty that he has managed, such as the Allman Brothers and the Police, two faces haunt him the most.

"There are people who you just never forget—you see them in your head all the time. Ronnie was one of those. Otis Redding was like that. When I first met Ronnie, he came into the room of our agency, and you were thrown back on your heels. It's not really a physical presence. Otis was a big, handsome, strapping man. Ronnie was a pudgy little fellow with thinning hair. But your eyes followed him around. He had that gut appeal. Soon as I saw him, I knew his band—and I didn't care who they were, even—was gonna do some serious damage. I didn't know how much damage they'd do to themselves, but you knew a band led by that guy was gonna push boundaries, break rules. He was troubled, you could tell, and maybe that was part of it. I mean, he was not a normal human being. You couldn't figure him out. And you couldn't wait for him to sing something so you might be able to try. That was the only way, 'cause Ronnie spoke through his music, the only way he felt comfortable doing it."

* * *

Ronnie had some important business to take care of before the trip to Muscle Shoals. The first was Larry Junstrom, who Ronnie suspected of something less than total commitment to the band—or not being enough of a bad boy—and was canned. Once "Stalin" had made up his mind about such things, there was no further discussion. Larry, who'd come a long way with the band, took it hard. "Can you believe it, man? They fired me. Skynyrd's fired me," he told a Lee High classmate. Junstrom was too good a bass player to go hungry for long. (He would later resurface as part of Donnie Van Zant's band .38 Special, which he still plays in.) And of course he would not be on that doomed plane flight. Junstrom was replaced by Greg T. Walker, who, when the offer came, quit his own band, Blackfoot—so named because all their members had some Native American heritage. But Walker, who is of Muscogee Creek descent, was mainly a placeholder for Leon Wilkeson, always Ronnie's first choice, who often was sidetracked for some reason or other.

Indeed, Ronnie had to vie with his brother Donnie for Leon's services. When Ronnie and Donnie's sister, Betty Jo Ann, married and moved to another neighborhood on the west side, her neighbors were the Wilkeson family. Leon, just fourteen then, was already an accomplished bass player; and when Betty Jo Ann told him that Donnie was starting a band, the Collegiates, Leon joined up with them first, before being persuaded by Ronnie to hang around as a sometime member of *his* band. But a problem arose when Leon's poor grades at Bishop Kenny High School led his parents to yank him from his bass and throw him into his studies. His presence with Skynyrd would be intermittent for the next two years, until he graduated, but even when he was part of the Hell House scene, he was apt to drop from sight, only to resurface drunk and incoherent. This of course put him in the line of fire of Ronnie's rules, but when Ronnie got in Leon's face, the latter often stalked out with a slurred "Fuck you." Rather than tear into him with his fists, Ronnie admired the kid's spunk and expected he would be back.

Next came a problem with Bob Burns, who had been a ticking time bomb for some time. When he was fifteen, his parents had moved to Orlando, allowing the tall, swarthy young man to remain in Jacksonville as he wished so he could continue playing drums with his band. Astonishingly, as Burns tells it, his mother and father simply let him fend for himself, apparently not caring enough to see to it that he had a place to live and could feed and clothe himself. Burns had dropped out of school in the eleventh grade, living the life of a nomad.

"I had no place to stay," he said. "I was crashing in people's bushes. I was crashing wherever I could. I hung on as long as I possibly could. I was borrowing clothes from the roadies to play shows with. I didn't even have any shoes, and it just got to me. Everybody was saying, 'Damn, man, what if [the band] don't make it, then what are you going to do? Your friends are driving Porches and 'Vettes, they're in college or making good money.' The rest of them were living with their parents or their parents were helping them out. I couldn't stay with any of them. Their parents didn't want me moving in with them. So I went to live with my folks in Orlando."

Ronnie, who had his own family baggage, was sympathetic. Rather than writing Burns off, he kept him on a leash, saying he would be welcomed back if he wanted to return. In the meantime, needing a drummer for the Muscle Shoals sessions, he reached out to another Blackfoot player whom he'd had his eye and ear on for some time, lead singer and guitarist Rickey Medlocke. Sioux by descent and son of blues banjo player Shorty Medlocke, who in the '50s had a local TV show in town, on which his son appeared, the Jacksonville native had been in New York City with Blackfoot, where the group's manager was quartered and demanded they make their base. It was the last place Medlocke wanted to be, having cut his teeth in Jacksonville bars. (Blackfoot had once been the house band at Dub's, a well-attended strip joint.)

When Ronnie called him, he asked if Medlocke would consider coming back home to play with Walker in Skynyrd—but could he play drums? Rickey hadn't done so in some time but was a brilliant musician, and homesick as he was, he promised he could step right in. After brushing up on the sticks, he arrived back in Jacksonville and was ready for Muscle Shoals, thus providing another much-needed benefit that Ronnie no doubt also had in mind: Medlocke was an accomplished songwriter, having composed much of Blackfoot's material. Skynyrd, needing good original songs from any source, could suddenly draw upon a catalog of them, most better than what they had come up with on their own.

There would be yet one more addition to the band that would pay off—Billy Powell, a wiry, affable guy who had been friends with Wilkeson since grade school. A navy brat born in Corpus Christi, Texas, and reared in Jacksonville, Powell had gone to Bishop Kenny High School then briefly studied music at Jacksonville Community College. He did a brief stint in a band called Alice Marr, in which a teenaged Donnie Van Zant sang. When Wilkeson moved deeper into the Skynyrd circle, he bugged Ronnie about hiring Powell, touting him as a superb boogie-woogie piano player, a rhythm element the band didn't believe it needed. Ronnie did hire Billy as a roadie for the time being, to help Dean Kilpatrick and another crony of the band, Kevin Elson, carry and set up equipment, and to keep a talented piano man within reach. Powell, who dug the band and wanted in, eagerly took the job, which paid exactly nothing. He too would go to Muscle Shoals and breathe in the ascent of a band he would soon be a major part of.

⋆ ⋆ ⋆

Alan Walden was more than a manager to Skynyrd; he was, for all the world, one of them. As if he could vicariously be the redneck he never was, he attached himself to the band by the hip, going to gigs with them, hanging out at Hell House, and calling band meetings that were more like pep talks. When they would break open a bottle of beer, whiskey, rye, whatever, he had his glass ready, even if he wasn't ever able to keep up with them. "I had drank with some of the best, with [soul singer] Johnnie Taylor, the best. But when I met Skynyrd, whew, I went under the table. Those guys could drink. Straight from the bottle—and they were still teens at the time."

He may have believed in Skynyrd, even loved them as manly southern men love each other, but when it came to financing them, he could offer them exactly nothing from his empty pockets. Skynyrd had to pay their own way to Muscle Shoals in the spring of 1971, and when they got there the only lodging they could afford was a fleabag truck stop called Blue's. So cash poor were they that they had to scrounge up empty soda bottles and cash them in for the five-cent deposits at convenience stores. Then came news that they wouldn't be recording at Muscle Shoals at all because more important acts had booked the studio. They would have to go down the road a few miles to the Broadway Sound Studio, owned by Quin Ivy, a former disc jockey and songwriter, who had benefited from the constant spillover of sessions from the FAME studio; it was here that Percy Sledge had recorded "When a Man Loves a Woman."

Ivy was affiliated with the Walden brothers as well as Atlantic Records. Rather than Jimmy Johnson, Ivy's in-house producer, David (another Johnson), would oversee the Skynyrd date. To Skynyrd, it was still a blessing, still Muscle Shoals. When the sessions began, David Johnson got them on eight tracks, which covered all the fresh material they had. By then Walden wanted to go further and cut an entire album, so more songs were needed. Jimmy Johnson, meanwhile, heard the rough tapes and wanted in. He and Walden agreed to produce a Skynyrd album at Muscle Shoals and cover the costs. If it bartered the band a record contract, Muscle Shoals would be reimbursed and become part of the Skynyrd arc as their home studio. Walden, of course, would own all the publishing rights to songs the band wrote.

Thus the possibility loomed that Muscle Shoals might be aligned with Alan Walden, and FAME with Phil Walden. Before accomplishing much of anything, it seemed Lynyrd Skynyrd was already at the center of a sibling rivalry—for now, only in Alan Walden's imagination—between two southern industry heavyweights. That of course only upped the pressure on the band to come up with some good material and blow the doors off the studio. The whole world was seemingly riding on these sessions when Skynyrd returned to Muscle Shoals early in 1972 after six months of intensive writing and rehearsing at Hell House. Looking back, Jimmy Johnson said that, after hearing their lead man sing live in the studio, "I totally fell in love with Ronnie Van Zant's fantastic voice," and that the now instinctively intermeshed guitar licks of Rossington and Collins were almost revelatory. "Gary and Allen," he said, "were doing solos that were twinned"—as if they were on separate tracks and mixed as perfect complements. Not that the other guys in the band didn't have their own vital roles, but to Johnson the sum and substance of Lynyrd Skynyrd was the skill and chemical interaction of its core; on the first day, he said, "I fell in love with those three guys."

* * *

Given this skew, it was almost insignificant that the band once again changed faces. During the follow-up sessions, Bob Burns came back for the time being. "I decided after I left that I would rather have nothing, no shoes or nothing, rather than not be in the band. I knew I had given up my dreams, my hopes, my everything. The first prayer I ever had in my entire life, I looked up at the sky, and I said, 'If there's a God there, I'm sorry if I've done wrong, but I want back in that band, it's just not working for me out here.' The next night, Gary called me up and said, 'Man, you want to play in this band or not?' I said, 'Yeah,' and he said, 'Be here about as fast as you can get here.' I left that night, hopped into my Corvair and went back to Jacksonville fast as I could get there."

Still having no place to stay, Burns made Hell House his home, sleeping there in a place so hot that, he says, "you could fry an egg there." As for food, "if I didn't catch fish," he says, "I didn't eat."

Leon Wilkeson, his schoolwork done, was also in tow, having been allowed by his parents to accept the long-standing invitation he had to be the permanent Skynyrd bass player. This meant that Greg T. Walker was excused, but Rickey Medlocke was too important to let go, having provided the bulk of the new stuff the band took to Muscle Shoals. He went back with them as a third guitarist, but more centrally, to take the lead vocals on his songs, which only he knew well enough to sing.

As Gary remembered it, from the band's standpoint, especially among those who suffered indignity at home, the experience was something like gaining an instant family. "They adopted us, took us in," he said. Although Rossington likely gilded the lily a tad later, saying that the tutorial they received from the Muscle Shoals producers was so revelatory to them that it was the first time they realized the bass and drum had to play in complementary tandem; when Johnson or his coproducer Tim Smith called out the downbeat—the "one, two, one-two-three" cue to start playing—as the tempo of the song, only then did they understand that was how it was done. Studio drummer Roger Hawkins worked with Bob Burns for *twelve* hours tuning his drum correctly. Johnson and Smith also imparted a critical method for accentuating Ronnie's vocals—having the band play in a lower key than the one in which he sang so that his voice would sound higher and harsher, something like his idol Paul Rodgers.

Like Peck's bad boys, they clambered in and proceeded to act like, well, themselves. David Hood recalls that "they'd have fistfights, actual fistfights. Someone was supposed to [play] a G-chord instead of an A-chord and boom, a fist would fly. That's how they settled their disagreements, they just fought." Those spats continued as if they *needed* such contretemps to clear the air and get themselves into the Skynyrd frame of mind. Cigarette butts littered the studio floor. But when Johnson called a take, mouths quieted, and heads snapped to attention. The singing and playing were sharp. There were limited retakes. Some wonderful counterpoint acoustic lines emerged among the electric guitar madness, with just the right echo and reverb. The sessions went smoothly and rapidly, and a few Muscle Shoals sidemen came in to play with the band, buffing and adding nuance to the scorched-earth quality of the Skynyrd sound. With the previous eight songs in the can from Quinvy (the Broadway studio), the band cut nine more, almost as if in a blur, by Johnson's reckoning; years later he seemed to think almost all of them went on for around nine minutes, including the second studio version of "Free Bird" and that "one thing I would not do was edit them." Here his memory is clouded a bit; the still-evolving "Free Bird" on these tapes ran seven minutes and twenty-six seconds, still long but still far shorter than the later versions, a couple of which went over *eleven* minutes. Eight of the seventeen tracks did run longer than five minutes—"One More Time," "Was I Right Or Wrong," "Simple Man," "Comin' Home," "Things Goin' On," "You Run Around," "Ain't Too Proud to Pray," and "Free Bird." As with "Free Bird," the tracks for "Simple Man" and "Things Goin' On," and an early version of "Gimme Three Steps," are historical curiosities, all instantly recognizable but obviously works in progress at the time, destined to see better days ahead.

The songs that all agreed were the best and that would go on a possible album of the sessions, were three Van Zant–Rossington songs—"Down South Jukin,'" "Was I Right or Wrong," and "Things Goin' On"—as well as the Van Zant–Collins composition "Comin' Home" and the Van Zant–Rossington–Collins original "Lend a Helpin' Hand." Three Medlocke songs made the cut—"White Dove" and "The Seasons," essentially poems turned into redneck rock, and "Wino," cowritten with Ronnie and Allen. For these, Ronnie willingly stood aside and allowed Rickey to handle the leads in his high falsetto, the only time any Skynyrd songs would be fronted by anyone other than its regular lead singer for the next five years. And Medlocke added an even dreamier tone to "Free Bird" with a soprano backing vocal, a role almost never again taken by a band member.

★ ★ ★

Amazingly, "Free Bird," which nearly everyone who has ever heard it says knocked them out, was *not* deemed worthy of the final cut. If there was one song judged to be a potential single, it seemed to be "Was I Right or Wrong," a tale of deep-seated angst producing high art—the narrative told of a young rocker living out his dreams and then returning home to find his parents dead, no doubt a nightmare that had jarred Ronnie awake more than once. Little wonder that the song, with Ronnie yearning to be a "restless leaf in the autumn breeze" and a "tumblin' weed," caused the rock critic Dave Marsh to opine years later that it was "hard to believe the song is only a fantasy."

But with Skynyrd, such breezes always led back home. As "Comin' Home" made clear, the long road just might be too long and full of "broken dreams and dirty deals." There were also the night-trolling comforts of "Down South Jukin'," the objective of which was to head to town trying to "pick up any woman hanging around," which would have to suffice as peace of mind. There was, too, a cautionary note in "Wino," which warned: "Wino, you wasn't born to lose. Sweet wine is making you a fool." Not content with presenting a catalog of redneck ups and downs, Ronnie took another stab at a message song. "Things Goin' On," with its honky-tonk vibe, took aim at an easy target, big government, for "too many lives" spent "across the ocean" and too many dollars spent "upon the moon." "They're gonna ruin the air we breathe," he seethes, ending on a massively ironic note, coming from a rock band: "I don't think they really care / I think they just sit up there and just get high."

Johnson was quite sure the songs chosen were valuable record label bait. Alan Walden, further leaning on the reputation of the highly respected Swampers, taking the approach that a hard sell wasn't necessary, went to L.A. with the mild-mannered Johnson and made the rounds of the big record company headquarters. Wincing still, Walden tells it this way: "Nine record companies had turned us down! I don't mean, 'We like you but you need better material.' I mean 'Not interested! No need to contact us again.' Atlantic, Columbia, Warners, A&M,

RCA, Epic, Elektra, Polydor . . . they all passed after hearing 'Free Bird,' 'Gimme Three Steps,' 'Simple Man,' 'I Ain't the One,' and about twelve other originals. Their comments were: 'They sound too much like the Allman Brothers!'

"Now, I ask you—put them on back to back and tell me they sound alike? We all came from the South, played hard, had long hair, drank and chased women. But we did not sound alike! The Allmans had their jazz influences, and we were a straight-ahead juking band! I remember one executive telling me to turn that noise off while I was playing him 'Free Bird.'" Says Johnson: "It hurt because the stuff was fantastic." When word got back to the band, recalls Rossington, "We were all angry, freaked out, thinking we didn't know what we were doing. Because those were the best songs we could write."

Out of frustration, they even took to blaming Muscle Shoals. As the house bass man David Hood recalls, during the trip out west, "somehow the tapes had gotten twisted up on the reel so when they'd play it, they'd be playing the wrong side of the tape, and it would be all muffled. So Skynyrd thought that Jimmy had done something to sabotage them. They were a little mad at us—at Jimmy, really—and we all felt real bad about it. Later on, they found out about the technical glitch, and they made up with Jimmy." To make good, Ronnie swore he'd make those Swampers famous by getting their name into a song. Hood laughed. Yeah, like *that* would ever happen.

5

★ ★ ★ ★ ★

DOWN SOUTH JUKIN'

In truth, beneath the anger was a hard reality: the Muscle Shoals tapes were definitively *not* the best songs the band could write, nor even the best they could record them, as would be made clear down the road when a chosen few, recorded more competently, would become hit fodder. It wasn't Johnson's fault. His role was not really to alter anything they did, just to get them on tape in a technically professional manner. The band simply wasn't yet good enough to get by on raw talent alone. They needed time to hone their sound and understand *how* to present this hybrid creature—rock with a country smirk and attitude but not necessarily a belch. To get to that point, they needed clever arranging and production under a sort of guru whose word was law, even for Ronnie.

As for the tapes, nine of the tracks, some of them having been embellished with additional guitar parts for potential release after the band exploded in popularity, would eventually appear on the posthumous 1978 *Skynyrd's First and . . . Last* album; a 1998 rerelease, retitled *Skynyrd's First*, carried all seventeen tracks, including "Free Bird" (despite its not being ready for prime time), "Gimme Three Steps," and "Simple Man." Amazingly, after the plane crash the thirst for any "lost" Skynyrd product was such that even these tracks were reviewed on the same level as their biggest albums.

The *Village Voice* music critic Robert Christgau's verdict upon the album's release was that "I expect more from Skynyrd than good white funk and second-rate message songs"—never mind that the songs had not been released for these very reasons. Some latter-day critics would have a fairer perspective. Stephen Thomas Erlewine of the website All-Music.com, conceding that their value was mainly as curios, nonetheless believed that "it's possible to hear Ronnie Van Zant coming into his own as a writer" on the early efforts.

* * *

The "white funk" of Lynyrd Skynyrd almost never came to the attention of the record-buying public. Though they may have positioned themselves as free birds, they were still strange birds in the overall rock milieu. At times they seemed painfully true to their image; perhaps a little too eager to play the redneck role, Ronnie would come out for gigs in his bare feet or in flip-flops, his eyes increasingly glazed by "poison whiskey." Still, it is of note that not a single Confederate flag was anywhere in sight—an important detail to keep in mind, as their original instinct was that the most egregious (yet for many the most prideful) symbol of the South seemed way too tasteless. If their native turf and themes of "down south jukin'" and simple men wistfully seeking flights of freedom but coming home to their kin and women weren't enough to pinpoint them as trailer-park friendly, emblazoning their venues with that symbol of human bondage—leaving aside labored alibis insisting it was about *heritage*—would be as subtle as a kick in the nuts, something they only wanted to accomplish through their music, not pedantry.

However, something had to give. With nothing earned by way of royalties or advances, the starving, Bohemian life of nomadic rockers getting nowhere was a dead-end street shared by many acts. For Ronnie, the thought of Lacy telling him "I told you so" was depressing enough, but having to keep working irregularly at menial jobs magnified the indignity. While he still went in every once in a while to the auto parts store, Gary and Allen actually had to take jobs at Clark's meat-rendering plant, their hair tucked under hairnets similar to what the ladies in the Lee High cafeteria wore. Rickey Medlocke grew so frustrated that, with his role becoming less defined, he decided to re-form Blackfoot, which he relocated to Jacksonville and would keep together until the 1990s, when the past would again beckon.

No one needed to remind Skynyrd that they were falling further behind in the southern rock derby. In 1972 Phil Walden signed the Toy

Factory—now renamed the Marshall Tucker Band, after a blind piano tuner the bandmates knew. So popular were their first two albums that their third was a double LP: one record of studio cuts, the other of live shows. All six of their Capricorn albums went gold, even though they wouldn't have a Top 20 hit until "Heard It In a Love Song" on the fifth album. This was certainly proof that the era of single hits as the overriding priority was over, opening a new market that Skynyrd would seek to exploit as well. Another band, Pure Prairie League, formed in Ohio in 1969 by Craig Fuller, had both critical and commercial success with five straight Top 40 albums.

Although the Muscle Shoals tapes did not click with the record companies that heard them, at some point the band may or may not have been offered a contract with Capricorn Records. A story, perhaps apocryphal, has been told that such an offer was in fact proffered but that Ronnie vetoed it because he didn't want to put his band in the shadow of the Allman Brothers. But this is not how Charlie Brusco remembers it. "Alan tried but couldn't convince his brother to sign them. Alan Walden was not Phil Walden. He was the kid brother. And Phil wasn't about to bail him out. It was a very difficult thing to get them signed. They weren't really a country-rock act—they were a three-guitar rock band in the country fold, and there just wasn't anything like that around. Phil never considered signing them, a decision I'm sure Phil came to regret."

Around the industry, it was taken for granted that Alan had no desire to run up against Phil; most of those who knew them both believed the kid brother was physically afraid of the bigger, elder brother, whose volatility and impetuosity were ironically much like Ronnie Van Zant's and who got himself into the same trouble with drugs, which would later cost him his music empire. In any case, Alan Walden says he never actually *asked* his brother to sign the group, and the point became moot one night when Skynyrd played the Grand Slam club in Macon. Not only were the Allman Brothers there that evening to watch them, but so was Phil. After the set, said Alan Walden, "I walk up to Phil, start talking to him. Well, he's arrogant as hell, acting like he's the shit. He says, 'Your lead singer's too goddamn cocky, he can't sing, the songs are weak, and they sound too much like the Allman Brothers.'"

In Alan's story, Phil made this critique (which was the same as that of the record companies that had rejected them) loudly so that Ronnie, lurking nearby, could hear it. But he couldn't quite. When Phil exited, Ronnie sat down next to Alan.

"What'd he say?" Ronnie asked.

"Nothing important," Alan lied, sparing him. "Let's go have a drink."

Putting a period on the story, Walden says, "And we went and had a drink—a whole bottle, actually. J&B Scotch."

Nothing more was ever said about Capricorn Records. But the hurt inside Alan Walden only grew deeper and more scathing.

Alex Hodges, who was the closest person to Walden, says, "Alan was so hurt by Phil that I don't even know if they ever spoke to each other after that. Alan felt that Phil had insulted him and he was pissed off. I remember Phil called me around that time and said, 'Alan won't speak to me.' And the fact is, it was Phil who had encouraged Alan to sign Skynyrd. Phil told me that if Alan didn't want to manage them, that I should. He said, 'Go talk to Alan about it.' And I had lunch with Alan to talk about it, and that's when he made the decision he would sign them. But when Phil rejected them, it blew a hole between them. And it became an obsession for Alan to get them a record deal, just to show Phil. Alan has spent half his life trying to get out from under the shadow of the great Phil Walden, and Alan has mishandled that, because he exaggerates so much. It's always 'I was the guy, I was the guy.' But there were a lot of guys who had a part in Skynyrd. I have never blown my horn, but I was right there every step of the way with them for the first five years."

Indeed, Alan Walden was no Phil Walden. But even though he was right about Lynyrd Skynyrd, and Phil wrong, he would have scant time to rub it in. And it might not have been Alan Walden but Fate who played the biggest role.

* * *

It seems unimaginable today that no record company was interested in Skynyrd. Charlie Brusco, for whom Alan Walden played the shelved Skynyrd tapes, was stunned by how good the band with the funny name sounded. "The guitars were just on fire," Brusco recalls. "It really was something that grabbed you by the ears and the balls." Yet it was that very metal overkill that easily explained the industry aloofness. Brusco indeed had the same barrier to scale with the Outlaws, charting new territory in the country-rock genre that was just too over the top as defined by the Allman Brothers' formula of not-too-heavy-duty rock.

Skynyrd, however, was close enough to the Allman Brothers' style and substance to ride on their coattails. It helped that the Brothers' roadhouse boogie blues cover of "One Way Out," the old Elmore James blues standard originally recorded by Sonny Boy Williamson, featured a transcendent bottleneck slide guitar line by Duane Allman and could provide some cover for their harder electric country-rock emphasis. There simply has never been a better slide guitarist than Duane Allman. Eric Clapton knew it too. He had been dabbling in country-rock sounds, touring with southern singers Delaney and Bonnie, and in 1970 when he came to Florida to record in Miami's Criteria Studios, he hired Allman to play the soaring, searing slide guitar lines of the pomp-rock opus "Layla."

Duane Allman would become a rock martyr when on October 29, 1971, the Harley-Davidson he was riding through Macon smashed into a flatbed truck. He was thrown from the bike, which then landed on him, pinning him and crushing him to death at age twenty-four. Amplifying the tragedy, just over a year later Allman bassist Berry Oakley crashed *his* motorcycle, only three blocks from where Duane had finished his final ride, and died as well. The Allmans carried on, with Dickey Betts taking Duane's place, providing the electrified blues guitar; two brilliant Betts compositions in 1973, the country/pop/rock monster crossover hit "Ramblin' Man" and the rollicking seven-minute instrumental "Jessica," among the greatest country-rock grooves ever written and played, created an almost visual sonic field. This assured the band's unbroken dominance—though this enormous success soon sowed the seeds of their destruction. Drummer Butch Trucks later said the band "got away from the music" with "country-fried hit records," creating egos that "ripped [them] all apart."

* * *

This aspect of fame, with booze and drug excess—one imitated by Skynyrd all too well—wrote an end to the Allmans' heyday, which would essentially be over by 1975, though their reunion tours would become endless. Still, their footprint was so large that FM stations had no compunction playing in full their live-album jams, which stretched as long as twenty-three minutes. Had they not broken radio's time barriers, a song like "Free Bird" never would have been written in the form it was. By that time southern songwriters had become the modern southern literati, and in their pens lay the definitions of a new reconstruction of the South and southern manhood. The classic stereotypes had taken a beating through the twentieth century, but certain instincts were inbred, such as a courtly kind of regional and sexual chauvinism in which southern women, as one historian notes, were "put firmly on the pedestal of an impossible purity."

If the songwriters' aim was to "recoup white male power, even as they admit[ted] that their terms of that power [could] never be the same," as southern historian Caroline Gebhard postulated in an essay in Anne Goodwyn Jones and Susan V. Donaldson's essential 1998 cultural analysis of the region, *Haunted Bodies: Gender and Southern Texts*, the new crop of native southern rock and rollers had to walk a fine line between racial rehabilitation and racial reversion, a very risky theme for any band. To Bartow J. Elmore, a noted history professor at University of Alabama, the southern rock idiom was "essentially reactionary," a bastion of "unquestioning traditionalism." To yet another, Ted Ownby, author of "Freedom, Manhood, and White Male Tradition in 1970s Southern Rock Music," it was "upholding traditions while they were at the same time, as young rock musicians, rebelling against authority" and thus espousing a sort of closeted liberalism. Still other commentators anointed southern rockers as the first role models of the region who were not evil or buffoons, providing young southerners with a new way of healing from the scars of their ancestry.

For Lynyrd Skynyrd and their cohorts, such arguments were nearly irrelevant. To them, they merely sang of bonding, extreme loyalty to God and family, and the land, and of being men who admitted to needing "all my friends" one day and nobody the next. The bad boys of Skynyrd had good cause to cast their own image in an Allman-like molding. Even so, major deviations in style and substance distinguished the two bands. Van Zant's writing was far more personally rooted in real-life yearning, pride, fear, and insecurity, and would grow even more so, a clear sign that none of his alienation ever eased. If he was after solace, all he could find was in his writing and singing about what he saw through the windows of his life, but he never really flew free like the bird he longed to be.

Needing to seem like a smart-ass whiskey-bar singer more than a blues singer, he wanted to sound as if he had just picked up the microphone after a stiff belt of liquid courage and a drag on an unfiltered cigarette. Mission accomplished, he decided that background vocals would not be sung by any band members, not just because they weren't polished singers or because as front man he wanted the spotlight all to himself—though that certainly was the case—but because the intricate guitar lines played by Gary and Allen might be disrupted if they had to remember lyrics and sing them into microphones. Thus most of their songs would be written without harmony parts—another departure from most every band of the day and, specifically, the Allman Brothers—and on those that benefited from a backup vocal, Leon would handle that well enough.

The anomaly of "Free Bird" aside—and the irony, given its influence on FM radio—Skynyrd was more attuned to cutting discrete hard-rock songs that were bar blues based and country themed and lasted three to four minutes, making their point and getting on to the next song, rather than letting a set flow into one big, interwoven jam session. Ronnie's thinking was that the Allman Brothers had done that, and only a band of fools would try to beat them on their own turf. His credo would be: Let's don't overstay our welcome. To Ronnie, it was all from the heart, the gut. The rules mattered only in how far they bent. After all, this whole thing was, as Paul Rodgers sang, a "rock 'n' roll fantasy."

"Ronnie Van Zant and those guys, they were totally independent from all the bullshit record-industry nonsense," recalls Alan Walden. "Ronnie was a leader—he wasn't no follower. Other bands I'd auditioned had misconceptions about how to act. They'd follow the magazine stories to try to figure out what to say and do to be successful. Not Ronnie. He was totally down to earth."

By the time the Allman Brothers Band self-obliterated, the band from Shantytown would be there to pick up the fallen torch of the New South.

* * *

The problem for Skynyrd was remaining on the upward path before they burned out. As it was, they were building a following in the Deep South, the absence of a record-label contract notwithstanding. With the next big break ostensibly waiting around each new corner, the grind went on through three years of, as Gary Rossington puts it, "just starvin' and payin' dues and stuff." It could be rough out there in the sticks. Rossington tells of the time at a nightclub when, from the stage, he witnessed "a guy getting his head blown off" in a typical sort of altercation, the reason unknown but probably a woman. It all went with the ambience of their existence, that of seamlessly stitched wasted days and wasted nights.

Walden, who kept reassuring them they would get their break sometime, could only pray he was right. As he recalled, "I had one hundred dollars in my pocket" at the time, and "I had encountered problems with some of the other partners and was looking at starting all over again. I got about thirty miles out of Muscle Shoals one day when the old Cadillac broke down with a bad fuel pump. The wrecker service left me out there waiting until after 5 PM so he could charge more. There went all but ten dollars. Add $90,000 that I was in debt back home, and you might understand how bad it was. I walked out into a cotton patch, shaking my fist at the sky, shouting, 'I am going to make Lynyrd Skynyrd happen even if it kills me!' It was my solemn oath."

Ronnie, who in the past wouldn't have given a hang about borrowing money, felt guilty as hell that he had to keep asking Judy to loan him enough to get to a gig. She had to take a job as a waitress, which was another thing he felt guilty about and probably one reason why he decided that, even if he had nothing in his pockets, it was time to marry Judy, lest he lose her. They took their vows on November 18, 1972, in Waycross, Georgia, her hometown, during another tour of the Atlanta clubs in which Skynyrd opened for Bob Seger's band on a few nights at the Head Rest club. When they got home, the newlyweds moved into an upstairs apartment in the Boone Park section of Riverside, at least symbolically far from Shantytown and metaphorically a million miles from Lacy Van Zant.

For some time, Ronnie's catchphrase had been to tell people that he had no doubt the band would make it—one day soon, they'd have it "made in the shade," he'd say, to the point where people rolled their eyes. He even wrote a song with that as the title. But where was the shade?

* * *

One little sliver of success came late in 1972 when they landed a critical gig opening for the Allman Brothers on some shows in Macon, the first time that the similarities and differences between the two bands could be gauged. Not that the Allmans had any particular reason to separate

Skynyrd from the buffet of southern rock bands Phil Walden hired as his meal ticket's opening acts—most of whom Walden managed and had given contracts with Capricorn Records, thereby goosing sales for them and profits for himself. Skynyrd of course was not on his roster, but the link with his brother gave the band a few advantages. And when they were allowed to play in front of the Allmans, they continued making their bones. Van Zant's gritty vocals and the stampede of guitars made for a very difficult act to follow, especially for a blues-rock band that didn't punch listeners in the face but instead wove trance-like spells with long, free-form jams. Skynyrd even had their own soundman traveling with them, mixing their sound to specification on the board. Record deal or no, they were making perfectionism a rule of what seemed like a no-rules, anything-goes act.

Seeing the fuss Skynyrd was causing, the Allmans started keeping their distance, perhaps afraid that the much more aggressive southern band might eclipse them someday on their home turf. Indeed, Gregg Allman rarely had anything nice to say about them and, even decades later, still seemed to be looking down his nose at them. In his 2012 memoir, he mentioned Skynyrd exactly once, in an oh-by-the-way fashion, with ambivalence and perhaps arrogance. "In 1972," he wrote, "we had a lot of Capricorn bands that Phil had brought to Macon opening for us—Eric Quincy Tate, Wet Willie, Dr. John, Alex Taylor, Captain Beyond, and Cowboy—and it was a very good thing for everybody. There ain't but one Allman Brothers, and there ain't but one Marshall Tucker. There ain't but one of any of those bands, so we weren't worried about them stealing our thunder or whatever." Interestingly, giving them credit for success they hadn't had at that point, he added, "I would imagine that Lynyrd Skynyrd had more hits than anybody else, but they sure ended up appealing to a real redneck bunch of folks."

Ronnie felt the sting of this condescension. Cameron Crowe—now a movie director, but then a wunderkind reporter for *Rolling Stone*—was privy to some of Van Zant's unguarded thoughts on the band's bus rides during long tours. Ronnie, he says, "didn't feel like Gregg was giving him too much back in terms of respect or acknowledgment. It wasn't a rift or anything, but I know Ronnie sort of wanted his props from Gregg, more than he was getting. . . . [He'd ask], 'Did you talk to Gregg? Did Gregg say anything?'" The irony was that by dissing the "redneck" audience they may have made Skynyrd more appealing to that crowd, establishing a building block to the latter's growing momentum. Gregg Allman's arrogance was duly noted by Ronnie and his band, generating a good deal of motivation for wanting to surpass the great godhead of the Allman Brothers.

Gregg, who still tours with the Brothers (or, like Skynyrd, a reasonable facsimile), can take pride in his unlikely longevity—after a lifetime of drugs and booze and having contracted hepatitis, apparently from dirty needles, he required a liver transplant in 2010 at age sixty-three. Yet even four decades later, he is no more generous to those southern rockers who followed in his path. "[T]here was some competition between bands—there has to be," he wrote. "But we weren't out there to sell southern rock, we were out there because we had the best goddamn band in the land. The Allman Brothers has had its bad nights, but we are some Super Bowl motherfuckers compared to all them other bands."

Allman may be a victim of his own hubris, but he did have a point when he noted that the term "southern rock" was so amorphous as to be meaningless, given how different the bands all were in terms of musical style and sound. Unlike most rock-and-roll idioms, country rock was splintered *before* it hit its apogee. And that left a door wide open to any band with a fresh approach to get through it. Skynyrd made the most of its opportunity. Their concert appearances were like Fourth of July parties, with half-naked crowds baking in the southern heat and getting off on the sonic fireworks on stage as Ronnie, affixed in place and never breaking character with any awkward dance steps or patter for the audience, stood nonetheless as a transfixing presence, spilling southern populist soul into the microphone amid the concretion of screaming guitars and pounding drums melting the air. The Allmans were no match for them in sizzle factor, no doubt a factor in the Brothers deeming that it would be better if Skynyrd didn't open for them anymore.

Skynyrd's time was nearing, even if the industry—even if *they*—didn't know it.

★ ★ ★

Fate was a stronger force than all of Alan Walden's designs and connections. For no reason other than pure chance, the man who would help bring Lynyrd Skynyrd to fruition crossed their path in mid-January

1973, during the same swing through southern Georgia on which Ronnie married Judy. That man, born Alan Peter Kuperschmidt but better known as Al Kooper, was in Atlanta at the same time that Skynyrd was playing in a club on Peachtree Street called Funochio's, a dim, suffocating cavern with a sign on it reading ATLANTA'S ORIGINAL HOUSE OF ROCK. There was almost no room between performers and audience, some of whom would sit on the foot of the stage during sets. As bands played, the crowds would dance as if on top of one another, and if there was a capacity limit or fire code, the owners seemed not to care.

Alan Walden, knowing pretty much all the dive bars in southern Georgia, calls Funochio's a "hell hole, a real fruit and nut bar. The booze was good, the women were wild and we stayed until I thought I would die there." On one Skynyrd date there, Ronnie's grandmother died, and he didn't want to sing. He and Walden went to see the manager of the bar, who was unmoved by their request to cancel the show. "The old bitch is dead, and you go on!" was his answer. It took all the self-control Ronnie had not to separate the guy from his spleen. He went onto the stage, burning hot under the collar. Then after the band played its finale—"Free Bird," as always—he snapped. Says Walden: "Ronnie started throwing amps onto the dance floor, smashing chairs, and breaking bottles. He totally wrecked the joint! People were screaming and running, cops rushing in. I reached him just as the cop was about to bust him with a billy club. I screamed, 'His grandmother died! Don't hurt him!'"

The cops just wanted to get Ronnie out before he could level the joint. "We got him outside," Walden says, "only to find out I had to go back and collect the money for the week." Seeing how crazed Van Zant could get, the manager paid up. What's more, Skynyrd had been so good that night, they kept on getting asked back. Kooper, an archetypal New York industry big shot, who had a list of music industry credits as long as his arm, frequented many such clubs. After visiting Funochio's for the first time, he regarded it as a "bucket o' blood," where "shootings and stabbings regularly took place, and bodies were routinely carried out"—in other words, the very sort of place where one might find some fairly cool music being played. Not since Haight-Ashbury in the late '60s, he says now, had he seen such a "fertile breeding ground" of music.

Kooper was in Atlanta at the time with a two-act band he had formed called Frankie and Johnny, whom he wanted to tune up for a recording session in the city by having them play some clubs. During his stay, someone suggested he hang at Funochio's, where he was given a private box with flowing booze and easy women to trifle with while listening to the music. Kooper had earned that kind of sway. Born in Brooklyn and raised in Queens, he was a prodigy at fourteen, playing guitar on "Short Shorts," the Royal Teens' twelve-bar blues riff that became a seminal rock-and-roll hit in 1958. Plying his skill as a songwriter, he composed the Gary Lewis and the Playboys smash "This Diamond Ring." A peripatetic presence, he was in Bob Dylan's backup band at the Newport Folk Festival in 1965; the same year, when Dylan cut his breakthrough folk-rock album *Highway 61 Revisited*, Kooper played the immortal, spindly Hammond organ line on arguably the most existential long-form rock song ever, "Like a Rolling Stone."

He had also played on Dylan's landmark *Blonde on Blonde* sessions in Nashville and would become involved with just about everyone in the rock sacrarium, either producing, writing for, or playing sessions with the likes of the Rolling Stones, Cream, the Blues Project, B.B. King, the Who, and Jimi Hendrix. He was a cofounder of the Blues Project, teamed up with super guitarist Mike Bloomfield and singer-guitarist Stephen Stills in several legendary live albums in the late '60s and somehow found time to found and produce the horn-driven jazz-rock unit Blood, Sweat and Tears. By 1973 the curly-haired Queens Jew with the thick "Noo Yawk" accent had seen enough of the percolating native southern rock scene and was so taken by the sanctuary the region seemed to offer from the industry jungle he despised that he considered moving to Dixie and creating a label similar to Capricorn. Kooper rhapsodized about a new South, saying that Atlanta had changed drastically in the three years he'd been away from it.

"It was looser," he said. "It wasn't so . . . *Southern*. There was a sociological gentrification in attitude. . . . The *rednecks* had long hair now. They were no longer the enemy. People got along better. I liked this. The women were beautiful and willing."

This was, of course, the South that bred a new music. Phil Walden's success with the Allman Brothers proved to Kooper that the timing was right for a rock retrenchment. Everyone, it seemed, was into rock forms that had strayed far from their original charter, and a heavy corporate canopy hung over all of it. The sterile nature of L.A. rock had seeped across the industry, in the formation of contrived, profit-geared "intellectual" supergroups like Yes, Genesis, and Emerson, Lake and Palmer. A polar opposite but equally contrived animal had also emerged—the glam rock of T. Rex ("Bang a Gong") and Gary Glitter ("Rock and Roll Part 2"), a tide that took the Rolling Stones into their mascara-caked "It's Only Rock and Roll" phase. Kooper envisioned an antidote to all the pretension and cerebral marketing strategies, something stripped down and from the gut and loins—"basic rock and roll," as Kooper put it, recalling the predominant music of the time as "schmutz," Yiddish vernacular for, well, garbage. Kooper had it exactly right when he said, looking back, that if a southern band didn't rate with Capricorn, "they were pretty much doomed, because no other label understood this phenomenon."

* * *

As a real mover and shaker in the industry, Kooper had the influence to get such a label up and running, as well as backing by the music label MCA. But he would need to have a strong act as his selling point. As fate would have it, Skynyrd would enter his purview with perfect timing, even if they were still rounding into shape—during a six-show run at Funochio's from January 15 to 20, club posters billed them as LYNYRD SKYNNYRD, an opening act for a band called Boot, along with another called Smokestack Lightnin'. But Kooper's first impression of them was ambivalent. Skynyrd might have sung about the pride of being a "simple man" of southern stock, but Kooper's snap judgment of them was much like that of most nonsouthern music people.

Seeing the front man on stage at Funochio's—"blond and barefoot, and sw[inging] the mikestand around like a majorette's baton"—Kooper admitted, "I hated Ronnie Van Zant upon first look at him. . . . He was so unusual. I never saw anybody like that—he was a very weird front man." The word *weird*, in fact, was Kooper's operative word for them. Rossington and Collins, he said, were "like two Cousin Its on stilts"—referring to the Smurf-like, mop-topped *Addams Family* character—"you literally couldn't see their faces when they played." The sound that emanated, he thought, was—again—"a weird amalgam of blues with second-generation British band influences." He wasn't alone in first-impression coldness. Even among those who paid to see them, there were sometimes crossed signals. While the band was determined to play "Free Bird" at every gig, the venue could make that dicey. Ronnie once recalled that at dance clubs, "they wanted to hear 'Knock on Wood' and 'Midnight Hour.' They said ['Free Bird'] wasn't a good dance song, and we'd get a lot of boos and things thrown at us."

As it happened, the first time Kooper walked into Funochio's, they were playing "Free Bird," and, he recalled, "nobody was paying attention." *That* would have been an off night, for sure, since it was the charge they put into audiences—in lieu of a record deal and hit songs—that kept them employed. But, like most audiences a tad baffled by Skynyrd, Kooper quickly warmed to them over three straight nights in his box, the "weird amalgam" suddenly making sense, such as when they played the song Kooper was taken with, "I Ain't the One." By night three, he thought "they had the sound I was looking for—that return to basic rock." Having been introduced to the band by the club owner before the show, Kooper asked if he could play guitar with them on stage. As aware as they were of major studio musicians, the band knew Kooper had played with Michael Bloomfield and Jimi Hendrix and made room for him, with no idea that Kooper saw them as a possible linchpin in his future plans.

For his part, Kooper says he was "flattered" that they had heard of him and would open their clique to the "Yankee slicker," as they called him with affectionate sarcasm. What he learned off the bat was that the redneck facade might have been their shtick, but they had a level of musicianship that impressed even him. He recounted his informal jam with the backwoods boys this way: "I strapped on a guitar and said, '*Let's go!*' [Van Zant] called out 'Mean Woman Blues' in C# [C-sharp] and counted it off. . . . In all my years of jamming, nobody ever called C#. It's a weird key between two relatively easy keys that would just as easily have sufficed."

Later, Kooper said, "I found out it was an intimidation process they dreamed up to keep jammers offstage." Realizing they were smarter than he had anticipated, Kooper didn't know if they were testing *his* renowned mastery or whether perhaps they were not as eager as they seemed to have an outsider on stage with them, no matter who it was. In any case, Kooper would proudly boast, "I could play fine in C#," and he continued sitting in with the band for three more nights, more than enough time for him to make them an offer to get them to commit to his incipient label. Following the last of those shows, Kooper was talking big.

"We talked and he said he'd make us an offer and he was interested," Rossington said, "but, actually, he didn't." Indeed, for all the attention he lavished on them, Kooper had also seen other acts to whom he had paid the same sort of attention and made the same promises—big talk being the most abundant and cheapest commodity a music nabob has. And there remains a fuzziness about how and when Skynyrd was in fact signed. Kooper, who has taken bows for having "discovered" them, liked to say that the opportunity was like "walking into a real funky bar someplace where you could get shot and hearing the Rolling Stones [and] finding out they weren't signed to anybody." Kooper says he offered to sign and produce them. "They said they would mull it over and discuss it with their manager. We said our goodbyes, and that was it. I hoped [their] manager would call me back." Soon Alan Walden—whom Kooper knew only as "Phil Walden's younger brother"—did.

But even now Kooper didn't push it, possibly because he wasn't particularly fond of Walden and vice versa. Kooper didn't mind who overheard him belittling the junior Walden for not being able to convince his own brother to sign his redneck rock act. Walden on the other hand saw Kooper as a northern sharpie stereotyping "dumbass Southern[ers]." And so nothing happened for three months. Kooper would later say this was merely because "they had to get to know me really well before they would sign," but if so, Walden never heard a price from Kooper that seemed satisfactory; the most he could offer, based on the ceiling given him by MCA for signing talent, was $9,000.

During the interim, Kooper didn't stand still. He moved from New York to the Atlanta suburb of Sandy Springs and opened his label—Sounds of the South (SOS), the logo of which was a two-hundred-year-old log cabin on the grounds. He went ahead and signed a number of other acts, his new favorite the Mose Jones band, who also played at Funochio's and sometimes jammed with Skynyrd there. Once signed, Mose Jones—who, as Kooper likely appreciated, had named themselves after Bob Dylan's Mister Jones—kept pitching Kooper to sign Skynyrd, says the band's drummer Bryan Cole. "We were close to them for a while," Cole said. "Ronnie actually asked me to join [Skynyrd] at one point but I think he was just pissed off at his drummer at the time. [Bandmate]

Jimmy O'Neill and I both told Al that he should check this group out. Even then they were tight and powerful and looked like stars."

Charlie Brusco, who kept tabs on Skynyrd's progress, sure that they were on the edge of a breakout, says that Kooper "was unsure about them. He had two or three bands that he was seriously interested in over Skynyrd. It wasn't a slam dunk. They were just so different. Again, no one in southern rock had that kind of hard-rock sound. It was a real gamble, and nobody was eager to take it."

* * *

Kooper indeed had his eye on many acts. He wanted to sign a hard-rock country group, Hydra, but they spurned him for Capricorn Records, as did country rock singer Eric Quincy Tate. And in a very odd choice, he did sign Elijah, the Latino horn-funk band hailing from East L.A., whom Kooper had seen playing at the Whisky a Go Go. Fudging the sequence of the Skynyrd signing, Kooper has said simply that he "also" signed Mose Jones, whose tight three-part harmonies and nearly pop hooks appealed to him. "Stylistically speaking," he said, "Mose Jones were my Beatles, and Skynyrd were my Stones."

Yet when he took Mose Jones into the studio early in 1973 to cut the first product on the SOS label, he didn't have his "Stones" under contract. All that changed when, at 2 AM one night in February, Kooper was awakened by the ring of his phone. On the other end, he heard a familiar husky voice—not cocky for once but despondent—with a request he felt he couldn't make of anyone else.

"Al," said Ronnie Van Zant, "our equipment van got broken into last night . . . We have engagements to fulfill immediately, and unless you can send us five thousand dollars by tomorrow morning, we're fucked!"

As Kooper remembered, there was no need to think it over. Whether or not Ronnie would ever be able to pay it back, five grand was a stiff but reasonable price to pay if it would break the negotiation logjam with Walden. "Where do I send it, buddy?" he said.

Grateful, a relieved Van Zant stunned him. "Let me tell you somethin'," he told Kooper. "You just bought yourself a band for five thousand dollars."

Walden, when he heard about this oral agreement, nearly fell down. He knew that Ronnie's word was good as gold, and he would never go back on it. That meant that any leverage Walden might have had was gone with the wind. Walden had known the band would wind up with Sounds of the South—there just was no place else for them to go—and as he says, "the band would not have survived" any longer without a deal. But he nevertheless believed he had turned over a fortune for peanuts—the same bargain-basement $9,000 advance that Kooper had dangled all along. What's more, Ronnie had vowed to pay back the money, southern men not being prone to charity.

So Skynyrd finally got their contract. It was drawn up by the MCA lawyers, dated February 5, 1973, and signed shortly thereafter. Kooper was quite pleased about having committed highway robbery—though in his purview it was the reasonable advantage he reaped as an industry veteran. The contract broke down the split of every dollar in sales royalties thusly: Kooper ten points, Skynyrd five. But five was better than 0 percent of zero, and Kooper still cackles about how happy the rednecks were "that they got a major-label deal, and they were braggin' about it." In truth, they were no fools. They knew how lousy the deal was, because Walden told them. The manager, justifiably uneasy about how much power Kooper might grab from him, was in the parking lot outside the Macon Coliseum, contract in hand, waiting in his pickup truck for the band to finish a show. When they came out, Ronnie came over and hopped into Walden's pickup truck. He asked Alan what he thought of the deal.

"It's the worst piece of shit I ever seen," Walden told him.

Ronnie, who had no intention of taking back his handshake agreement, also understood there was no other option, "What else we got?" he asked, knowing the answer.

"Nothin'," Walden said.

"Gimme the goddamn pen," Ronnie told him.

Walden looks back on that moment with not much glee or pride. Lynyrd Skynyrd, he says, "signed away two million dollars that day."

But they'd make up for it. Lord knows, they would make up for it.

6

★ ★ ★ ★ ★

ENTER ROOSEVELT COOK

The men—no longer boys—of Lynyrd Skynyrd saw the money for a fleeting, giddy moment. As Ed King recalled, having been told of it by the band when he joined, "Ronnie cashed the check from Kooper and literally brought all the money to Hell House. Once we were all there, he threw the money up in the air and [they] just sat there for a while looking at it laying everywhere while drinking some beer." However, after rolling around in the green, cold reality set in, and every dollar of it, King noted, "was poured back into the band for equipment and for those that needed money to get by," which was actually everyone. For the time being and until the advance was earned back, there would be no additional bread; when—if—they earned out, they were told they would be put on a weekly salary. Thus, little changed for them materially. They were still starving artists, living hand to mouth, still selling auto parts and packing meat in their nonband hours. King could be glad he was in Greenville, North Carolina, earning his own money.

"If I had been in the band twelve months prior to Kooper signing the band," he says, "it would've been *very* frustrating. You have to recognize how much Collins, Rossington, and Van Zant believed in and supported each other in those early days."

Of course, Al Kooper, too, had no way of knowing if there would ever be any sort of return on his investment or whether he and MCA would in the end take a $9,000 bath. To test the waters of his newly signed act, Kooper, with his New York connections, landed them a one-shot gig as the opening act for Black Sabbath on February 25 at Long Island's

Nassau Coliseum. It must have seemed like a good idea at the time. Sabbath, fronted by the not-quite-all-there Ozzy Osbourne, was touring the United States in support of its *Sabbath Bloody Sabbath* album, a brilliant, widely praised milestone in metal, and would play in April at the California Jam before two hundred thousand people on a bill with the Eagles, Deep Purple, Black Oak Arkansas, and Emerson, Lake and Palmer. Yet Sabbath fans were a loony lot, and so was Osbourne, who in the '80s would legendarily bite the head off a bat at one concert. To the fruitcakes in the Long Island audience, there was no accommodation to be made with Skynyrd.

First they threw bottles at the stage. That was not new for Skynyrd, but then, recalled Kooper, "the audience came at them." Guards had to intercept several fans before they reached the stage. Not knowing what they might do, Leon Wilkeson had worn a holster with a gun, loaded with blanks. As Skynyrd played their set, their ears stinging from catcalls like "You guys suck!" and "Get the fuck off the stage!" and "Ozzy rules!" Wilkeson, Kooper said, "pulled out his gun and fired off a blank but convincing round right at them that caused a few wet pants in the crowd and an immediate cessation of catcalls."

Score one for the Thumper. He was let alone by the cops when it was learned the gun had fired blanks, but the band, shaken by the experience, surely had to wonder, flying home after the show, what the hell they had gotten themselves into.

* * *

As it happened, however, the deal Skynyrd had signed with MCA was so weighted in the company's favor that it was highly unlikely that Kooper or anyone else beside the band would suffer. As Alan Walden recalled, "I knew from the beginning we needed MCA on our side. I made sure we gave them a deal that would give them a chance to make millions. We recorded [the debut album] for $22,500. Can you believe it? We did not try to borrow a lot of money. We did not call [MCA] every day. We were a working machine fully tuned and oiled. Independent!" Indeed, the MCA honchos wondered why the band and Walden were so detached from the pomp of signing a deal with a big company. "When I met [MCA Inc. president] Mike Maitland, he was shocked," Walden goes on. "I was all business and not into hanging out in the Hollywood scene like most." Nor did Skynyrd particularly care about going out west and shuffling their feet down Sunset. Right after the Nassau Coliseum debacle, Kooper got the group into the studio, in this case Studio One in Doraville, just outside of Atlanta, where the owner of the studio, Buddy Buie of the soft country rock band the Atlanta Rhythm Section, gave him the run of the place. The session, at which Kooper would produce tracks for a debut album, was scheduled for March 26, 1973. Skynyrd tuned up for it by playing a seven-date engagement back at Funochio's—the first three still as a backup act, to the headliners Blackfoot and Hooker, before getting top billing as "Lynyrd Skynyrd" for three shows and then returning to backup for Orpheum Circuit and Kudzu.

By then Kooper had filled their heads with garrulous promises of what he could deliver them, no less than superstardom. One night, Kooper, as always looking to sample the charms of southern women, found himself invited home by a girl he'd met in a club. When he got there, he had to rub his eyes when he saw Allen Collins, who had also been invited, possibly for some sort of rock-and-roll ménage à trois. For Collins, the encounter was a tad awkward, what with his recent marriage. Kooper, meanwhile, jumped not on the girl but on the opportunity to butter up Collins, telling him that Skynyrd was "the missing link" in rock's evolution. Kooper remembered that "we forgot about the girl and talked all night."

This rendezvous with Kooper wore down the group's initial wariness of him as a sharpie and user. Ronnie—still grateful about the loan, rip-off or no—had grown to respect Kooper as he did no other industry figure. He was impressed to no end with the MCA signing, boasting a year later that "we were the first southern group to go with a label that wasn't in the South." It's not at all clear, however, whether Kooper ever really *liked* the band members or just tolerated them for his own purposes. But then, who knew how long he, as an industry bumblebee, would even sojourn in the South before taking off on another conquest somewhere?

* * *

Just as with Skynyrd's trip to Muscle Shoals, personnel adjustments had to be made before the Doraville sessions. Leon Wilkeson, who, if he didn't bitch and moan about *something* during any given day, caused Ronnie to give thanks, began acting crazy during the three-month writing and rehearsing period at Hell House. He frequently came in piss-faced drunk, muttering about Jesus, the devil, and rock and roll stealing his soul. Little got done, and with the band about to take a road tip to Saint Augustine for a gig, Leon said he might not be a-goin'.

Ronnie, steaming as he was, did not want to cut Leon adrift any more than he'd wanted to cut Bob Burns, knowing his value to the band. So he cut Leon slack so the bassist could make up his mind, but insisted he teach the bass lines he had developed for the new songs to another bass player. And it seemed they got a real break when Larry Steele, a real heavy hitter, agreed to play with them until the Wilkeson matter was settled. Steele had played sessions for a staggering range of artists, including Cat Stevens, Al Stewart, jazz organist Jack McDuff, and blues guitarist Stefan Grossman. Recently he had contributed to Elton John's *Honky Chateau* and Stephen Stills's eponymous solo album. He had far more experience than Leon but played good soldier, patiently taking direction from the boozy, barely coherent kid. Both made the trip and roomed in a hotel—ironically, the Headrest—getting drunk and running up excessive room service tabs that Ronnie had to empty his pockets to pay for.

Now *really* steaming, Ronnie thought *Steele*, not Wilkeson, was the bad influence. Plans had been made for Bob Burns to pick up Larry for the trip to Doraville; he waited on the side of the road for Burns, who never came around. That was Skynyrd's way of firing Steele, who chalked it up to bad judgment on his part, wasting his time with a bunch of two-bit redneck punks. He has hardly suffered for it; he's been working constantly in the years since, including regular gigs playing bass on and writing songs with both the Johnny Van Zant Band and Donnie Van Zant's .38 Special. Leon, shaky as he was, got himself together enough to go to Doraville, though Ronnie could not go without a backup ready to step in if—when—Leon got crazy again. That man turned out to be an old ally. A few days before, knowing Steele was a goner, Ronnie had called Ed King at his home in Greenville, North Carolina, and invited him to join Skynyrd, not on guitar but bass. King, who'd wanted to get just such a call from Skynyrd ever since he'd first met up with the band, was surprised nonetheless.

"I mean, you would think there would have been a bass player in town that they could have called. Larry Junstrom, I know he was the original bass player, and Larry Junstrom is like one of the best bass players. Matter of fact, when they played 'Need [All] My Friends' way back at the Comic Book, Junstrom's bass part was just, it was miraculous. It was just genius. So I don't know what Ronnie saw in me. There was no logical reason for me to be in that band when you think about it."

King drove to Jacksonville, rehearsed on the bass with Wilkeson, and went to Doraville ready to play the four-string but just as likely to be utilized as a third lead guitar, something Ronnie had hoped would give as much kick to the Skynyrd sound as possible. For King, a grand learning experience was beginning. And by now Billy Powell had gotten the promotion that *he'd* been waiting for. For a time, as he carried out his job as a roadie, it seemed as if the band had forgotten that they had a classically trained pianist in their camp. Then after a Skynyrd concert at the Bolles School in Jacksonville, Powell dropped onto a piano stool in the auditorium and began noodling a keyboard embellishment for "Free Bird." Ronnie, hearing it, was taken aback. "You *play*? You been workin' with us for a year and you didn't tell us you played?" he asked Powell. A few more bars and he was in the band, a move that would have a profound effect on the Skynyrd sound.

* * *

Powell was among the pilgrims who assembled before Al Kooper on March 26. Kooper, though a hands-on producer with great ears, always allowed the artists he was recording the breathing room to record their songs as they wanted them to be. Right from the first downbeat, he realized he wouldn't need to do much by way of producing Skynyrd. The band, he would later say, "was years ahead of their time. They were twenty year-olds playing like thirty year-olds." This was, he insisted, just as he wanted it, since "I'm not interested in producing anybody I can't learn from." He had told them to come in with all of their songs, literally *all* of them, including whichever tracks from the Muscle Shoals sessions they were fond of enough to rerecord. They would have fourteen of them, with "not a bad apple in the bunch," according to Kooper. He found them "incredibly well rehearsed," their guitar solos arranged beforehand, leading Kooper to call them "the best damn arrangers I have *ever* worked with" and to acknowledge that "their mental discipline was *everything* to them. They understood music organically, not by the book."

After getting them in the controlled environment of the studio, Kooper's judgment of Van Zant was much the same as his original one. Although he still thought Ronnie had "a rather pedestrian voice," he conceded that Van Zant had a "unique sound" and "remarkable leadership skills" that seemed to give that voice a swagger; in his view, the vocals were undeniably commanding. Kooper loves to relate the time when Ronnie amused himself during a break by crooning Johnny Cash's "Hey Porter." Just as he sang the first line—"Hey porter, hey porter, would you tell me the time"—a janitor sweeping up checked his watch.

"6:08, son," he said.

Light-hearted moments like that were rare. While the sessions ran smoothly enough, the bandmates were as thorny as ever, "always getting in fistfights," Kooper said. "If they couldn't find anyone to fight, they'd fight each other." Having King and Powell surely made things easier. Wilkeson managed to get through the day, freeing King to pick up a guitar and contribute that third lead-guitar part, which to Kooper was gravy, given that Rossington and Collins were already near-perfect complements. Gary, he thought, was a "curious mix" between the great folk-blues guitarist Ry Cooder and Free's Paul Kossoff, aping the latter's honkish, vibrato style; while Collins had an "Eric Clapton–like approach," presumably a reference to Clapton's self-described "woman tone," amp cranked to the max, wah-wah pedal creating a thick, distorted sonic blast that poured out of speakers like quivering cake batter.

In developing and rehearsing songs, there was apt to be a fight over who would play what part. Rather than deciding on some intellectual reasoning about style, Rossington says, "Most of the time we just knew whose rhythm or lead style would fit. On occasion it was more rough and tumble: whoever thought they had a cool approach would jump on it, and if the other guy thought he could whup him, he would just try to take it."

For Ed King, the new guy, such a claiming of turf was rare. Usually he would gladly accept a rhythm part, bridging the other two, and then dive into the three-guitar solo breaks when all three would play the exact same notes; yet even then, their distinct styles would lend depth and a "real" feel that could never have been created by Gary or Allen overdubbing their own parts. To Kooper, King was "the icing, [a] James Burton," referencing the legendary studio guitar man for Elvis. "It's ridiculous," said Kooper, "they had every kind of guitar playing covered." King was just beginning to figure out the quirks and habits of his new bandmates, which extended even to the guitars played by Rossington and Collins—indeed a curious duo. "When I first met them, Gary was playing a white SG and Allen a gold-top Les Paul with mini-humbuckers," says King, using the vernacular of musicianspeak. "When I joined the band, they'd switched! The Les Paul you hear on the [first] album is that gold-top Paul." Both of those guitars, he notes, were later stolen out of Collins's hotel room during a 1974 gig in San Francisco, by which time the band's supply of guitars was such that they could have freely switched them to match their clothes if they chose to.

King, the ultimate pro, echoed both of the guitars with his own, broadening the texture of each and the sonic field as a whole, seeming to solder the sound into a cohesive pulp, with not a note out of place or wasted. Billy Powell's funky, bluesy, honky-tonk piano also added depth. If there was a weak link, it was Bob Burns, but he did what was asked of him, playing drum parts that were written for him by the others with an inherent "Skynyrd" feel, having been there from the start. Being in the Skynyrd "gang," as Kooper put it, was like having taken a blood oath, one that could only be broken, it seemed, if Ronnie allowed it to be.

* * *

March 26, 1973, was a long and beneficial day, fourteen crisply recorded demo tracks done. Kooper and the band listened to them, and eight songs were chosen for inclusion on the album. Ignoring that one of them, "Things Goin' On," had been in the projected album rejected by numerous labels and that four more—"I Ain't the One," "Free Bird," "Gimme Three Steps," and "Simple Man"—had been among the outtakes, the band chose these songs to make up the bulk of their first official album. "I Ain't the One," Kooper's favorite, was tabbed as the first cut and "Free Bird" the last. In between, the new songs would be "Tuesday's Gone," "Mississippi Kid," and "Poison Whiskey." Skynyrd went back home to rehearse the songs, planning to return to Studio One early in April for more polished takes of the tracks. By then, Wilkeson was again coming unglued, adding uncertainty that Ronnie didn't need. He had Ed King make sure to take a bass along with his six-string Fender Stratocaster. As it happened, Leon would make it through two tracks before getting up and walking out the door, with not a word to anyone. Kooper, seeing this bizarre behavior, believed that Wilkeson "was actually frightened of all the responsibilities that would be forthcoming" and created an exit scenario. In any case, he hitchhiked back to Jacksonville, leaving King to step in, which he did seamlessly, having memorized all of Wilkeson's bass lines to the chosen songs.

Kooper was delighted that King not only played the lines but added "little flourishes, slides and grace notes that made the difference between bass playing and art." As the sessions went on, Kooper would make further use of King, as the third lead guitar. It was little wonder that when people first heard these songs the guitars leapt out of the radio and off turntables. With Kooper doubling the guitar tracks, a massive, coiled font of sound erupted, through which certain notes seemed to climb out of a distant, dewy mist and move from one stereo channel to the other and across the aural spectrum—the nearly *visual* nature of the Skynyrd sound that would be their signature. The other newcomer, Billy Powell, was another pleasant tool for Kooper, his nimble, bluesy piano accents—"all the textures," Kooper called them—an effective counterpoint to the deafening din of all those guitars. On "Tuesday's Gone," a hazy ballad mourning the things left behind in the course of a man movin' on—e.g., "My baby's gone with the wind again"—the guitars gently weeped. It was one of the last songs recorded, and Powell had come up with a solo that Kooper called a "beautiful little sonata." Kooper got in on the session too, playing the mellotron, the keyboard/synthesizer contraption that creates an orchestral sound from recorded tape segments—the forerunner of modern studio sampling.

He also played on "Mississippi Kid," a jug band–style rag with the requisite tale about crossing the state line into Alabama to "fetch" a straying woman, with the ominous vow that "I'm not looking for no trouble, but nobody dogs me 'round." Kooper hired his old Blues Project/Blood, Sweat and Tears compadre Steve Katz to add a wailing harmonica part. Kooper also heard the need for a mandolin. Obsessive as he was, he called every mandolin player in the musicians directory, in vain, and then scoured music stores in the area until he found a mandolin selling for forty bucks and taught himself the chords of the song. (Pertinent to Skynyrd trivia freaks is that Bob Burns, who took ill, didn't play on this track; Atlanta Rhythm Section drummer Robert Nix took his place.)

Knocked out as he was by Powell, whose solos he says were "truly unique," Kooper did have to temper Billy's tendency as a classic pianist to overplay with his left hand, which at times drowned out some of the more nuanced guitar notes. Improvising, he had Powell play with his left hand *tied to the piano bench*. Billy was none too pleased, but when the band would chafe at some Kooper direction, Ronnie would intervene for the producer, if with a little dig.

"Awright, wait a second," he said during one session. "I think that idea sucks too but I will listen to everything Al says. Maybe once in twenty times he'll have a great idea, but I will suffer the other nineteen times because that twentieth one will make us sound better, so go easy on the old guy!" Never mind that, at the time, Van Zant was twenty-five and Kooper all of twenty-nine. Ronnie always did live in his own reality warp. And when *he* had an objection to a Kooper directive, the "old guy" knew he'd have to back down. That happened most emphatically when Kooper didn't think "Simple Man," a rare Ronnie reference to the down-home wisdom of Sis Van Zant—"Take your time. Don't live too fast / Troubles will come and they will pass"—was strong enough to go on the album.

"You guys are not gonna cut that song," Kooper told them.

Ronnie was not about to argue the point. He took Kooper out to the parking lot and opened the door to Kooper's Bentley. "Get in," he said. Too petrified to resist, Al slid into the driver's seat. Ronnie, standing outside the open window, had just one thing to say.

"When we're done cuttin' it, we'll call you."

Recalls Rossington: "We cut the whole tune without him."

This is another of those slices of Skynyrd BS lore that likely didn't quite happen. Although the band and the producer had numerous run-ins, and arguments were de rigueur, Kooper need not have been banished that day; rather, he gave in on "Simple Man"—"it did fit, and I was wrong," he later said, adding, "I'm glad it did go on the album"—and also played organ on the session. Kooper's role in buffing, tweaking, and polishing Skynyrd's backwoods rock with technical proficiency, even perfection, without compromising its essence and character is one of the great rock triumphs of all time. Not an ounce of what came out of his studio was either under- or overproduced, nor was any element more or less spacious or more or less biting than was intended when the band composed and played it. Needless to say, he couldn't have made chickens out of chicken poop. Not just any band could have been buffed into the next big thing in rock—Skynyrd was not just any band. Thus, everything that came out of these sessions constituted the ingredients of what made Skynyrd into *Skynyrd.*

Yet Ronnie, being Ronnie, never would see completely eye to eye with Al, one departure being that he thought Ed King's bass playing was not up to snuff. This was something that King would find out soon enough. But his guitar sorcery would keep him in the fold, feeling not entirely accepted and almost lost in the shuffle among the indigenous rednecks, but quite nearly indispensable, at least for a while.

⋆ ⋆ ⋆

The song that Kooper had first heard them play, to a tepid reception, ate up the most studio time, as it would have to, given its length. "Free Bird" had by then become a running soap opera in itself. When Rossington and Collins first erected the melody, Ronnie couldn't make it work lyrically until Allen simplified the chords. Rather than because of any artistic or rule-breaking consideration, the long instrumental break and fadeout came about because Van Zant, the only singing voice on every song, needed to almost literally take five to keep from losing his voice. Thus he had no objection to standing on stage with little to do but caress the microphone and catch his breath. There would be no forced participation, no banging on a tambourine, no leaping about or swiveling of the hips; like Jim Morrison had done during the extended break of "Light My Fire," all Van Zant need do was to look cool, something he could manage quite well.

Kooper let his version run to a stupefying 9:09 when the song was cut on April 3. Until then, the intro through two previous recordings had been Gary's straightforward lick, joined by Allen's mournful-sounding slide guitar. But when Ronnie heard Billy Powell's off-the-cuff piano swirls at Bolles, he had a different idea: to kick the song off with a similar riff. Kooper, however, heard the song as an anthem of redneck royalty and decided that it needed a regal, gospel-like feel, similar to what had been created so effectively by Keith Emerson's Hammond organ on Emerson, Lake and Palmer songs like "Hoedown," not to mention the contributions of Booker T. Jones, the Doors' Ray Manzarek, and good-old Texas boy Doug Sahm in the Sir Douglas Quintet ("She's About a Mover").

Such a feel, played beside Powell's delicate piano line, Kooper said, could give "Free Bird" an opening like the reverent, fugue-style chorale intro of "You Can't Always Get You Want." Indeed, Stones fan that Ronnie was, all it took for Kooper to convince him was to mention for the hundredth time that he had played on Stones sessions, as if he could transfer some of that same magic to a hillbilly band. The organ, of course, was an instrument Kooper was rather familiar with, having made a particular Hammond B-3 accompaniment a rock-and-roll staple eight years before in Bob Dylan's studio. And so he came onto the floor and played as he had back then, on feel and instinct, creating for himself yet another link to rock immortality, joining southern-fried rock and Bob Dylan. Kooper would list himself on the album credits in code as "Roosevelt Gook," something he had been doing for years whenever he played a session.

Kooper's main task was to make the song's waves of guitars ring in balance, none louder or more commanding than any other, a real challenge given the sheer overload of it all. Both Rossington and Collins doubled their own parts on a separate track, making for a faintly echoing quality to their lines. Yet it was all interwoven, all firing in unison, each seeming to challenge the others during a particular segment, and then each receding in turn to begin another mounting wave. It was so over the top that no one inside the studio that day believed the song would ever be released as a single. When MCA saw that 9:09 in the tape can, executives sent word to Kooper to cut it down to a reasonable length; but he knew better than to ask Ronnie to do that. Besides, he believed it would play right into the maw of the now entrenched long-form FM radio formats.

"Free Bird," however, was not considered for the album's first single. Instead, "I Ain't the One" was thought to be the best choice. Van Zant and Kooper cut it as the album's "Free song," one reserved on each LP for Ronnie to try to sound like Paul Rodgers, though it usually came off more like ZZ Top than Free. Its catchy beat and funky acoustic and electric guitar pickin', along with Ronnie's bluesy, throaty vocal and brief spoken rap formed a real platform for the lead man, whose bad-boy image was aided by the provocative, metaphoric line: "I never hurt you sweetheart, oh Lord / Never pulled my gun." That line, analogizing the penis to a gun, would make the song a concert favorite. The song sounded so good that, even though a guitar part was played slightly out of time, the band ordered Kooper to go with it anyway.

The consensus pick, however, became "Gimme Three Steps," the first song recorded on March 29. It sprung from a once scary but now humorous incident at a Jacksonville club—usually assumed to be the Little Brown Jug on Highway 17 (thus "the Jug" in the song)—that had occurred early in their existence. (Rossington seems to think it was the West Tavern on Lenox Avenue.) Ronnie, self-deprecatingly described in the song as the "fat fellow with the hair colored yellow," took a woman, "Linda Lou"—a nod to Allen Collins's aunt, a onetime country singer who had sung under that name—onto the dance floor, only to have her boyfriend break in. Suddenly the fat fellow was "staring straight down a forty-four" and making one request: "Mister, gimme three steps toward the door."

The band liked to have fun with the tune on stage. Ronnie's line that night in the bar was actually, "If you're going to shoot me, it's going to be in the ass or the elbows. Just gimme a few steps, and I'll be gone." The classic rock structure of that tune—simple three-chord repetition, intro, chorus, break, and fade, sung and played with brio and pickle brine—would be the song template for the life of the band; the rejected Muscle Shoals song "Was I Right Or Wrong," for instance, is a virtual note-for-note copy. The only sound not played by the band on "Three Steps" was a faint bongo part by former Motown percussionist Bobbye Hall.

With the album in the can and the first single chosen, the last order of business for Kooper was one that no amount of personal cache or begging would make the band budge on. His intention was to get them to change their name, which he loathed. "Lynyrd Skynyrd" struck him as unpronounceable and abstruse, and left him concerned that it might be impossible to market. Kooper says he "hated" it and that it "didn't make any sense" and "certainly didn't conjure up what their music was about." But left no choice, he set out to make it work. With the self-effacing cheekiness that would become their sine qua non, the album was named *(pronounced 'lĕh-'nérd 'skin-'nérd)*, thus addressing the dual need to clarify the name and provoke curiosity about what it meant. The "nerd" part was a hoot, the mark of a band with a sense of humor, though if one were to judge by the album jacket, they could be taken for Allman Brothers wannabes. On the cover shot they struck the same pose the Brothers had on College Street in Macon for their '69 debut album, unsmiling and looking a trifle pissed off. The shot, taken on Main Street in Jonesboro before Wilkeson split, was nonetheless the one they went with, keeping faith with Leon, who as it happened gave the photo its only panache, wearing aviator shades, a constable hat with badge, and a T-shirt emblazoned with a lightning bolt decal.

The back cover featured a photograph of a cigarette pack reading LYNYRD SKYNYRD'S SMOKES next to the eight-song listing. (The 2001 rerelease added five demos from Muscle Shoals as bonus tracks.) The band's name was lettered in bones on the cigarette pack, above and below a skull and bones and surrounded by a ghoulish blood-red umbra, thus merging the imagery of rising heavy-metal bands like Black Sabbath with the nicotine stains of Tobacco Road. One could hardly have imagined how, in a corridor of America where southern Christian conservatives marched in lockstep behind Billy Graham, Jerry Falwell, and Oral Roberts, folks could also get behind leather-clad merchants of devil worship. But then again, Skynyrd's was not the South of their grandfathers.

As contrived as such imagery was, Kooper knew the industry and the imperative of getting attention in a swarm of similar acts. He also knew the target audience of restless youth with a thirst for restless rock. Most of all, knowing Skynyrd as he did, as a bunch "always getting into fist-fights," he would say, "I decided to paint a rough-house image for them." As a $100,000 ad campaign approved by MCA rolled out, promotional albums sent to radio stations were bundled in packages engraved enigmatically with the question WHO IS LYNYRD SKYNYRD? Full- and half-page ads were bought to run in the hippest of counterculture newspapers like the *Village Voice* in New York and the *Free Press* in L.A. Snobbish big-city music critics who might otherwise have ignored a backwoods band of pigpen rednecks took notice; maybe this band was actually made up of southern apostates, a hint of a new wave happening in Dixie, with rock and roll the elixir of liberal notions bubbling down there in the trailer parks and swamps. Stoking such suppositions would be critical to their breakout, and whether it was jive or not, the men of Skynyrd were ready for some altered realities as the price of inordinate fame.

7

★ ★ ★ ★ ★

"CHICKEN-SKIN MUSIC IN THE RAW"

Al Kooper was so demanding about making *(pronounced 'lĕh-'nérd 'skin-'nérd)* a reference point in a new order of rock and roll that he took the master tapes to New York three separate times to mix the album to his satisfaction at state-of-the-art mixing facilities. During the process, he threw a kickoff party for himself and his label on July 29, 1973, at Richard's, a posh nightclub on Monroe Drive that billed itself "Atlanta's finest rock club," with "full theatrical lighting and 360-degree sound." Kooper invited executives at MCA Records to hear the band they were paying for, and to position Lynyrd Skynyrd as a welcome addition to the label's enormous parent company, Music Corporation of America Inc. For Skynyrd to be associated with this gigantic megacorp seemed a fable in itself. MCA's entertainment conglomerate had grown into a dominant role across the show business terrain under the storied leadership of the prototypical Hollywood power broker Lew Wasserman. MCA Inc. had already gobbled up movie studios like Paramount and Universal and publishing houses like G. P. Putnam's Sons, and its music division had annexed labels like Decca and Kapp. The company even purchased the Danelectro guitar company.

In 1972 MCA Records had, after consolidating all its sublabels, gone worldwide with its first release, Elton John's "Crocodile Rock." Seeking all manner of acts, its executives were quite receptive to Kooper's southern rock designs, and for the coming-out party of Sounds of the South, plunked down $10,000 without blinking to arrange and cater the night's festivities. One of the company's most valuable artists, Marc Bolan of the English glam-rock band T. Rex, was a guest. Even though the event was on a Sunday night, the company's éclat was such that the Atlanta police waived the blue law against serving booze on Sundays, just this once, or until they wanted to do it again. Gary Rossington surmises that Kooper wanted Skynyrd to perform at the party so that the suits could validate his ardor for a band of freaky redneck hippies and he wouldn't be left out on a limb if they flopped. "He invited all the MCA reps and everybody down to hear these three Southern groups that he had found," Rossington explains. "And so the other two went out and played, and we were last."

Throughout the spring and summer of '73, Skynyrd had returned to the clubs and dive bars, the album garnering them nothing more ornate than dates backing up the bands Traktor and Mose Jones (Kooper's "Beatles") at the Great Southeast Music Hall in Atlanta and taking them back to Funochio's where they backed up Mason and Traktor. Knowing the stakes for them at the Richard's party, they had a good gimmick ready, a song called "Workin' for MCA," cowritten by Van Zant and King, about their rise coinciding with that of a certain "Yankee Slicker": "Worked in every joint you can name, yessuh, every honkytonk / Along come Mister Yankee Slicker, sayin' maybe you what I want." Kooper loved every word, especially the lyric that went, "Nine thousand dollars, that's all we could win / But we smiled at the Yankee Slicker with a big ol' Southern grin." It wasn't merely a gimmick either; it was a damn good song, those frontal guitars on fire. The MCA boys loved it as well, rising from their seats, loosening their ties, and stomping around to the band's molten, ear-splitting, three-guitar assault and Van Zant's riveting voice. Kooper knew right then that he had it right about Skynyrd: they had a cheeky impudence and cleverness and could play with the fire and play *loud*.

Kooper was beaming that night. Skynyrd, he said, "stole the show. They mustered up all of their inherent discipline and put together a show that *floored* these people." Suddenly, his "Beatles," Mose Jones, were on the back burner. Everything was about Skynyrd now. So triumphant was the evening that Gary Rossington recalls it as the very moment Kooper asked to sign them, saying that he "brushed the other two groups off and said, 'Hey, you're signed.'" Of course, as with many Rossington recollections, this is way off target, but the gig was certainly productive; having passed this audition of sorts, they were booked to play six more shows at Richard's and then again in September opening for Bonnie Bramlett.

Prepared to bank everything on Skynyrd, Kooper had already convinced MCA to throw all of its promotional clout behind them, including $100,000 for those skull-and-bones-dotted promotional and ad campaigns. MCA's creative directors could hardly imagine how the image fit a bunch of dusty rednecks and a lead singer who just sang. But they trusted Kooper and went full steam ahead. By the time the album was released on August 13, 1973, the L.A.-based public relations agency Norman Winter Associates was hired to ensure the name was actually pronounced correctly, preferably when record buyers walked into music stores and asked for the album. That week, a very expensive two-page ad ran in the music trade papers, *Variety* and *Billboard*.

By then, too, Ronnie had made it his business to talk Leon Wilkeson back. Toward that end, he had insisted that Leon be in the group shot on the cover of *pronounced*, allowing him to enjoy a rank he hadn't really earned by playing on just two tracks. His name was also on the back cover's album credits. Indeed, as with the prodigal Bob Burns, Wilkeson was never written out of the band, and he would be given a one-seventh share of the royalties from sales of the album—a hell of a better payday than he'd earn stuffing ice cream cones for sniveling kids, as he was doing at the Best Dairy in Jacksonville. In Ronnie's value system, a bandmate he judged to be worthy of the Skynyrd brand—as opposed to, say, Larry Junstrom—was a bandmate forever. Skynyrd was more than a band to him now; it was an all-for-one, well, *confederacy*, born of a blood bond that went beyond even family and had less to do with music than it did with honor. Thus he had no trouble bringing Leon back into the ring in time to play on the next album, never again to stray from the fold.

* * *

For the Skynyrd rollout, nothing was left to chance and every advantage was sought. In planning their first tour to sell the album, Kooper's connections stretched a long way. Putting the word out across the rock meridians that Skynyrd would be available to open for a big act that might be concurrently touring, he received an invitation from Alice

Cooper née Vincent Furnier, the leather-covered, face paint–streaked rocker who was more shlock than shock. It seemed to be the best they could possibly do—but only until Kooper was in L.A. on business and happened to be in the MCA offices. There he ran into Pete Townsend and fellow Brit Peter Rudge, whose management firm, Sir Productions, managed the Who's world tours, as well as those of the Rolling Stones.

MCA had just subsumed the group's longtime label, Decca, and their first release on MCA Records in the States would be the Townsend-composed rock-opera double album *Quadrophenia*, to be released in late October when their new world tour would begin, a humongous event, to be sure. Kooper, who had done session work in London and had even planned to move there before catching the Dixie bug, struck up a conversation with Townsend and Rudge about his new southern band. As Kooper recalled, "Miraculously, the timing was perfect. The Who were looking for a young buzz act that they felt could sell whatever seat deficit was left over from their own fans." This was important since such an act would reduce the Who's red ink, which would be plentiful given the enormous budget they would foot for their battleship-sized stages and elaborate light show.

Rossington, with his usual abbreviation of the facts, recalled that Townsend listened to their album "and he said, 'Hey, I like this group here, get them to open for us.'" Rudge listened too and agreed. Kooper then ran the idea by the band, who knew there was no way they could let the opportunity slide yet were still abashed. "Up until then," said Rossington, "we had been playing clubs, like three hundred people, one hundred people, and the next day [Rudge] said, 'You wanna do this tour?'" Adds Ed King, "Everyone else was scared shitless for us. [MCA] was a little leery. I mean, they took us to a Who gig with Mylon LeFevre, the opening act, and he was just booed off the stage. He got eaten up." LeFevre was also a southern act, albeit a gospel-blues singer, and the reaction could not have helped his state of mind; a few months later, he died of a heroin overdose.

Recalls Alex Hodges, "It wasn't a slam dunk, I'll tell you that. Alan [Walden] likes to boast that he made the tour, but, you know, that's Alan, thinking of Alan. There was a lot of dissent about it; it wasn't only that it was a daunting thing to go out there with The Who. I remember I had booked about fifteen dates for Skynyrd and Black Oak Arkansas, and those were for a lot more money. Skynyrd was already making $2,000 a night, and the Who tour paid us $750 a night. But I told Alan, 'You gotta do it.' We'd get them into bigger arenas, move up into a bigger league. It was a career decision. And Alan ultimately made the decision to go. He said, 'OK, but if it goes wrong I'm blamin' you.' He was jokin', of course, but that's how concerned he was that we weren't ready for that kind of heat yet."

And so, leery as they were, Skynyrd pulled out of the Alice Cooper deal and became the latest victim, er, opening act for the Who. The first thing they did was get drunk—not for the first time and definitely not the last.

* * *

The Who tour, which would hit the United States on November 20 in San Francisco, would propel the Skynyrd rollout onto a higher level, putting them into the biggest arenas and stadiums. Getting their feet wet, they worked toward that, playing another week at Richard's and then taking it on the road: headlining at the Cellar in Charlotte, North Carolina; backing up the New York Dolls at the Lion's Den in Saint Louis; headlining at the Paramount Theatre in Palm Beach, the Peabody Auditorium in Daytona Beach, the Fine Arts Theater in Augusta, and the Mill Hall in Athens; then up to the northeast, to the Capitol Theatre in Passaic, New Jersey, dates in Rochester, New York, and Portland, Maine; on Halloween night, their first *big* venue—Avery Fisher Hall in New York City—for two shows, opening for Kooper's Blues Project; heading back south, to Birmingham, Alabama, and Charleston; and finally up to Jersey again to play at Princeton's McCarter Theatre.

The Atlanta gig, at the recently opened Omni Coliseum, was as much a show of their mettle as their metal. This was the first of a number of concerts at which they, as the opening act, had to salvage a pay date. As Hodges remembers, "Blue Oyster Cult was the main act that night. But the place was new—it wasn't even fully built. And the sound system for the building hadn't gotten there yet—there was no amplifiers. So Blue Oyster Cult said, 'Fuck it, we ain't goin' on.' The promoter didn't know what to do. He was thinkin' he was gonna have to give back sixteen thousand refunds. So he called me and put Ronnie on the phone. And Ronnie says, 'The fans are all here, and we're all set up to play—but there's no sound system, the rig didn't come, the other guys went home. What do we do?'

"I'm thinking, 'Thanks for puttin' all this on me, pal.' I just winged it. I said, 'Ronnie, is there a PA system in that building? You can hook microphones into it and sing and play through the PA. It won't be great, but you can do it.' I said, 'Look, it's gonna be your call, but I will tell you exactly what'll happen. You'll go up on stage, grab a microphone, and tell those people, 'I want to talk to you for a second,' you'll tell 'em the headliners aren't there but that Skynyrd's gonna play without amps. You're gonna ask them, 'Do you want us to play?' Because I knew they'd scream, '*Yeaaaahhhh!*' I said, 'You're already big in Atlanta. This will be something the fans will never forget. They'll love it. You'll walk off that sage, and you will own Atlanta forever.' And they played, and that's what happened. I had to feel pretty good about it. I didn't really know it would work—I was just pullin' somethin' out of my butt to get 'em to play."

They had been scheduled for a six-show run at Kenny's Castaways in New York City, which would have been a huge step, but with the Who tour about to commence, the run was canceled. Gearing up, they flew cross-country to meet up with the superstar band at the Cow Palace in San Francisco on November 18, with a buzz about them. That month, *Cashbox*, another trade paper, was one of the first to take note of them, its reviewer writing, "Watch for this band. Tight, mean and rough, they're one of the few rock acts in the business that really get it on." The bisection of the bad-boy Brit whitenecks and the bad-boy Deep South rednecks was a devil's bargain in itself. By being brought into the circle of one of the world's biggest acts, the country rockers were turned up all right, and turned on. They were able to observe and hang with all-time great rockers and self-abusers, drinking in—literally—the lifestyle of rock icons, as well as invaluable tips on showmanship, musicianship, and the mandatory misbehavior methods of the contemporary rock culture.

At that very first show at the Cow Palace, Keith Moon, a sprite with an endless capacity for self-destruction, consumed massive quantities of brandy and tranquilizer pills meant for zoo animals. He passed out on his drum stool during "Won't Get Fooled Again" and, after a break backstage, did it again during "Magic Bus." When Moon was carted off again, Townshend, looking more resigned than angered or concerned, having had to do this before, asked the audience, "Can anyone play the drums?—I mean somebody good?" A nineteen-year-old audience member, Scott Halpin, did so, legendarily, and the show went on. By contrast, Skynyrd, nervous as they were, having graduated from two hundred–seat clubs to a hall with twenty-two thousand screaming people, had preceded them and given their usual overheated performance, with no forced theatrics, no one falling off a stool, and no one stumbling about the stage in a drunken shamble. Their "light show" was the passion they had for the music, carried across in Van Zant's anchoring voice and those three guitars that didn't need to be set ablaze to sound like they were on fire. That first night, playing a set limited to thirty minutes, they nonetheless caused such a stir that the audience begged for an encore.

Kooper, who had been watching from the wings, recalled Townsend and Rudge as "incredulous," quoting Rudge as saying, "I have *never* seen this happen with any Who opening band."

Kooper had little time to observe. He had taken an active, hands-on role on the tour, dropping himself behind the sound mixing board during their time on stage, a chore he would not trust to Kevin Elson, their usual soundman. Such were the stakes on this tour that the aural shadings of the songs had to be perfect. This was a rather amazing sight, a record company executive mixing the sound—as Kooper would say, "Let's see Clive Davis do this!" What's more, he had to do it in unorthodox fashion, with the board not out in the audience so as to hear if the band was being amplified loud enough, but in the wings. This was per Townsend's orders; if he thought *his* soundman, Bob Pridden, messed up, he could walk over and attack him, verbally or even physically, something he did regularly during the tour. To ease the task, Kooper hired people to filter through the crowds and report to him on the sound levels via a walkie-talkie telemetry system. Again, nothing was left to chance.

* * *

Billy Powell nearly didn't survive that first night. After Skynyrd was done with their thirty-minute set, Billy meandered to the foot of the stage so he could watch the Who, just as the security staff was trying to clear the area. Massive bouncers were bodily picking up stragglers without backstage passes and throwing them over a barrier behind the stage. Powell, whose pass was in his coat pocket, was next. When a bouncer grabbed him by the hair, Billy told the guy, "Hold it. I'm in the Skynyrd band." He tried squatting down so he could reach into his pocket for the pass; but the guy wouldn't let go, and Billy threw a punch at him.

Standing nearby was the promoter Bill Graham, a man who watched over his shows like a hawk. Graham, née Wolfgang Wolodia Grajonca, was as famous as many big rock acts. The acts he promoted in the late '60s included the Grateful Dead, Jefferson Airplane, and Janis Joplin. His shows at the Winterland Ballroom and the Fillmore in San Francisco and the Fillmore East in New York all but created the era of arena rock, and he promoted the Rolling Stones' 1972 American tour, which set the standard for road-show depravity, as well as the outdoor Watkins Glen festival headlined by the Dead and the Allman Brothers. Seeing the commotion, the swarthy, scowling Graham, as Powell remembered later, "came running down the ramp and punched me in the mouth. I mean with full momentum. Knocked me about ten feet. He knocked me silly. I was bleeding everywhere, and I was about to pass out."

As if in a scene from *Animal House*, Leon, also in the area, leapt into action. "I go running to Billy's aid," he once said, "and here comes Ronnie, Gary, and we're all up there," mixing it up with bouncers, fans, whoever. Somehow in this melee Powell was able to get the pass from his pocket, upon which Graham turned contrite. "He apologized, swear to God, ten times," Powell said. Still feeling badly two months later, Graham would send a five-foot floral wreath and bottles of Jack Daniels to the Whisky a Go Go when Skynyrd was booked to play there. If they could draw an apology from Bill Graham, it must have felt like the world really was in their hip pocket.

Ronnie was also busy that night working the press. The young Cameron Crowe, covering the Who on tour for *Rolling Stone*, was backstage after the concert when a thick-chested guy with stringy blond hair sidled up next to him. "I can really relate to you," he said, "because you're a young guy starting out and I'm a young guy starting out." Crowe recalls Van Zant as "the first musician that crossed the line and talked to me like I was an artist or a writer. It blew me away. [He was] a straight-ahead, sensitive guy. No agenda. He didn't ask me to write about him." But Crowe did write about him, went on the road with the band, contributed liner notes to one of their albums, and in 2000 wrote his first movie *Almost Famous* about coming of age and then some with them (in the guise of the fictitious band Stillwater, an amalgam of Skynyrd, the Stones, and Led Zeppelin). Smart as the leader of the band was, gaining exposure in the Yankee-dominated rock media was a piece of cake, done with a dollop of charm and a load of bull.

★ ★ ★

The most obvious Who "thing" was their dance of nihilism, smashing their instruments at the conclusion of a concert, an exhibition of senseless mayhem that would send crowds, who by then expected it as part of the show, into a sometimes frightening frenzy. Jimi Hendrix had been so impressed with that dynamic of postmodern beatitude by anarchy that he started setting his own precious guitars on fire at the epochal 1967 Monterey Pop Festival, as if to outdo Townsend's earlier destruction of his own guitar by smashing it to bits, a routine he had begun in 1964. Not that Skynyrd would ever, *could* ever, have done this, even when they were rich enough to, not those gorgeous instruments of their craft that meant so much to them.

Still, there were plenty of other lessons they eagerly sucked up—including their introduction to drugs in addition to the usual booze, booze, and more booze. It was on the *Quadrophenia* tour that Skynyrd encountered cocaine, heroin, pills of many sizes and colors, and God knows what else, all readily available backstage and at the hotels where both bands stayed. As Leon Wilkeson said, getting shit faced had nothing to do with acting the part of rock rebels; it was because "we were terrified to go up on the stage and perform before The Who." But the problem with the drinking, he said, was that "we never stopped." Seeing them at close range, Rudge's assistant, Chris Charlesworth, formed an immediate image in his mind of the country boys. They all, he recalls, "drank like fishes, took all known illegal drugs, fucked anything female on two legs, and liked nothing better than to fight with their fists, either against others or amongst themselves." Ronnie, he added, "was the toughest of the lot and he could more or less silence any of the others with the threat of a beating."

Another infamous part of the Who playbook offered additional comfort: satisfying the primal urge to blow off steam by trashing hotel rooms and having the record company pay for it among the overall travel "expenses." Billy Powell remembered how, as a kind of rite of passage into rock stardom, starting on that tour they would throw half-filled cans at the back of the TV until the alcohol soaked the tubes and set them on fire. "We'd watch it blow up," Powell said, still amused by such a simple pleasure. Another one was heaving beer cans out the windows and into the swimming pool below. Back in L.A., MCA would find bills, often running into the thousands, from promoters and hotels seeking recompense for the damage done by the label's new investment. Kooper could only shrug and point out that it all went with the territory of rock. Somehow, both bands were able to get it together at show time. What else mattered?

★ ★ ★

However, at times during the tour they seemed to be progressively coming apart at the seams. There were so many complicated components in trying to recreate the densely layered studio effects on the Who's *Quadrophenia* that something was apt to go wrong and often did. They brought with them a score of tapes that had to be played on the sound system at precisely the right time, and if one wasn't, the timing and texture would be thrown off. Soon, Townsend slapping Pridden wasn't good enough. The Who actually *stopped* playing songs from the album in favor of the simpler songs from the past, which required no technological appurtenances; but those who had bought the album in droves, not to mention the critics, were baffled. Right from the start, the enormous pressure that Townsend put on himself to make the tape sequencing and light shows work—and the emotional outbursts that followed when something screwed up—provided the Who with one of many excuses to unwind by wrecking themselves and, famously, whatever hotel harbored them. Such wreckage had become their signature, an all but obligatory part of their persona.

And they didn't disappoint on *that* count. Once, after a show in Montreal, they were so out of control and caused so much destruction to their hotel room that the Canadian Mounted Police were called. They were arrested and bailed out, and as usual let their managers and accountants pay for the damage. Because of the negative publicity, promoters in Denver canceled the six shows the Who was to headline there. Stepping into all this madness and chaos, Skynyrd, Billy Powell would say, "blew

The Who away." Ronnie, however, didn't con himself into believing that. By tour's end, he would recall, "We were playing good and still getting our asses kicked by The Who." He said of the tour, however, "I really dug it. It was like a challenge. . . . And we didn't have to change our show any. We're still doing what we did in the clubs."

If the Who were grateful for Skynyrd getting audiences jacked up and perhaps a little less apt to find fault with the main attraction, they apparently were not thrilled about being upstaged. Yet those were the times when the boys from Britain would rebound and put on some of their best performances, as if to keep pace with the rubes from Florida. All in all, the bizarre juxtaposition worked to benefit both bands—even if in order to keep the tour rumbling on night after night, the Brits and the good old boys needed constant numbing. "The drinking was crazy," agrees Rossington, "but we'd just wake up the next morning and go for it." It was so crazy that it openly became part of the act. Wilkeson once noted that "we decided to take the bar atmosphere on stage. We had a little portable bar up there and everybody was drinking."

Still, they won grudging admiration from the Who, and on Rossington's twenty-second birthday, December 1, Townshend came into his room with booze and a cake and, Rossington recalls, "mashed the cake in my face," apparently a ritual of acceptance. Skynyrd got even when Roger Daltrey happened into the Skynyrd dressing room just as a bottle of beer was thrown across the room for someone, sending a sudsy spray all over him and ruining his expensive, tailored vest. The increasingly besotted tour stumbled from the Forum in L.A. to the Dallas Memorial Auditorium to the Omni in Atlanta to the Saint Louis Arena to the International Amphitheatre in Chicago to Cobo Hall in Detroit to the Montreal Forum to the Boston Garden to the Spectrum in Philadelphia to the finale at the Capital Centre outside DC on December 6. Then Skynyrd, on their own again, jumped back to their originally planned tour, headlining with Black Oak Arkansas, Canned Heat, and Brownsville Station at the Palladium in Hollywood, opening for Blue Oyster Cult at the Long Beach Arena, and finally, headlining a sold-out New Year's Eve show back in Atlanta at the Sheraton-Biltmore Hotel.

Keeping the iron hot, instead of going back home to Jacksonville to chill, they immediately headed back to the studio with Kooper for their second album. According to their contract, they would need a new one every nine months. This time they recorded not in Doraville but across the continent at the Record Plant in L.A., a logical choice since a California tour, with them as headliners, was to begin in San Diego on January 12, allowing for recording on off days and performing at night. The backbreaking schedule would test their endurance and whether they had the right stuff. To Skynyrd, though, it was business as usual, as long as they had gigs and bottles of hooch to comfort them, not to mention vials and little paper envelopes filled with a certain white powder to keep them from collapsing.

They had picked up something else from the Who as well—a future manager. Pete Rudge had seen enough of them on the tour to decide he wanted to run their affairs and bring them even further into the rock elite. But there was a minor complication: Skynyrd already had a manager who went everywhere with them. Down the road something was going to have to give—something named Alan Walden.

* * *

Despite the band's to-kill-for gig with the Who, the rock media fairly ignored *pronounced.* If Skynyrd's presence on the tour provided a crucial lift for them—and their performances indeed killed—they were still a long way down the rock roster, more a novelty for the young, northern college-bred editors at the increasingly upscale *Rolling Stone* and even for the more fanzine-style rags such as the C trinity—*Circus, Crawdaddy!*, and *Creem*, the last of which had the brass to call itself AMERICA'S ONLY ROCK 'N' ROLL MAGAZINE. In fact *Creem* was the first of the crowd to give the band any media attention, a July 28, 1973, note about Kooper's bash at Richard's. Oddly, it was the teeming British rock press that found more space for them. The October 31 issue of *Sounds* magazine smartly perceived the LP as "a raw blend of hillbilly, country, and British boogie packed with typically Southern flavor; moaning slide guitar, country-pickin' mandolin, aggressive guitars, driving rhythm section . . . and dry, thirst-parched vocals. . . . Van Zant's lyrics completed the geographical picture with tales of disapproving daddies, guns, trains, rides, ghettos, the Lord, and getting high on dope and booze."

It was hard to get a handle on them. Rossington, when asked what they were, could only reply, "We were kinda rebels." Indeed, they were *kinda* a lot of things: nonhippie hippies, but far more prone to crush flowers under their boots than wear them in their hair, more Harley hog than Magic Bus, kinda hard, kinda soft—and both in one song, their own "Stairway to Heaven," a compost of nice 'n' easy and nice 'n' rough. Decades later, *Rolling Stone*'s album guide decided that *pronounced* "boiled down its potent regional influences—blues, country, soul—into a heady, potentially crippling homebrew. They liked to play; those three lead guitars weren't just for show." Robert Christgau's review in the *Village Voice* read, "Lacking both hippie roots and virtuosos, post-Allmanites like ZZ Top, Marshall Tucker, and Wet Willie become transcendently boring except when they get off a good song. But in this staunchly un-transcendent band, lack of virtuosos is a virtue, because it inspires good songs, songs that often debunk good-old-boy shibboleths."

Critics have noted the tie between redneck and metal rock in songs like "Tuesday's Gone" and "Poison Whiskey," which, as a 2012 review on the *Ace Black Blog* said, "exude animated danger festering at rock's far reaches. . . . Solid examples of the best elements of southern rock reaching for the solidity of metal, the vocals of Ronnie Van Zant perfectly suitable for stretching into metal, and the guitars of Gary Rossington and Allen Collins more than willing to follow. . . . The good material succeeds in outweighing the bad, and the greatness on the album is pronounced 'Free-Bird.'"

Others look back at Skynyrd's flowering through a cultural lens. Historian Barbara Ching points to the album, which Van Zant always said was Skynyrd's best, as something startlingly new for its time, "the mock-didactic title . . . suggest[ing] that the band came from a South so deep that even the language was incomprehensible"—which in this case only worked in their favor. Indeed, all future cover art and publicity photos of the band would reflect the tableau of that Deep South, which as Ching put it, "displayed sullen and grungy members in kudzu-choked landscapes." *Uncut* calls the LP "all spring-tight riffage, jukin' country and delinquent boogie . . . chicken-skin music in the raw. On 'Simple Man' and 'Things Goin' On,' Van Zant emerged as a lyricist with a common touch, making monuments of everyman while decrying the political hypocrisy that kept them poor."

But all this was a taste of still-cooking stew. On the way was the song that would make them the only thing anyone would need to know—*Skynyrd.*

The one-story wood-frame house that Lacy Van Zant built for his brood at 1285 Mull Street in "Shantytown," the hardscrabble neighborhood on the west side of Jacksonville, stands pretty much as it did when Ronnie Van Zant was young. CAMERON SPIRITAS

Here, at Robert E. Lee High School, which still stands stately on South McDuff Avenue, the Shantytown boys ran afoul of crusty gym coach Leonard Skinner for wearing their hair too long, which earned them suspensions and inspired a ready-made name for their band. CAMERON SPIRITAS

In perhaps the first-known photo of Lynyrd Skynyrd, the bandmates play onstage at Atlanta's dingy Funochio's club on July 21, 1972, with bass man Leon Wilkeson singing lead, while Ronnie Van Zant looks on. Gary Rossington strikes a chord while Allen Collins, his face hidden by hair, focuses on his own guitar. CARTER TOMASSI

Few would know that a slice of rock history was made in this drab warehouse at 2517 Edison Avenue, which in the early 1970s housed the Little Brown Jug, where Ronnie was inspired to write "Gimme Three Steps," the semitrue tale of a flirtation gone very wrong. CAMERON SPIRITAS

Copping an Allman Brothers' pose, Skynyrd lines up on a Macon, Georgia, street and shows some attitude for the cover of *(pronounced 'lĕh-'nérd 'skin-'nérd)*, which would eventually go double platinum. From left to right are Leon Wilkeson, Billy Powell, Ronnie Van Zant, Gary Rossington, Bob Burns, Allen Collins, and Ed King. GETTY IMAGES

In this shot from May 6, 1973, taken during sessions for Skynyrd's debut album at Studio One in Doraville, Georgia, Al Kooper, in the glasses, works the control board as Ronnie and Gary try to lend a hand and engineer "Tub" Langford stands by. GETTY IMAGES

During Skynyrd's 1973 tour with the Who, trying to keep up with the manic-eyed Keith Moon (left) Ronnie hoists a J&B in front of Allen's face while Gary appears to look for something to ingest from a candle bowl. GETTY IMAGES

Lacy Van Zant, who dubbed himself the "father of Southern rock," poses here with son Ronnie in 1975. DAVID M. HABBEN

If Ronnie was apt to take a swing at all the others in the band at any given moment, he had nothing but admiration and even some envy for the clean and sober guitar virtuoso Steve Gaines, who became Skynyrd's newest member in 1976. AP

The essence of Skynyrd in a single image: Ronnie Van Zant, front and center, flanked by the guitar firepower of Allen Collins and Gary Rossington, the thunder of Leon Wilkeson's bass rolling in from stage right and Billy Powell's funky piano swirls from stage left—and a giant Confederate flag hanging over Artimus Pyle's booming drums. GETTY IMAGES

Ronnie and Gary rock out under blue skies that are so blue, not only in Alabama, but in Oakland, California, where this concert occurred. RALPH HULETT

October 20, 1977: Southern rock died in a swamp in Gillsburg, Mississippi, with the twisted wreckage of Skynyrd's rickety Convair CV-300 strewn between the trees that tore it apart, killing Ronnie Van Zant, Steve Gaines, Cassie Gaines, Dean Kilpatrick, and its two inept pilots. Miraculously, the other nineteen passengers on board survived. AP

A simple headstone in Jacksonville's Riverside Memorial Park marks the grave of Skynyrd's front man and of the southern rock movement. The original grave site was vandalized in 2000, necessitating that Ronnie's remains be moved to a concrete vault deep under the stone. DAVID M. HABBEN

The "Father of Southern Rock," as truck driver Lacy Van Zant dubbed himself, was laid to rest in 2004 alongside his wife, Marion Hicks "Sis" Van Zant, in Riverside Memorial Park, the same grounds where Ronnie Van Zant is buried. DAVID M. HABBEN

March 13, 2006: Oft-denied, Skynyrd was finally elected to the Rock and Roll Hall of Fame, giving the band a chance to bask in pride—though the body language of everyone but Billy Powell betrays the hurt feelings that still existed for Gary Rossington, Artimus Pyle, Ed King, and Bob Burns. AP

The Freebird Live Cafe on Jacksonville Beach—owned by Judy Jenness, Ronnie's widow and the executor of his estate—is the sort of place where the fledgling Lynyrd Skynyrd might once have honed their sound. CAMERON SPIRITAS

One of the many tributes to Jacksonville's most famous native son is Ronnie Van Zant Memorial Park, an eighty-five-acre stretch of greenery and crystal blue lakes in the Penney Farms area—the sort of spot where Ronnie might get away to fish, though he likely would have disobeyed the NO CURSING signs. CAMERON SPIRITAS

8

★ ★ ★ ★ ★

WE ALL DID WHAT WE COULD DO

Al Kooper had assembled the band at Studio One back in June 1973, a month after the *pronounced* album sessions had concluded but before Kooper's party at Richard's, to record a song that Ronnie swore to all that was holy just had to be a hit. It had come about a few weeks before at Hell House from a riff Ed King liked to say came to him in a dream but that, he says now, really began with him joining in on an idle Rossington riff. The way Ronnie incubated a song, King had come to learn, was most unusual. When such a riff was played for him on a guitar or piano, his brain would go into overdrive, but the others in the band wouldn't know until he had a microphone before him what he would sing.

"I never saw him write a lyric down," says King. "It was all in his head, based on the groove. If you ever showed up at rehearsal the next day and couldn't recapture the groove—you might have the chords right, but if you'd lost the groove—the lyrics were gone forever. One time he said, 'I can't remember it.' We go, 'What happened?' And he said, 'You guys lost it, man.' So you know, that song was gone. But that didn't happen anymore. We'd stay there till dark, playing stuff over and over until we were playing it in our sleep. No wonder that solo came to me in a dream, because we just played and played and played.

"Listen, Ronnie Van Zant really wasn't a redneck. He was a very sophisticated guy. I mean, people think he was just this rowdy, whiskey drinking, going out, gathering other women, but Ronnie had a level of sophistication that even early on just grew so fast. Every day you'd see a change. So I wouldn't, didn't even classify him as a redneck. But the thing about him that appealed to everybody is you could tell by listening to him sing that that's exactly what he was like in real life. I mean it's exactly him. All you had to listen to was six Skynyrd songs, and then you'd have the whole gist of what that man was about."

"Sweet Home Alabama," as this one was called, coalesced when King locked into Ronnie's lyrical progression, which from somewhere deep in Ronnie's thought process developed as an answer to Neil Young's scalding couplet of Dixie ragging, the 1970 "Southern Man" and 1972 "Alabama," eviscerating all southern men who didn't explicitly condemn the vestige of their "heritage" that had caused black men to hang from trees on nooses. "I saw cotton and I saw black," Young had sung on the former, a huge hit, "tall white mansions and little shacks. Southern Man, when will you pay them back?" In the latter song he further mocked the hypocrisy of men not compelled to "do what your good book says": "You got the rest of the union to help you along / What's going wrong?" Ronnie, who thought such generalizations ignored the obvious debt being paid to black music by country rock bands like his, decided to pay back the man he greatly admired. Indeed, he came to regard Young's 1972 smash "Heart of Gold" as a template, with its mourning slide guitar and thumping beat. He had a drawer full of Young T-shirts, which he often wore on stage and would continue to.

Ronnie, in fact, was squeamish about taunting Young. He later recalled that "I showed the verse to Ed and asked him what Neil might think. Ed said he'd dig it; he'd be laughing at it." And so he went on, repaying Young in kind, his lyrics just as stinging, sticking up for southern manhood. There was some soft soap too about the rush of being carried home "to see my kin" and the peerless Swampers up in Muscle Shoals, who've "been known to pick a song or two." But then there were the references that at first listen seemed affectionate about George Corley Wallace—"In Birmingham they love the Gov'nor"—followed by the most cryptic sequence of stray thoughts ever in rock: "Boo! Boo! Boo! We all did what we could do. / Now Watergate does not bother me, / Does your conscience bother you? (Tell the truth!)"

Just what this all meant was anyone's guess. Indeed, the references were in some ways outdated or predated. Wallace at the time was not quite the roaring lion. He was recovering from the near-fatal wounds he had suffered while campaigning for the 1972 Democratic presidential nomination, when the drifter Arthur Bremer shot him five times at a Maryland shopping center. After a hospital stay, Wallace returned to the governor's mansion, no less adamant in his support for, as he once infamously said, "segregation now, segregation tomorrow, segregation forever." Even in a wheelchair, he was still a hoary segregationist.

The reference to Birmingham was pointed, but it had been a decade since the city had witnessed the horrendous Ku Klux Klan church bombing that had killed four black girls—way back in 1963. As for Watergate, Ronnie was behind the curve. The scandal had grown and was closing in on Richard Nixon. The lyrics, then, were a weird hash of scattered, unfocused thoughts, something not surprising given that Ed King describes Van Zant's writing process as less than disciplined. "Basically," King says, "Ronnie didn't think real hard about what he was writing. He wrote from his heart; he was a guy who wrote his feelings into songs."

Artimus Pyle, after he later joined the group, believed he could play it with more conviction on the drums if he knew what Ronnie had in mind. As Pyle recalled, "Ronnie explained it to me he was telling the Southern Man that the Southern Man is not to be blamed for something that happened two hundred years ago. He was saying, 'I don't have anything against African American people,' and Ronnie didn't. He'd give the shirt off his back to anybody, black or white. Ronnie was not a racist."

Extrapolating all that from the lyrics of this song is impossible, and to be sure, Pyle would have more than one fanciful explanation about Skynyrd matters big and small. For his part, Rossington, believably, says that the picking of a fight with Neil Young was "completely fabricated. We all loved Neil. Ronnie used to wear Neil Young T-shirts all the time because he loved him and was really inspired by him. He just wrote those lines about 'Southern Man,' which seemed cute at the time, almost like a play on words." But the constructions that began to take hold about the overall intent of "Sweet Home Alabama" would not be so easy to dismiss as innocuous folderol.

* * *

While cutting the first vocal take of the tune, Ronnie, having trouble hearing the rhythm track in his headphones, instructed engineer Rodney Mills to "Turn it up!" For Kooper this must have brought back fond memories of playing his impromptu organ line on "Like a Rolling Stone," one that the record company executives in the studio hated but were overruled on by Bob Dylan barking, "Turn the organ up!" Perhaps feeling sentimental and because it caught Ronnie's sense of conviction, he left it in, prefacing King's prickly guitar intro, which repeated through the song—and which would be, ahem, appropriated four years later by Joe Perry on Aerosmith's "Walk This Way." So profound was King's riff that the Fender Stratocaster he used that day, the same one he'd originally played the riff on at Hell House, is in the Rock and Roll Hall of Fame—despite the fact that King liked it least of all his guitars. "It was a horrible guitar," he later said. "It was the banjo-like tone that prompted Ronnie to write about Alabama, like 'I come from Alabama with a banjo on my knee.' But I still hated it."

Kooper also got into the swing when, after the opening lines about hearing "Mister Young" sing about the South, the producer sang a line from the Young song—"Southern man, better use your head"—in harmony. Ronnie didn't care for it, but Kooper left his rendition in, though he mixed it so low that it was "nearly subliminal," he says. The band played at a honky-tonk blues pace, the three guitars pealing high and twangy, so sharply recorded by Kooper that they could tear off one's eyebrows. Prepared and on target as they were, they nailed it in one take, though Ronnie, who never liked anything the first time he heard it, demanded a second take to make sure. And Kooper wasn't through with it yet either. When he and the band went out to the coast for the Who tour, he brought the tape of the song so he could continue tweaking it, including adding a horn overlay at an L.A. studio. He also hired a trio of female soul singers, Merry Clayton, Clydie King, and Sherlie Matthews—proof enough to some that the song was hardly a celebration of Old South racism—to juice up the hooks; this was the second song of note Clayton would dress up, having sung a withering harmony with Mick Jagger and the unforgettable solo about "rape and murder" being just a shot away on "Gimme Shelter."

Finally calling it done, Kooper had in hand a fisty, smug, funky, hard-rockin' ode to the New South struggling to get out of the shadow of the Old Confederacy. With its clever and catchy title hook, a listener could get lost in a dreamy milieu where "the skies are so blue" and the words "Lord I'm coming home to you" could make it actually *feel* like the South was one's home, anyone's. But those throwaway lines about the "Gov'nor" and the most stigmatized of all Southern cities were going to be heard too—loud, if not exactly clear. Kooper was sanguine about it. "I think they were proud of where they came from," he said breezily. "Racism didn't come into it." Still, he had to admit that lines like "We all did what we could do" were "ambiguous." And even Ed King says he didn't know what Ronnie meant by it, especially in relation to Watergate. Kooper's interpretation of that line somehow was: "We tried to get Wallace out of there," although nothing in the maddeningly ambiguous song supported that point of view.

Feeling so good about the tune, as well he should have, Ronnie did not forget his promise to Jimmy Johnson. That night he called Muscle Shoals. "Hey, man," he told Johnson, "we put you guys in a song."

Johnson was duly flattered but had to wonder: Would anyone ever hear it?

Ronnie had no doubts about it. "Well, Ed," he told King when they wrapped up recording, "that's our 'Ramblin' Man.'"

* * *

"Gimme Three Steps" was released in November, backed with "Mr. Banker," one of the Kooper demo tapes that hadn't made it onto the album. Although the band was a hit out on the Who tour, the single made little penetration, failing to crack the charts or rouse concert audiences. Clearly, as a light-hearted pastiche of redneck life, it was more suited to be a change of pace after a hoped-for string of hits. Indeed, the buzz about Skynyrd was centered on "Free Bird," which was igniting audiences, and "Sweet Home Alabama," which they made sure to perform at every show and which etched their identity. The amazing thing was how tight the guitars were, how spectacularly they meshed, and how close to the Kooper studio versions these live performances were, confirming Kooper's initial conviction that he had never run across a band as polished and rehearsed to perfection as this one. On "Alabama," absent background singers, Leon stepped forward from his usual place hanging around the rear of the stage to execute a harmony vocal, something that delighted Ronnie once he learned that Wilkeson actually had a decent singing voice.

Having sung "Free Bird" hundreds of times already, Ronnie had developed a routine for what could be up to ten minutes of guitar onslaught. Having remained true to his vow never to try any hip-swiveling moves or flounce around like the bare-chested, Spandex-and-fringe-wearing front man of the hugely successful Black Oak Arkansas, Jim "Dandy" Mangrum—not that he *could* with all the beer he put in his gut—Ronnie would float between the guitarists or merely hang back by the drum, digging the groove. In his hat, jeans, and bare feet, he was still a riveting, engaging front man, even doing nothing.

Kooper and the MCA boys were satisfied. They had cautiously set a target sale level for the album of four hundred thousand copies, and with gathering momentum it had cleared one hundred thousand by the end of the year, which was punctuated by a show the band headlined in Atlanta at the Sheraton Biltmore that sold out its five thousand tickets and was a success even though the power went down for a few minutes during the set. They met up with Kooper at the Record Plant in Burbank with a full sheaf of new songs for the second album—though at first glance their visit might have been confused with a getaway at a spa. The studio was one of three with the same name, the others being in New York and Sausalito, California—all owned by Jimi Hendrix's former recording engineer Gary Kellgren and Revlon cosmetics executive Chris Stone. A radical departure from drab "dentist-officey" studios, as Kooper put it, the L.A. Plant was like the Playboy Mansion with recording gear. With a Jacuzzi room, three plush bedrooms, and hordes of nubile young women everywhere (and clothing purely optional), it was little wonder the Plant was *the* studio among the big L.A. bands.

Indeed, when the Skynyrd sessions commenced in one studio, the Eagles were in another cutting their magnum opus *Hotel California*, and the two bands mingled during breaks that were more like playtime. This was decadence of the highest order and lowest instinct, something the Eagles' Don Henley and Glenn Frey wrote and sang of in their new work but which Ronnie would claim was a turnoff to the Dixie boys more accustomed to back porches and fishin' hole contentment. He too would write of the L.A. mise-en-scène, not as a magnet but a mine field. None of the Skynyrd boys felt much like prowling the back alleys of Sunset; instead they spent almost all their time in the studio or in the Jacuzzi between takes, snorting piles of cocaine.

The growing success of the debut Skynyrd album gave Kooper more leeway, and his budget for the new album was upped to around $30,000. The band kept faster company now as well, a fact that was underscored when during the sessions John Lennon, during his three-year "lost weekend" separation from Yoko Ono, dropped into the studio and hung out (though in his perpetual drunkenness he may not have known who *he* was, much less this band from the South). By comparison, Skynyrd was all business. They had come in with seven songs well thought out, arranged, and rehearsed to perfection at Hell House. Kooper, looking for the same formula as that of *pronounced*, was amazed at the versatility of material before him. In a real tour de force, they gassed up Oklahoman blues troubadour J.J. Cale's 1972 ballad "Call Me the Breeze" into slick, *loud*, foot-stomping biker-bar blues, with sizzling solos by Rossington on slide guitar and Powell on piano. Another eye-opener was "The Needle and the Spoon," a Van Zant–Collins tune confronting the bane of heroin, with Ronnie's vocal cutting to the bone:

> I've been feelin' so sick inside
> Got to get better, lord before I die
> Seven doctors couldn't help my head, they said
> You better quit, son before you're dead.

They also had written their best pure blues song, the Van Zant–Collins original "Ballad of Curtis Loew," in which Ronnie spun a fictitious yarn about selling soda bottles as a boy to pay to hear "an old black man with white curly hair" play his "old Dobro." That man, given the name Curtis Loew, was a composite of the great Delta guitar masters and "the finest picker to ever play the blues." Kooper kept the arrangement to a minimum, with Ed and Gary alternating on slide and Al playing piano and acoustic guitar and singing backup vocals.

For the first two weeks, with no gigs to get in the way of recording, they raced through the album. Kooper found a place for the parody riff he liked so much, "Workin' for MCA." Besides "Sweet Home Alabama," a good candidate for release as a single was "I Need You," a valentine from Ronnie to Judy—and to Paul Rodgers, given that the tune was intended to be the album's Free soundalike. "What more can I say / Ooh baby, I need you / I miss you more everyday," he crooned as sinewy multiple guitars rang behind him. Every song seemed to come up a winner. Another, the Van Zant–King "Swamp Music," was a heartfelt wish to flee "them big ol' city blues" and spend long days huntin' 'coons with hound dogs, and it throbbed to the beat of Eric Clapton's "Lay Down Sally." Al Kooper was pleased to note that no attempt was made to do "Free Bird II."

The album, called *Second Helping*, rounded out the rough edges of *pronounced*, an objective that could be seen in the cover art. The bone design of the Skynyrd logo was smoothed into more of a *Flintstones* look than a Black Sabbath one by mod artist Jan Salerno. In a psychedelic, pastel-colored Peter Max–style collage Salerno inserted the band's rotogravure faces into something resembling a church window or a honeycomb around which were images of birds' wings and leaves that could have been cannabis. The jacket sleeve had individual black and white, Scavullo-esque shots in various cool poses, and one of the group tossing Kooper into a pool during a birthday party at his house. They did manage to throw in some satirical, frat-boy touches, listing among the album credits a string of pseudonyms—Wicker, Toby, Cockroach, Moochie, Punnel, Wolfman, Kooder, Mr. Feedback, and Gooshie—the band's pet names for each other, Kooper, the soundman Kevin Elson, and chief roadie Dean Kilpatrick. "Wicker" was Ronnie's nickname, one that stemmed from, Ed King says, "the name of a gay guy in a movie." Van Zant liked how it sounded and adopted it, daring anyone to infer he was gay. *That* would have been dangerous to someone's health, for sure.

★ ★ ★

Images aside, there were deeper issues to be resolved. As Kooper recalls, "I sent them the mix, and they went bonkers. Too much cowbell here, not enough vocal there." Fighting a deadline for the album's release, he took the tapes to the Record Plant in Sausalito to mix, aided by Ed King who came up just days before a six-day Skynyrd run at Whisky a Go Go. When Ed arrived, he found Kooper in a house provided by Stone and Kellgren, which was crawling with drugs and bouncy young things. King, who came up with his wife, was disgusted. Once, when Kooper was playing music in his bedroom at ear-splitting levels in the middle of the night, King walked in and tore the arm off the record player. Another time, seeing Al and a friend snapping pictures of a naked woman, King, as Kooper recalled, "just walked outside shaking his head."

Despite all this, what they finally came out with was another remarkable piece of vinyl, one that *Rolling Stone* retroactively observed "served up the band's feisty hard-rock twang to a broad national audience." Stephen Thomas Erlewine of Allmusic.com regards Van Zant's work on this album as a tour de force, "at turns plainly poetic, surprisingly clever, and always revealing" and credits him for "developing a truly original voice." In *Crawdaddy!*, Bud Scoppa wrote that the album "cannily and positively draw[s] a distinction between Skynyrd and the Allman Brothers, a key distinction for them."

As big a gift as Kooper had in "Sweet Home Alabama," he decided to hold it back, not, he insists, out of any risk the band would be stereotyped as too regional but because he wanted it to be a killer follow-up to a first hit. Thus the first single was "Don't Ask Me No Questions," written by Van Zant and Rossington on a fishing trip, always a head-clearing interlude, that had Ronnie hating on the pressures of the record industry; integrating that theme into a typically macho dismissal of a suspicious woman's inquiries about where he'd been, he sang with his best sneering arrogance, "Don't ask me no questions and I won't tell you no lies / So don't ask me about my business and I won't tell you goodbye." Kooper put a lot into the song, including a full horn section with longtime Rolling Stones sax man Bobby Keys, and played piano and sang backup. The single went out on the market in April backed with "Take Your Time," a song that had been left off the album; and amid a heavy ad campaign Skynyrd set sail on another long, long trek called the Second Helping Tour.

But while the album began to sell well, the single failed to chart. And the tour itself was becoming something of a bummer as well, the high point being perhaps when they played Nassau Coliseum on February 25, the first time they'd been back on Long Island since the Black Sabbath fiasco. This time, they were the headliner, and the sold-out show went perfectly. Fortuitously, the schedule then took them to their home turf, playing gigs around the South, for the next month and a half. But they needed a jolt, lest they become yet one more band with promise who simply couldn't cut it in the marketplace. As it happened, they had the jolt they needed in their hip pocket—"Sweet Home Alabama" had become even more of a fan favorite, available on record, and was getting more airplay from the disc jockeys than "No Questions." Now, Kooper knew, it *had* to come out as a single, and the future of the band was riding on it.

★ ★ ★

"Sweet Home Alabama," with the flip side again "Take Your Time," hit the stores on June 24, 1974, and began to scramble up the chart, stopping at number eight on the *Billboard* Hot 100 chart in late summer. On its way up, it did more than give Lynyrd Skynyrd its first and only Top 10 hit. It unfurled the symbolic pennon, and the accompanying baggage, that they have carried ever since. Even before it was released as a single, it had become their virtual theme song out on the hustings, so it was only logical to develop some sort of stage atmospherics to help frame it as such. Thus came the entrance of the highly contentious monogram that still causes delight and consternation to this day.

There is no agreement about who exactly made the decision to pin the literal Confederate flag on Skynyrd's figurative hide. After it began to appear, it drove redneck fans into a frenzy and nonrednecks into a state of revulsion that an American band had adopted this long-shunned symbol of intolerance at a time when de facto segregation was still extant in the South. When the sharp divide became apparent, Ronnie was not prepared to fall on a Confederate sword—not when it might cut to pieces Skynyrd's carefully crafted mainstream appeal. Finding a convenient fall guy, he put the blame squarely on the bosses. The flag, he said, was "strictly an MCA gimmick . . . you know, Southern band, drunken fighters and all that. They put out that publicity. Hype, nothin' but hype."

Gary on the other hand maintained that the flag entered the picture as a result of their corporate owners *not* caring much about contributing any ideas or angles for the band to use. "MCA didn't promote us," he said. "*We* promoted us. We were from the South and our audience always had rebel flags, flying 'em and putting 'em on stage. One night we just said, 'Hey, let's just get a big one and put it behind us.' It was just that simple. We didn't mean nothing by it. There was no meaning; like the flag means this, or we're against blacks. We're just from the South. It wasn't no big thing to us, it's not a 'Hell no, we ain't forgetting, let's be rednecks' kind of thing."

Although Alan Walden boasted that he and Mike Maitland had sat down and put together a "brilliant marketing plan" for Skynyrd, neither took ownership of the flag idea. Putting the onus back onto the band,

Bob Davis, an executive at MCA Records who in the 1980s became vice president of the label, said, "I don't [believe] that MCA as a company, from a policy point of view, was in any way involved in decisions as to stage presentation, whether or not Confederate flags or anything were part of the presentation of the live show. That being said, that doesn't mean there were not people out in the field, whether they were sales or marketing people, promotion people, who weren't making suggestions . . . in connection with marketing a record."

Those people would have had a great influence on a fairly wide-eyed band in the maw of free-wheeling, free-ranging record company lackeys, either under contract or as loosely affiliated promotional leeches and lemmings—think Artie Fufkin, Paul Shaffer's bumbling record-company stooge in *This Is Spinal Tap*. People just like that swarmed around bands on the rise, meeting them backstage or in hotels looking for an in, the pockets of their faux-satin baseball jackets stuffed with envelopes of cocaine. Not only were such supplies liberally dispensed to Skynyrd, fueling their descent into an addiction inferno, but the yes men, amoral as they were, eagerly endorsed the Confederate flag as a marketing tool, on the assumption that racism could be cool.

Certainly, Skynyrd needed *something* to enliven a rather static onstage persona. Davis thought they were "very bland" and wanted to add pizzazz. And Al Kooper had perhaps unwittingly opened the door for something more daring than an image of long-haired rednecks when he applied the skull-and-bones motif to their album and subsequent promotional materials; soon T-shirts with that motif were selling quite nicely at arenas. Adding one more promotional tool might put them over the top, and it surely made sense to some at the record company that the Stars and Bars conveyed some sort of nativist pride, if seen in the narrow context of southern "heritage." When Skynyrd would enter the stage to "Dixie" playing through the hall and a giant Confederate flag covering the entire back wall, there was surely a surge of regional pride in the air—but also a surge of anger.

This helped them in the South but elsewhere left a decided unease and instant revulsion. For many African Americans and for northern liberals, including the most respected music critics, the flag was tantamount to a swastika, and defending it was a very tricky business, as the band would learn. Ronnie, who would usually act on gut instinct and say the hell with whoever disagreed with him, burned up the phone line with calls to Charlie Daniels, his confidant, concerned the band was asking for big trouble. Daniels told him to keep it in the act, that it would do more harm than good to remove it, and that the issue would recede when critics came to size up Skynyrd as a nonpolitical bunch with a regional angle that cut to the heart of the South's identity—not as racists but good, decent folks keeping the faith with its traditions sullied by civil war and opprobrium for its mistakes. Skynyrd's songs were, after all, about just those elemental themes.

Or *most* of them. With "Sweet Home Alabama" they would inject a new element, taking them into deeper water. Indeed, the first manifestation of the flag was the jacket art for the single release of the song, featuring an image of a young woman's beckoning lips, onto which were stuck a color image of the Confederate flag. This put the race angle in blatantly sexualized terms, always the most incendiary of all in matters of race, not long separated from the days of Emmett Till when a black man could be lynched for merely looking at a white woman. As squeamish about it as the band was, when the lights went up on their shows, audiences went absolutely crazy. There would be deafening shouts of *yee-haw!* and others cries that sounded like they emanated from barnyard animals. On the opening guitar bars, feet stomped, hands clapped, and the building shook. When Ronnie sang, "Big wheels keep on turning," a mass sing-along would erupt. Emotions would keep rising until the great climax of "Free Bird" left everyone limp.

The phenomenon was unlike anything they had seen, and it helped manufacture an institutional engraving for the song. As Ed King says, "I'm sure Dickey Betts disagrees, but 'Sweet Home Alabama' is the Southern anthem." But, as it happened, part and parcel of this was that most southerners and those who *felt* like southerners listening to Skynyrd took the lyrics of the song as a cue to release some not-so-courtly feelings. The easiest thing for the band to explain was the fight they had picked with Neil Young, who for his part refused to take the bait and indulge in a cheesy "feud." He expressed no ill will and said he greatly admired Skynyrd, which he proved in future years when he said the lyrics of his that Ronnie had objected to were "condescending and accusatory" and "not fully thought out." Indeed, Young had some repenting to do; in 1972 the soundtrack of his pseudodocumentary *Journey Through the Past* was released with cover art depicting hooded horsemen carrying cruciform staves and an inset photo of Young glaring at a Confederate flag. If Van Zant wasn't pissed off by *that*, he may as well have walked away from his birthright.

Al Kooper helpfully confirmed that Young "loved" the Skynyrd song. And proving that there never was a schism between them, Van Zant and Young began discussing collaborating on future songs. Ronnie pointedly wore T-shirts on stage screened with Young's face. Neil would wear a Skynyrd/Jack Daniel's T-shirt. After Ronnie's death, Neil Young would perform a cover version of the very song that had taken him to task.

* * *

Not so easily dispensed with was the reaction to those confusing lyrics about Wallace and Watergate. With people in his circle beginning to wonder if he had produced a racist band, Al Kooper suddenly was not so sure about what the song said. "Hey, you have to be more careful when you write a song now," was his revised opinion. Skynyrd might have wanted to say to him, "Hey, Al, nice of you tell us that *now.*" Pissed off that they even had to address the issue, they acted as if anyone who asked was an idiot. Ronnie, far from what he told Artimus Pyle later, called it a "joke song" and "a party tune" that he never thought would ever be released as a single, and that when it was, it "hit Top 10 and we've been paying for it ever since," though they also had been *paid* for it ever since, quite well. "We're not into politics," he said. "We don't have no education, and Wallace don't know anything about rock n' roll."

Ed King, however, doesn't toe the company line these days. Contrary to what Van Zant may have told Pyle, King says, "Ronnie was a big fan of George Wallace. He totally supported him. We all did. We respected the way Wallace stood up for the South. Anybody who tells you differently is lying."

What Van Zant was trying to do was clear the biggest hurdle for any Southern Man: separating the concept of "standing up for the South" from the chaff of innate racism. It would seem impossible that he could have worked Wallace into these lyrics as he did without realizing that the man was a breathing synonym for intolerance. Wallace himself would need to go to great lengths later in his life to remove the stigma, saying in 1998, "I was wrong. Those days are over, and they ought to be over." The need for Van Zant to walk the racial tightrope was unavoidable, especially after his own record company had put him up there on that high wire. If the crackers embraced Skynyrd, it was still incumbent on him—not on the suits at MCA but the band's leader—to assure the record-buying public that nothing racist was meant by "Sweet Home Alabama." And, no matter his feelings about "the Gov'nor," he did so, with great contrition.

"Of course I don't agree with everything Wallace says," he said. "I don't like what he says about colored people"—yet the fact that he used a pejorative term for African Americans while insisting nothing had been pejorative in the song only underscored the quandary of acting southern without malice carved out of southern conditioning.

He went on, "We're southern rebels, but more than that, we know the difference between right and wrong. . . . My father supports Wallace but that doesn't mean I have to. . . . I've heard him talk and wanted to ask him about his views on blacks and why he has such poor education and such a low school rate there, such a low housing rate," meaning for African Americans.

His best case for proving that the song was actually a sly rebuke of Wallace lay in those three repetitive syllables in the verse that he explained were the key to understanding the entire song. "The lyrics," he said, "were misunderstood. The general public didn't notice the words 'Boo Boo Boo!' after that particular line, and the media picked up only on the reference to the people loving the governor."

Not everyone bought it. As was the case with the rest of the lyrics, the "*Boo! Boo! Boo!*" refrain could be construed any way the imagination wanted. If he had been serious about debunking Wallace, why not *say* it, in words, something like, say, "In Birmingham they love the Gov'nor / Well, that ain't something they should do." Why go with a guttural ballpark response to an umpire's bad call? Still, it provided plausible deniability, though that was not really needed; in fact, the murky connection with Wallace seemed only to add another whiff of outlaw chic. Skynyrd might have been pissed about the brouhaha, but they could live quite nicely with having a hit. And if anyone needed a period to put on the end of the sentence, Leon Wilkeson offered it. "I support Wallace about as much as your average American supported Hitler," the inscrutable bassist said.

* * *

Wily bush dog that he was, Van Zant likely was apolitical, it not being worth the aggravation of lecturing people who just wanted to hear him sing, not talk. The only endorsement for a candidate he ever made was still on the horizon, support he would offer when another son of the South ran for president—a *Democrat*, of all things, a clear case of regional loyalty being political enough for him. He did know that he had a tightrope to walk, playing to type in his writing and stage persona while avoiding any taint of too-literal Confederate status; it was already a heavy enough lift for MCA's radio liaisons to get Skynyrd played on FM stations in the North. And in fact, Ronnie *was* a different sort of Confederate soldier, as was Wallace, who despite his segregationist stance never got on board with standard right-wing doggerel about the underclass being, in the contemporary vernacular, "takers"; indeed, by then Wallace had won a certain fealty among Alabama's black underclass, having raised taxes on the rich to sink money into the ghettos.

That was the Wallace with whom Van Zant related. "To me," Ed King says, "Ronnie was a proud, working-class southern man, and George Wallace represented proud, working-class southern people. To Ronnie, Wallace was not just a man who wouldn't let blacks into a college, he was a man who spoke for poor, uneducated people who didn't have a voice. It's right there in ['Sweet Home Alabama']." Still, it was never easy to split hairs when it came to Wallace. The "Gov'nor" so loved the song that when Skynyrd and the Charlie Daniels Band played a gig in Tuscaloosa, Wallace appeared on stage to present Skynyrd with plaques making them honorary lieutenant colonels in the Alabama State Militia—another symbol of racial grievance, since the militia had imposed martial law during the civil rights marches. Rather than steering clear of the "honor," they eagerly jumped at the chance to be deputized. Indeed, agreeing with King, Charlie Daniels recalls that Van Zant "had great respect for George Wallace. Ronnie was a southerner, man [and when] they got plaques from the governor . . . they were just tickled to death about it."

Yet here too Ronnie had to backtrack, calling the interlude a "bullshit gimmick thing," neglecting to say that the band kept that hardware and their "commissions" in the militia. And decades later, when the song was made into the state motto, no one in the band calling itself Lynyrd Skynyrd threw *that* fish back either. Al Kooper tells of the time when, during the recording of *pronounced,* he brought to the studio a guitar that had been given to him by Jimi Hendrix. Someone he identifies only as "one of the Skynyrd boys" began fooling with it, saying, "Hey, Al, this guitar plays nice." From across the room, Ronnie said, "That guitar used to belong to Jim Hendrix," whereupon the guy, Kooper says, "let it fall out of his hands onto the couch. '*OOOO . . . I just got some nigger on me!*' he screamed irreverently."

"You better pick that guitar up," Ronnie said, "and see if you can get some *more* of that nigger on ya."

Naturally, such palaver was meant in jest, but it did show how easy it was for men of the South to fall into racially offensive dialogue odious to northerners and progressive southerners. One Yankee journalist, Jaan Uhelszki, who was sent to write a piece about Skynyrd for *Creem,* claimed the experience made her feel like she needed to be deloused. After meeting Rossington, she said she expected him to tell her "some juicy tales of nigger skinnings." Mark Kemp, then a southern music journalist and later an editor at *Rolling Stone* and vice president at MTV, wrote in his 2004 book *Dixie Lullaby* of visiting Ed King and asking if anyone in the band had ever uttered racist thoughts. "When King's wife, who was sitting at the table with us, chimed in, saying, 'Oh, please, I remember Gary making a comment just a few years ago,' King immediately interrupted her." Choosing his words carefully, King then told Kemp, "I don't have any personal experience with that. But I can tell you this: unlike the Allman Brothers, we never had any black people hanging around Lynyrd Skynyrd at all. At all. I mean, none at all."

Yet, as if King himself had been bitten by the routine, quotidian expression of racism during his time with the band, he too betrayed some rather acrid opinions during the highly charged debate surrounding the Trayvon Martin killing in 2013. King wrote on his Facebook page that young black men were "lazy," "thugs," "killers," and "thieves," and that blacks in America have "had their reparations." Kemp, who had believed King was the "enlightened" one in Skynyrd, took that label back.

"I thought he had more insight than other right-wing rockers. I was wrong. . . . Who the hell does this ex-southern rocker think he is to moralize so generically and condescendingly about 'blacks' he doesn't even know?" (King later scrubbed the offensive remarks from his page.)

As much as Ronnie craved black recognition for Skynyrd, a few bluesy numbers did little to ameliorate centuries of cultural and racial conditioning.

* * *

While MCA had gotten down with the flag and was feasting on "redneck chic," fashioning the band's name in promotional materials and record jackets out of pieces of the Confederate flag, Ronnie began to feel the heat over it. Asked to explain what the flag meant to the act, he did his damndest to deflect the issue by folding it into his general beef about the "establishment"—the "gimmick"-hungry record company. "It was useful at first," he allowed, "but by now it's embarrassing." Years later, *Rolling Stone*'s John Swenson bought into this construct that by flying the flag Skynyrd was actually making their own antiestablishment stand, the Old Confederacy being among that establishment. The flag, he wrote, had "some kind of complex relationship to the Confederacy, but it's not about states' rights or slavery; it's something very personal. It's closer to the whole idea of the Declaration of Independence. This was their version of it, being a rebel."

It was a tortuous rationale, assuming a whole lot, but it did make some sense given the Skynyrd inferiority complex that would never end; as high as they got, they always saw themselves as mutts—dirty dogs—never accepted as anything more by the cultured rock Brahmins and thus never under any obligation to act like anything else. It was a self-serving prophesy and shield, giving them license to act like dogs. If the problem areas of the flag and "Sweet Home Alabama" were thorny, Skynyrd might deflect criticism but embrace the notoriety. In fact, rather than merely let the flag be an avatar, they went even further. Soon their sound equipment was painted battleship gray, a "Confederate" hue that blended in with the backdrop of the flag. Ronnie even strode onto the stage one night clad in a Confederate officer's coat and hat—though he later laughed it off as a "showbiz stunt," his way of sending up the whole kerfuffle about the flag.

With so much at stake, all they could do was follow along with it and hope that lame clarifications about the "gimmicks" would keep the fallout off their backs. However, as time went on they almost became *prisoner* to that flag, even consumed at times by it. The first time Skynyrd took their show across the pond to Europe—a two-month trek beginning in mid-November 1974 with dates in Glasgow and Edinburgh, two weeks in England, three days in Germany, one day each in Belgium and France, and the finale at the Rainbow Theatre in London on December 12—the flag came too, though Europeans had not the slightest notion of the mortal insult it was to African Americans. As Ronnie reported, patrons such as those the band played for at venues like Britain's Saint George's Hall, Theatre Royal, the Kursaal, Theater An Der Brienne Strasse, Jahrhunderthalle, and Ancienne Belgique "really like all that [Confederate] stuff because they think it's macho American"—which of course it was in a good part of America as well.

On one night during the well-attended and well-received tour, Ronnie happened to drop the flag onto the floor; he freaked out, as if he had committed a great sin against the motherland. Reaching for the phone, he called Charlie Daniels back home. The rotund fiddler, who himself had taken to wearing jumpsuits at his concerts covered with the Stars and Bars, recalled that the band had gone as far as to take the flag out to an alley and burn it, in accordance with antebellum protocol for flag desecration.

"Do you think it would be all right if we went on without the flag?" Ronnie asked him. "Certainly," Daniels replied.

Ronnie sighed in relief. The symbol he insisted was a gimmick and an embarrassment had not been sullied on foreign soil after all. The honor of the South lived on.

9

★ ★ ★ ★ ★

YOU DON'T GET NOTHIN'

"Sweet Home Alabama," the big bang of an already explosive act, didn't quite cause a seismic sonic boom nationally, but it did give Skynyrd the only Top 10 hit they would ever have, which at the time was a must, as even an FM-oriented band needed at least a decent-sized hit single regularly to keep album sales at a peak. Despite rising no higher, it seemed to be heard endlessly wherever one went, and also went to number six in Canada and made the charts in Germany, Austria, and Switzerland. The next single wouldn't need to be released until late November, when the band allowed a four-minute version of "Free Bird" to go out, which would be further edited down to three and a half minutes on some AM stations. Though hardly reflective of the glory of "Free Bird," it still got to number nineteen in the United States and to thirty-one in Britain. Meanwhile, the two albums sold apace—*Second Helping* hitting number twelve, *pronounced* reaching number twenty-one, both soon to go gold. This cascade seemed to revolve around "Sweet Home Alabama," the success of which unsealed Skynyrd to the masses and further honed their professionalism and raised the bar for them.

Gradually, they occupied more and more space in the music press, with the Brits genuinely fascinated by them, even if not quite getting some details right. Playfully echoing the marketing campaign, the headline WHO THE HELL ARE LYRNRD SKYNYRD? ran in the February 1974 *Disc and Music Echo*, a UK version of the teenage-geared fanzine *Tiger Beat*, tracing the roots of the band back to "a used-car salesman somewhere in Florida," meaning Leonard Skinner, who was never a car salesman. Another English rag, *Melody Maker*, told of Al Kooper's triumph with the band in a profile titled SWEETHEART OF THE SOUTH. Perhaps the earliest American music magazine to start spreading the news was the short-lived, Florida-based *Zoo World*, which in April wrote of them as "an alcohol band . . . steeped in southern blooze [who] create that perfect sleazy barroom atmosphere both in concert and on record." However, once "Sweet Home Alabama" hit, the big rags fell in line. *Rolling Stone* reviewed *Second Helping* by, mandatorily, comparing them to the Allman Brothers, saying that while Skynyrd lacked the Brothers' "sophistication" the work had a "certain mellowing out that indicates they may eventually acquire a level of savoir faire to realize their many capabilities." And Robert Christgau called it the work of a "substantial, tasteful band" that "will expose you to their infectious putdowns of rock businessmen, rock journalists, and heroin."

The album has lost none of its sheen over the years. The *Rolling Stone* album guide calls it "the consummate Skynyrd platter; the guitars sigh and sting like a stiff breeze as Ronnie Van Zant draws a line in the dirt."

★ ★ ★

After completing their second exhausting US tour, opening for acts like ZZ Top and Savoy Brown and capping it off with a boisterous headline gig in Memphis's cavernous Liberty Bowl Memorial Stadium on July 28, they could barely take a breath before they were back in the studio with Al Kooper. In early August they cut at Studio One a song they'd been asked to write for the Burt Reynolds movie *The Longest Yard*, director Robert Aldrich's black comedy about a prison-yard football game between prisoners and guards; with a song needed for a scene involving cops with guns drawn, Ronnie and Ed King worked out something much more significant, which took form when Ronnie had King play a riff over and over until, from somewhere in his soul, Van Zant came up with the line "Two feets they come a creepin' like a black cat do." Says King: "I was just amazed by that—it was brilliant. That was Ronnie at his best as a songwriter."

The verse continued, referencing three grim tales of people reaching for no good reason for a "Saturday Night Special," the cheap, poorly constructed .38 caliber Smith and Wesson handgun, the kind that flows so freely in the United States, no less now than they did then. Ronnie likely was unaware that the pejorative nature of the term derived from "niggertown Saturday night special," a term coined by fearful whites about blacks who armed themselves in fear of *whites*, though by the 1970s it pretty much applied exactly as he used it in the lyrics, as a way to end a drunken Saturday-night argument. Thus did he define the most salient argument for avoiding guns altogether, that far more likely than preventing a tragedy, a gun will *cause* one—though this was *not* an induction he bought entirely. In fact, he had a few of those .38s himself and had bought one for Judy to protect herself with when he was on the road. Rather, Ronnie, who'd had his share of run-ins when he was looking down a barrel, and often worried what he might do with his own pistol if he was provoked and drunk enough, simply regarded a .38, unlike a hunting rifle, as completely useless for anything but killing people.

It was a radical position for a redneck band to take in a song—indeed, when Donnie Van Zant formed his band in 1974, they took their name from the weapon—but Ronnie had something to say, and as always he said it. His chorus hook, grim and sung as if with clenched teeth, could make one shiver: "It's a Saturday night special, got a barrel that's blue and cold / Ain't no good for nothin' but put a man six feet in a hole."

Just so the point wasn't being missed, he had another killer line—"Hand guns are made for killin', ain't no good for nothin' else / And if you like to drink your whiskey, you might even shoot yourself." It was a seething, riveting alter-ego argument, coated with balls-to-the-wall rock and an ominous undercurrent that was so convincing, when Kooper noodled a dark-sounding passage on the synthesizer, Ronnie remarked that it sounded "like an airplane crashing." He was satisfied that he had done something against the grain, even if its unambiguous meaning would be lost for some who heard its stew of overwrought guitars and bone-jarring bass and drums—"heavy-metal-under-funk," Christgau called it—as a seal of *approval* for keeping a gun concealed in one's pants. *The Longest Yard*, which made $43 million and was one of 1974's most successful films, whetted the appetite for Skynyrd, enough that the song would be released as a single nine months later in May 1975 and become so entrenched in pop culture that it would also be used on the soundtrack for the 1978 Richard Pryor film *Blue Collar*; when *The Longest Yard* was remade in 2005, the song was there too. Some songs and some causes never get old. "Special" was immediately earmarked for the third Skynyrd album, sessions for which were set for January 1975—but this album proved so difficult to make that it would send Al Kooper fleeing from the South.

* * *

First, though, there would be Skynyrd's landmark first trip to Europe, an obligatory act since there now was the exigency to expand their sales profits in the important European market—and a chance to play for American soldiers on the German dates. England in particular was a natural for any American band with a new sound carved by either soul or country music, which Britons were continually fascinated by. Indeed, the Eagles' first two albums, their most country-flavored work, were recorded in London, produced by erstwhile Beatles engineer Glyn Johns, a country-music buff. English rock audiences, notorious for showing displeasure by means of catcalls, streams of spit, and sundry objects thrown at performers, mainly had a jolly old time with the strange new American band, even if few knew just what they were supposed to do when they were cued onto the stage by "Dixie" and that unfamiliar flag was lit up on the wall behind them.

Skynyrd couldn't have sold out the tour alone and were booked as an opening act for most dates. In Glasgow they opened for the veteran Dutch band Golden Earring, who'd had their first US and UK hit, "Radar Love," in 1973, but a review in *Sounds* said that Skynyrd ate Earring's lunch. That pattern continued when they stole shows from Humble Pie—then two years into its post–Peter Frampton era and heard often on the FM album rock stations—in Belgium and Paris, and even from Queen in Hamburg, though this may have been the last time Freddie Mercury would ever be upstaged, his band still a year from its international breakout with their *A Night at the Opera* album, which included "Bohemian Rhapsody." Indeed, at the first show at London's Rainbow Theatre, when they were to open again for Golden Earring, the promoter flipped the acts, making Skynyrd the headliner.

However, while they came back home triumphant, they were also short a drummer. In Paris, Bob Burns had become a casualty of the pressures and his own mounting troubles. Never having resolved being abandoned in childhood, Burns had been slipping downhill for some time. Months before, driving on Jacksonville's Buckman Bridge, he had collided with another car, killing the driver. It was ruled an accident but Burns came away shaken and with no time to get his head together before having to go right back on the road. After a gig at New York's Avery Fisher Hall he polished off a fifth of Jack Daniel's in one shot, went berserk in his room, and ripped a sink off the bathroom wall.

The last thing he needed was the long, hectic trip to Europe. Once there, he behaved more bizarrely, his behavior apparently worsened by mixing up his drink of choice, whiskey, and codeine. Having just seen *The Exorcist* in a theater at one stop, he began screaming that he saw the devil in the eyes of a cat and threw it from a hotel roof to its death below. Then, in Paris, he saw the devil again, this time in soundman Kevin Elson, whom he began to chase down a street with an axe he had somehow found before someone restrained him. With only one date left, at the Rainbow in London, Ronnie told the band they'd need to find another drummer when they got back home, and told Bob he was out, at least until he got himself some help. While all of them would have benefited from that advice, Burns was undeniably the worst off. When he did seek help, he says, "My parents put me in a hospital in Jacksonville, and they found the problem. They found that I was bipolar. They gave me medication, antidepressants, lithium—the stuff people who went crazy used to be given—lithium, whatever." Not until after Prozac was approved for prescription in 1987 did he begin to finally recover, saying, "I've been a free man ever since."

As he fought to gain his sanity and equilibrium, Burns never asked to come back to the band. For one thing, he cringed at the very thought of getting caught up again in the meat grinder of pressure, drugs, and drinking. "Everybody was doing it in the band and they were going in one direction with it and I was kinda headed off in another, because my bipolar was pulling me in a different way," he says now. "But nobody understood what in the world was going on. We were like best of friends since we were like four or five years old yet we didn't see what was happening to us until it became something that literally threatened to kill us all."

* * *

Burns for many reasons can feel he saved his life when he quit the band, and on some level Ronnie and the others probably envied him and wished they could have dropped out for a while, something that was impossible by then. Skynyrd in fact had already found a new drummer before Burns split. Back at the time of the session for "Saturday Night Special," Burns had begged off, saying he was too exhausted from touring to do justice to the song. Seeking a fill-in, Ronnie asked Charlie Daniels if he knew of a drummer, and Daniels touted a guy with the lyrical name of Thomas Delmer Pyle. Born in Louisville, he served in the marines during the Vietnam War and then studied music at Tennessee Technical College. There, some classmates oddly dubbed him "Artemis," after the ancient Greek *goddess* of the wildland, the hunt, and wild animals, apparently because of the long, wavy tresses that fell halfway down his back and his tendency to behave, well, wildly. He adopted it willingly, and then legally, though he changed the spelling to the more Americanized "Artimus."

Threading his way through the country-rock scene, Pyle had played gigs with Daniels and the Marshall Tucker Band, and unlike most drummers was not content with going unnoticed. Instead, he was indeed a wild man. Looking like Jesus with his long beard and endless hair parted in the middle, he threw his elastic arms around like pick-up sticks, his legs churning as he beat on the bass drum, yet for all that, he kept a steady beat and was able to downshift from loud banging to delicate pawing at the snare and cymbals. Ronnie was impressed and had Pyle play at a gig at Jacksonville's Sergeant Pepper's Club and then took him to Doraville to play on "Saturday Night Special," which opens with a splendid Pyle shuffle beat. Now, he was called in for more on-the-job training, as the new Skynyrd drummer on their third album. And given Ronnie's precise specifications, he had very little slack. When Allen told bassist Larry Steele of the Burns breakdown and the importation of Pyle, he raved to the great bass man, "You gotta hear this guy! He kicks that sound like machine guns—and he takes *acid* before he goes on stage!"

Larry laughed. "And you're tellin' me *Bob* is actin' crazy?"

* * *

The sessions for the album began in early January, but Al Kooper's participation was uncertain. Months before, with his Sounds of the South deal with MCA due to expire in a year, the parent company wanted to buy him out, thereby giving them ownership of the SOS catalog—though all they really wanted was Skynyrd. MCA had already dissed Kooper by taking his imprint off Skynyrd records since *pronounced*, and they were prepared to put the new album in jeopardy to force him to sell out. First they threatened to withhold Kooper's royalties from the first two Skynyrd albums and then keep him from producing anyone else for the duration of the contract until he came around. But Kooper could play some hardball himself. His manager, Stan Polley, was a man whose name made industry people shudder or want to kill themselves—indeed, the latter actually happened when he managed the British band Badfinger in the 1970s, when Kooper had played in the band and been represented by him. When Polley, who was rumored to have mob connections, was unable to account for an escrow account that held Badfinger's earnings, guitarist Pete Ham committed suicide, leaving a note that read: "Stan Polley is a soulless bastard."

Kooper, however, had not severed ties with Polley, and now he sicced him on MCA. Kooper would sell, Polley informed them, but only if MCA shelled out a cool million dollars. And there was another nonnegotiable demand: the royalty rates for Skynyrd and Kooper—the band getting a puny five points, and Kooper, ten—would need to be flipped. This was Kooper's way of keeping his word to Ronnie that he would take care of them down the road, but MCA stalled, apparently hoping Kooper would eventually fold. MCA went ahead and rented an Atlanta studio, Webb IV, for the Skynyrd album. The studio was owned by Bang Records, which had recently moved to the South, mainly to accommodate Paul Davis, a Mississippian and the label's top act.

Kooper would not fold—MCA did. It took almost right up until January, but they made the deal on Kooper's terms. Suddenly, he was a million dollars heavier, and Skynyrd had a doubled royalty rate. As Kooper giggled, "Things were *very* good. Everyone was *extremely* happy—except probably Alan Walden." MCA people who were there disagree with Kooper's version of this history. Bob Davis said the decision to buy the producer out wasn't the company's but a ploy by the group to land a hefty advance. As Davis tells it, "The Skynyrd people came to MCA and said, 'We really need you to help us out. What we'd like for you to do is buy out [SOS] so that we could then begin a direct relationship with MCA."

The million-dollar buyout of Kooper, the band explained, according to this version of events, would be an advance on future royalties that Skynyrd would make back in half the time—provided their royalty rate was doubled. That rate, they said, "would be more consistent with artists of our stature." Said Davis: "There was no doubt that the deal was made with MCA by Skynyrd's representatives." In any case, figuring he had done enough with, and made enough from, southern rock, Kooper was ready to move on again, now to the happening scene in L.A. Then, with the date of the Skynyrd sessions creeping up, Ronnie made another demand of MCA—the band wanted Al to produce the album. This was quite a concession by Skynyrd, all of whom had grown weary of Kooper's hectoring in the studio. Working with him, Wilkeson once said, "became such an intricate thing. He was telling us what to do the whole time." Leon also went as far as to say, "It was Al Kooper who actually started the whole rowdy image for us"—a laughable contention, to be sure. Yet feeling they could not shoulder a failure at this stage and with scant time to look for another producer, they needed the security and familiarity of the egoist with the white-man's Afro and the goggle glasses.

Over a barrel, MCA, which had been at war with Kooper, sheepishly called and asked him to take the gig, which Kooper was all too happy to do, as it would earn him royalties on a third Skynyrd album that was sure to go through the roof. He hastened to Webb IV studios, happily anticipating another wealth of Skynyrd material. Instead, he found nothing. With the band having spent so much time on the road, there had been no time for writing and rehearsing, a condition that would be the norm from then on. They had a deadline of one month to record the album, meaning that, starting from scratch, they'd need to compose and cut eight strong songs right there in the studio. Kooper may have pondered whether he should have gone off to Los Angeles after all. Adding to his misery, after meticulously setting up the microphones for the first session, he walked in the next day and found they had all been rearranged by Bang engineer Dave Evans, who had convinced the band to do it his way—a violation of studio protocol, according to which the producer generally rules.

Kooper was livid and, out of spite, said *all* such decisions would be made by Evans. As the difficult sessions went on, Kooper said, there was "incredible tension" and little got done. Trying to get things off square one, Kooper, who was also facing jail time on a drug possession conviction at the time, decided the best thing he could do was leave the band alone and go party in New York. He told Ronnie, "I trust you and believe in you, I know you can do it." When he returned, the band had only two weeks to get it done, but Ronnie, whom Kooper calls "a man among men," had indeed taken charge, writing all the necessary tracks. As Ed King recalls, "We all worked together and had ideas and wrote songs on the spot. We were tending now to go in a bit more simple direction than we had in the past."

With "Saturday Night Special" in the can, the first song to be cut, on January 11, was the Collins–Van Zant track "On the Hunt," the new album's tribute to Free, who had recorded a song called "The Hunter." Kooper found it to contain "Ronnie's most misogynistic lyric ever"; Van Zant sang, "In these two things you must take pride. That's a horse and woman . . . both of them you ride." A close second in misogyny was the next song in line, the blues ballad "Cheatin' Woman," in which he considered gunning down his unfaithful woman, à la "Hey Joe." "You won't bother poor me no longer," he threatened in this tune. Kooper earned a writer's credit for it with Van Zant and Rossington, as he played organ and electric piano on the song. Then came the Van Zant–Collins original "I'm a Country Boy," a sweaty, bluesy kiss-off to both coasts with their cars and smoke "chokin' up my air." In King and Van Zant's "Railroad Song," its chugging beat aided by a frenetic harmonica line by Wet Willie's Jimmy Hall, Ronnie testified, "I'm goin' to ride this train, Lord, until I find out / What Jimmie Rodgers and the Hag was all about" ("the Hag" being Merle Haggard).

With the deadline closing in, sessions were lasting sixteen hours at a stretch, and when Kooper was gassed out, somebody, he said, "slipped some speed into my can of soda." With all of them speeding, the last three cuts fell in place. There was Van Zant and Rossington's "Am I Losin'," which showed off Ronnie's soft, sentimental side and was sympathetically written to Bob Burns. Kooper thought the ballad, featuring a smooth vocal, acoustic guitar, and banjo, was "the mellowest, most country thing Skynyrd had ever cut"; it included Kooper on background vocal, there being no time to hire any backup singers. Then, appropriating Shorty Medlocke's old adage, Van Zant and King cowrote "Made in the Shade," a hillbilly rag with a spoken Van Zant preface—"Well when I was a young-un, they used to teach me to play music like this here"—followed by a jug-band melange of mandolin, dobro, honky-tonk piano, and synthesized tuba.

The last track was "Whiskey Rock-A-Roller," which gave Billy Powell a credit with Van Zant and King, its honky-tonk noodling and muscular guitar licks a breath of fresh air. Kooper would overdub a second piano part by the producer David Foster when he mixed the album in L.A. in early February, his last official act as producer for Lynyrd Skynyrd.

★ ★ ★

In many ways, the content of the album was antithetical to the band's desire to break out of old molds; indeed, the work, called *Nuthin' Fancy*, can fairly, and ironically, be called Skynyrd's "country album." Much of it was mindless and to the gut—exactly what they were going for, given the lack of thought-inducing time they all had. And as it turned out, it was probably exactly what Skynyrd needed after all the hoopla about "Sweet Home Alabama." Clearly, though, MCA was thinking of something else; they had worked up a cover that repositioned the band as All-American megastars, neon replacing sawdust. The art no longer used subliminal similarities to the Allman Brothers nor paleontological parallels to Black Sabbath. Their name was printed not in bones but with futuristic letters that looked like florescent bulbs.

The group's idea for a cover photo, however, was intriguingly and decidedly unglamorous. They stood perched on a brick wall under, not the blue skies of Alabama, but the thick cloudy skies of Georgia. It was as stark as the back cover was a lighthearted hoot, depicting them striding down a dirt road, Billy Powell's middle finger upraised. The credits included baubles like "Ronnie Van Zant: Lead Vocals, Lyrics and Lots More J&B," "Allen Collins: Gibson Firebird and Trout Voice," and "Artimus Pyle: Drums, Percussion and Determination." And on the inner front sleeve, within a photo montage of the band, was a sign reading: FOR SALE, LEONARD SKINNER REALTY, 389-1396—a debt of gratitude now repaid. The old gym coach had left coaching to go into real estate in Jacksonville and, good egg that he was, allowed them to use the sign gratis.

Alan Walden was probably not amused by the jab he got, though; he was left unthanked. Listed among those singled out for "special thanks," however, was *Phil* Walden, for Jimmy Hall's turn on "Railroad Song" and

"Made in the Shade." The album was dedicated to Lacy Van Zant, Shorty Medlocke . . . and Peter Rudge.

The album done, and released on March 24, Kooper bowed out, a very wealthy man. Looking back at the kind of punishment he had just come through, he told them when he left, "I would rather remain your friend than your producer. . . . We damn near killed each other on this one." They laughed and hugged and then said good-bye, everyone relieved all around. While Skynyrd were tight with Kooper personally and enjoyed being linked with a cool industry icon, they had clearly come to loathe him as a producer. Billy Powell once said, "We fought all the time. He wanted to be the keyboard player, the producer, the director. . . . We finally got fed up with it after three albums. That's when we released him." Ed King agrees but insists that *Skynyrd* had set up the confrontation, for no better reason than that Kooper was "a northerner. They made it a North versus South issue. They just don't like Yankees and [wanted to] make Yankees look like idiots."

Allen was terse about Kooper. "I'm not saying anything against him," he said at the time, "but we ain't gonna use him anymore."

* * *

Kooper went on to live la dolce vita in L.A., occupying and getting way too high in a playpen he liked to call the Free Bird Mansion. And he would claim that, while he had beaten MCA, the company had gotten even—not with *him* but with their top-earning act. "Later," he said, "I found out they charged the million to *Skynyrd's* account!" In time he would also have to deal with the same thing Badfinger had when, a few years later, he would have to come after Polley for royalty payments the manager never made.

Ed King came away from the sessions calling *Nuthin' Fancy* "the best we've done so far," after the album he called "probably the worst." As he explained, "The music has changed, but not too much. We're aware of whatever basic element we have that makes us what we are and makes people like us." But Ronnie wasn't so sure. Having been forced to write songs rather than nurture them along at Hell House and then at clubs, he would lament that the band could not possibly come up with another "Free Bird" on deadline. "We haven't really progressed that much in the past two or three years because we haven't been given the time. . . .

Nuthin' Fancy was probably our poorest showing." The culprit, in his estimation, was the "record company putting so much pressure on us. . . . There were some good spots on it, I thought, but . . ."

With their tour of the continent a success and another album in the can that was sure to be a hit, they could finally enjoy some income in their pockets, each having received a good-sized royalty check for the quarter and a weekly salary, more like an allowance, of $300, according to King. Even at ten cents a record, big checks were still a ways in the future. Yet "Sweet Home Alabama" had clearly put them on a higher stratum, en route to building their empire—yes, their *empire*, ruled by only one emperor, the one with no shoes.

"One time in Birmingham," recalled King, who had a bit of a cushion from receiving royalties on "Incense and Peppermints" and who had lived the high life before, "we experienced our first limo ride from the gig back to the hotel. Big time stuff. When we got there, Ronnie demanded the night's take from our road manager, Russ Emerick. Russ told Ronnie he had the money but taxes had to be paid along with other expenses. It still came out to $15,000. Ronnie took the cash and gathered us all in one room. He held the money in his hand peeling off hundreds, saying to each of us, 'You two played pretty good tonight, you get a thousand bucks each. And you did ok, too . . . you get a thousand bucks. You did what you were told, that's worth a thousand. You played some good licks . . . here's a grand.' Then, he said, 'You'—I won't say who it was but he wasn't talking to me—'you played like shit. You don't get *nothin*.'" Ronnie paid himself two grand. Lesson learned."

The lesson was that Skynyrd might have landed in the big time but Van Zant still ran the show. And because he was getting itchy about the money being siphoned before it got to the band, he was about to make a change, one that would give Alan Walden the shock of his life.

10

★ ★ ★ ★ ★

TORTURE TOUR

Pete Rudge, a long-faced, motor-mouthed bloke with a big smile and a terrible chain-smoking habit—usually around *sixty* cigarettes a day—seemed to fall deeper in love with Skynyrd every time he heard them. Never much of an American country music fan, Rudge was so smitten with the new idiom in rock that he urged one of his top-shelf bands, the Who, to sprinkle some backwoods influences into their repertoire. His other top band, the Rolling Stones, of course, had already heard the call when they came to record at Muscle Shoals. Pete Townsend would subsequently put some redneck into "Squeeze Box," the Who's 1975 hit, by adding banjo and accordion parts.

Rudge approached Lynyrd Skynyrd gradually and cautiously but with some urgency after the Who became disenchanted with him due to all the attention he was giving the Stones, prompting Rudge to turn the Who's management over to an assistant and to inveigle himself into the affairs of the country rock band he was taken with. His company, Sir Productions, which certainly sounded more classy than Alan Walden's Hustlers Inc., had an office suite in New York, under the name Premier Talent, on the sixth floor of 130 West Fifty-Seventh Street, right next to Carnegie Hall. Everything about Rudge screamed "big time." Accordingly, it didn't take much for Ronnie to move in his direction. Indeed, to some in both camps, there was the assumption that Rudge was *already* managing Skynyrd; one of his adjutants at Sir, former British music journalist Chris Charlesworth, believes his boss had taken over the band back in *1973*, during the tour with the Who. In reality, Rudge dearly wanted them but never made a move, figuring they would come to him. And he was right. He never had to sell himself or bad-mouth Walden, seeing how worked up Ronnie was getting over the paucity of money that was trickling to the band out of the millions they were making MCA.

For his part Walden was quite content with the way things were—not that 30 percent of the band's royalties was getting him much, but his cut of the *publishing* royalties was a growing fortune. He also thought the band should be indebted to him for taking a good portion of their money and investing it, which he believed—correctly—was necessary because, with their backwoods way of divvying up money and spending it indiscriminately, they would lose it all down the line. Whenever anyone in the band asked for some cash, Walden peeled off some bills. But even a doubled royalty rate meant little if the royalties were being siphoned off. None of them could buy a trophy car or move into a spacious crib. They all still lived in apartments in and around Jacksonville, with Ed King and his wife sharing space with Ronnie and Judy at their duplex on Rayford Street, along with Dean Kilpatrick and his girlfriend. Walden hung out there so much it was as if he lived there too, and because he and Skynyrd had come through so much together, never did he think they would ever turn on him.

Walden boasted of their relationship, "We became the Ten Musketeers! All for one and one for all! Wild, crazy, drinking, fighting rednecks with a capital R and proud of it!" While the band wondered where the money was, Walden says now that none was squandered and that Ronnie simply could not understand that, without prudent money management, they'd be out on the street. "I did very career-minded booking while their manager," Walden says. "I had the long run in mind constantly. I caught a lot of crap from the band sometimes because they wanted to make a certain amount all the time. Once we played a $10,000 date, and they thought all the dates should be $10,000. Well, we might play Nashville for $35,000 and the next day be booked for $3,500 in a market undeveloped. Then another time they said they wouldn't play for less than such-and-such, then they complained of working the same cities over and over.

"Listen, they should have concentrated on the music and the shows and left the bookings and business to the pro. It amazes me how bands hire a manager and as soon as they get hot want to tell him how to do it. Or fire him because he is too smart for them. They should stick to what they know best. *Music!* And so I was thinking of their latter days when they would no longer tour. . . . I had set up profit sharing and pension plans for their older years. I got them life insurance. Things they did not want to keep at that time. They wanted it all in *cash*.

"On one of my road trips with them, I discovered $90,000 in a briefcase. I took it home and straight to the bank. I tried to remind them it wasn't that long before that we all had been broke. The wheel of success had turned, and now I was the miser. In their minds, they just knew the success would never stop. It was all going perfectly. *Pronounced* was a hit, and with *Second Helping* moving up the chart, MCA was thrilled and had reps meeting us in every city. Both smash albums were made for under $50,000. No wonder MCA loved us so much. And I was setting them up for the kill. We had not borrowed money, and it was a prime time to renegotiate their recording contract. It would have been a multimillion-dollar deal. We were getting prime concerts now, with the Allman Brothers in Atlanta at Braves Stadium, Clapton in Memphis, ZZ Top in Nashville, and heading to pick off the Eagles at the Orange Bowl in Miami. The band was now the showstopper! They killed and killed. No one could hold up behind 'Free Bird!'"

Yet it was right then and there, at the Orange Bowl on March 26, 1975, two days after the release of *Nuthin' Fancy*, that the sky fell on Alan Walden.

* * *

What Walden didn't know was that Ronnie had gone behind his back and contacted Peter Rudge on his own, a line of communication that Rudge intended to keep open. As Artimus Pyle observes, Rudge was "very manipulative." While he didn't ask to manage the band, he *did* make sure to say what he would do with them *if* he did: big-time things, worldwide things, things that would spurt big money. And the drip-drip-drip of those conversations filled Ronnie's cup of ambition to the brim. Skynyrd, he became convinced, needed a big-time manager.

He had a point too. Despite Walden's protestations about protecting their long-term security, the band was even then paying out of their own pockets to get to some gigs. When Gary Rossington said in 1977, "We weren't makin' anything, we were just surviving, and we were still having to pay thirty percent to a manager," it was obvious that they had come to see Walden not as a Musketeer but as a maggot. "We didn't think anyone would fuck us over, we just thought that if somebody said something, we'd take their word for it, because that's the way we were. We didn't know what kind of rat race this really is. But we started learnin' real quick."

Their thinking was evident: if managers screwed people by nature, they needed one who would screw not them but *other* people *for* them. Not by coincidence, Rudge came down to Atlanta just days before to attend a picnic Phil Walden threw at Capricorn. Seeing Ronnie and Gary sitting by a lake behind Phil Walden's house, Rudge ambled over and sat down next to them. "We just talked the whole afternoon," Rossington recalls, "and we really wanted to go with him. . . . He said, 'If you want to come with me, I'll be your manager.'"

A handshake agreement was made. The next step was to deep-six Alan Walden. When it happened, the Musketeer felt like he had walked into a fist.

"We were at the Orange Bowl with the Eagles, and I was doing an interview with *Creem*. They had spent two days traveling with me, and this was going to be the big story. Ronnie told me he needed to talk to me right after the show, and he and I went back to the room together. The conversation began with that they wanted me to move to California where I could pursue getting their songs and them into movies and further their career more in that direction. At the time, I was very happy living in a three-room log cabin in Round Oak, Georgia. My reply was, 'Ronnie, I can't stand California. When I'm there I'm afraid to go to sleep at night because I am afraid some guy might think I have a gold tooth in my mouth and kill me just to steal it!' I only trusted Mike Maitland and Bill Graham out there!

"Then he proceeded to tell me how Lynyrd Skynyrd was a well-oiled machine now and that the brotherhood of the band no longer was a big part of it. I told him that was one of the main reasons I had signed the band, and that maybe I no longer fit in."

That was Ronnie's opening. "At that point, he informed me the band had voted to replace me as the manager of the band. The wind went out of my sails. I was shocked, but more confused than hurt. I had done a superb job for this group. Here we were with the whole world at our feet and now—boom, it was over. I must admit that I also felt like a concrete block had fallen off my shoulders. Now I did not have to worry about their future, which had been a full-time job because of how they lived. But no one was looking after my future, or seemed to care.

"This had been my whole life for the last four years. No one loved the band any more than me. Ronnie had been best man at my wedding and the only people I invited were the band. I thought of Ronnie as my closest friend. And he felt so bad about it that he said I could beat the hell out of him, that he would just cover up the vitals and let me have a go at him. He was serious, too, but I couldn't. He also asked me if I wanted to know who voted what. I didn't want to know."

Walden, however, refuses to this day to call it a firing but something more like a reset. "I said if there was a separation that I would like to have a say in the whole matter, that I should help choose the next manager rather than the band and end up in a horrible lawsuit and court battle. Ronnie had told me he had met with [the Eagles' manager] Irving Azoff and another manager. I told him Irving was not someone I would recommend at all, and that I did not know who the other manager was. I told him I would lean toward Peter Rudge. I figured if he could deal with Mick Jagger's ego and Keith Moon's insanity, he could surely manage my little southern band." As it happened, of course, this decision had already been made.

Now, with the details to be worked out, Walden had every right to crack nuts with the band over terminating his contract. But he was still in a stage of denial, hoping the whole thing might blow over and things would go on as they had. "They said I was a miser and I do count money well—isn't that what a manager's job is?—but I did not want to see some idiot come in and totally ruin everything I had worked on and I wanted him to have to buy my contracts. So I waited a couple of days, prayed over it and then called Ronnie. I offered to meet with them and try to correct any problems and I did go out to see them. Ronnie and I ended up in a room alone and I won't go into details but I lost it with him. Here was the guy whose back I had been covering for four years even when we were up against very bad odds. And now he's letting them all stab my back. I knew Ronnie could kick my ass one-handed but I had to hold myself back, and after I had my say I saw a tear coming down his face. Then I lost it and left with tears flowing, too."

The soap opera had become so drawn out that Alex Hodges recalls still going on booking Skynyrd for Paragon even after he was told Walden had been sacked. Then a call came from Rudge's office ordering him to stop doing so. "That was not a good day," he muses, "but it was a lot worse for Alan. I had been booking a lot of acts for both Phil and Alan, all the big country rock acts, Marshall Tucker, Black Oak Arkansas, Charlie Daniels, everyone. But Skynyrd was the only act Alan had, and now, he had nothing. From that moment on, I was working only for Phil Walden."

Yet even with having his magic carpet pulled out from under him, Alan Walden retains all the bravado a man who fools himself can have when he insists on one point, a point he would never give any ground on: "I left Lynyrd Skynyrd," he says, "but I was never told I was fired—by anyone!"

★ ★ ★

Whatever the semantics and emotional delusions, Walden was out, with a severance deal to ease his sadness—a $1 million buy-out and co-ownership with MCA in perpetuity of the publishing rights to all Skynyrd songs to that point. Walden, downplaying the deal, says, "I took their offer of some cash and retained the publishing on the old songs that had already had their big earning days. The cash did not equal what I would have made off the negotiation of the record deal alone. It was a drop in the bucket compared to what I could have made in the next three years. It would equal about one-hundredth of what I would have made."

What with all that dough and future profit, word began to get around that it was *Walden* who had wanted out so he could reap his bonanza. "Rumors spread that I only wanted the money," says Walden. "I find that ridiculous and totally untrue!"

And so, in sauntered the elongated Pete Rudge, full of plans and schemes for how to make Lynyrd Skynyrd one of the world's biggest bands. To the band's delight, Rudge quickly won from MCA a fifty-fifty split of the publishing rights the music giant had shared with Walden. Starting with the next Skynyrd album, the publisher of the songs they composed would be listed as "Duchess Music Corp./Get Loose Music Inc.," the latter the perfectly apt name for Lynyrd Skynyrd's brand-new publishing company. Rudge drew up a touring schedule even more hectic than the one before. New studio sessions were set for early September at the Record Plant in L.A., with an as-yet-undetermined producer, and a new European tour was scheduled for October and November, with a

TV appearance booked on the BBC's *Old Grey Whistle Test* music series, along with *another* jaunt to England in February 1976 to share the bill with the Eagles. They'd also play some venues in the United States for the first time, including one show each in '75 and '76 at Bill Graham's Winterland Ballroom in San Francisco and at New York's Beacon Theatre, where the Allman Brothers seemed to have a key to the front door. A long-awaited, live double album was planned for mid-1976.

The plans, made by Rudge and the band in numerous meetings at his New York office, got bigger and more ambitious, fueled by mass quantities of substances legal and not. Rudge assistant Chris Charlesworth remembered, "Group meetings in Rudge's big office were all day and night affairs at which bottle after bottle of Jack Daniel's was consumed, piles of coke snorted, and carton after carton of cigarettes smoked. Voices were often raised and the language was as bad as you could hear anywhere. Anyone who'd crossed them was dead meat. MCA Records threw a party for the band that summer at a bar near Nathan's Restaurant which almost got out of hand when someone made a loose remark to one of Skynyrd's women."

Charlesworth encountered Skynyrd's quirks as a study in American sociology. "Before their shows," he has said, "Skynyrd liked to psyche themselves up in their dressing room, winding themselves up by breathing deeply together like US football players, passing the Jack Daniel's around in a ritual drink, willing each other on to perform as if their lives depended on it. Rudge, a sports fanatic, encouraged this."

But the purge wasn't over. With Walden gone, Skynyrd faced a brave new world, richer, famous, and with a need to show that they could rid themselves of anyone they deemed excess baggage. The next in that line of fire was in the band of brothers itself.

* * *

"Saturday Night Special" might have caused a few heads to be scratched in the South, but this was nothing fatal to the record. MCA, as usual getting as tasteless as possible in the ads for the band, ran one that showed a skimpily clad babe in a garter belt holding a .38 between her legs. By the early summer the song had gotten to number nineteen as the new album's first—and, as it turned out, only—single, that being enough for their purposes. The album, against the grain as it was, received uplifting notices, mainly for revealing Ronnie's taken-for-granted vocal range, about which Robert Christgau marveled: "Ronnie Van Zant has never deployed his limited, husky baritone with such subtlety. Where Gregg Allman is always straight, shuttling his voice between languor and high emotion, Van Zant feints and dodges, sly one moment and sleepy the next, turning boastful or indignant or admonitory with the barest shifts in timbre. I mean, dumb he ain't." The closest thing to a dissenter, *Sounds*, the Brit weekly, called it "rather disappointing. . . . Rightly or wrongly, you expect a band like Skynyrd to wipe the floor with you every time."

Skynyrd went out on a backbreaking tour, a ninety-day, sixty-one-date ordeal, during which came the Walden firing. But in contrast to the professional highs of the previous two album tours, the "Torture Tour," as they would privately call it, left a trail of fistfights, wrecked hotel rooms, sloppy performances, and canceled shows when Van Zant's unfiltered Marlboro-and-booze-punished vocal cords gave out.

Naturally, the brunt of it was taken by their hotel rooms. Van Zant said, "We get a lot of publicity about busting up places or being really mean . . . but you just get really tired . . . really nervous . . . just about to flip out and go over the deep end, just say the hell with it, I quit. Well, instead of doing that we're just liable to knock a hole in the wall."

Pete Rudge, going over the bills from the road back in New York, loved the "bad boy" ink they got, but had to keep a reserve fund separate from the routine expenses just to pay off property damages, which often were $10,000 per town when it got out of hand, but could go much higher. A hotel where they stayed in Nashville incurred terrible damage when an exercise room was set on fire, for which they held Skynyrd responsible. And Rudge could only write out a check, deducted from their account.

Charlie Brusco, like Rudge, saw the effects of the damage firsthand. "I remember at the end of one tour with Lynyrd Skynyrd, it was them, the Outlaws, and Golden Earring. The last show was in Cleveland, and we stayed at Swingos Hotel, where all the big rock bands stayed then. And I heard the number batted around that there was $10,000 worth of damage to the hotel, and that was in '75 or '76—that was a lot of money then. To their great regret, the hotel put Skynyrd in no less than the Frank Sinatra Suite, which had a big piano in it, and it was opulent—until they got through with it. We had a party to celebrate the end of that tour, and it went on not a few hours but an extra *day.* I don't think anybody got out of there to make flights the next day, we were all so hung over. We had done a hundred shows together in a six-to-eight-month period of time and that was the last show." With a pause and a wan smile, he adds, "Boys will be boys."

While all three bands were involved in trashing the suite, it was Skynyrd that got hit with the bill. That was the logical move, to go after the richest band. And Rudge's rule was "Do the damage, pay the toll." During the Torture Tour, Ronnie remembered, "Our manager hit me with a bill the other day for $29,000 worth of damages and I tore that up without even thinking about it"—though of course Rudge had to pay it and dun the band the same amount. By rote Ronnie explained the carnage as being somehow necessary to "let off steam. . . . We're a bunch of hyperactive people gettin' with it. If we don't let it all off at a gig, we're gonna make a hotel a wreck. We usually wind up gettin' thrown out owin' money."

It helped that they had the luxury to do that, write a check, and move on. But for Ronnie, it was never even that easy. He was just as ready to use his fists on people as on walls. In June 1975 he used them on an innocent bystander, Brusco. "I thought I'd gotten to know Ronnie pretty well, but you never really got to know him well because he could turn on you no matter how tight you were with him. He turned on Gary all the time. He'd pop him out of nowhere, *bang*, and both he and Gary would just go on about their business like nothing happened.

"Gary was used to that. I wasn't. After the show at the Beacon Theatre in New York, we were out late and Gary and I were a little loud in the hallway and Ronnie decided that he was gonna square off with us—with *me.* You know how for a fight you have a bell? Well, I got hit before the bell rang. That was Ronnie's way, he didn't waste any time. He just came up to me and *boom*. I went down, lights out. And Gary didn't even bat an eyelash. He just went to his room, leaving me there on the floor, not out of meanness but because something like that was an everyday occurrence.

"Nobody really got hurt when Ronnie did shit like that. If he wanted to kill you, he could. He just wanted to clock you, to keep you in line. He was very good at creepin' you—that's what they called it, that Ronnie was creepin' you. I got up in a few minutes, the damage mostly to my pride. I figured maybe Ronnie only did that to people he liked."

Of course, that term—"creepin'"—was the creepy way Ronnie had described that ominous black cat in "Saturday Night Special." He obviously believed it fit him just as well. In truth, *he* was the black cat. When he crept up on you, he was bad luck. Rossington seemed to be his favorite target. Once, everyone in the band was draining bottles of Schnapps, and "somehow," Rossington said, "a bottle got broke and I ended up with slashes across my hands and wrists. But the next day, we were the best of friends again. That's how it was, like a family."

As Powell learned, it was a family one might only see in horror movies. His operative phrase for Van Zant was "Jekyll and Hyde." "I remember arguing with him once, after a few whiskeys, about Allen Collins' volume and tuning up onstage," Powell said. "Next thing I know, I got four of my teeth knocked out." Ed King, not being in the circle of Jacksonville boys, observed Van Zant almost as a dispassionate outsider and came to see him as a threat to anyone around him and to himself.

"It was always a perplexing thing to me, why they descended to violence and craziness," says Alex Hodges, "because living the demented rock lifestyle wasn't what it was about to them. It was more that they had all these weird backgrounds and never had a sense of normalcy, even from a young age on. They had dark impulses, and they just flashed without warning. I didn't want to get too close to what made them that way because I didn't understand it, didn't *want* to understand it. If you got too close, you might wind up like Charlie Brusco, out cold on the floor and with a busted lip. I was lucky. 'Cause Ronnie never looked at me cross-eyed, so I must have been doin' something right."

The unfortunate ones clearly weren't, at least according to Ronnie's warped value system. Ed King tells of a frightful incident when Ronnie came into the hotel room he was sharing with King, "drag[ging] a young woman and beating her senselessly. He threw her head into a nightstand three or four times—I mean, he really fucked her up."

"Ronnie!" Ed shouted at him. "What the hell did she do, man?"

"She swallowed my yellow jacket," he said, meaning a yellow-colored speed pill.

It was as good a reason as any for Ronnie Van Zant, rock-and-roll star, to act like a raging, abusive asshole.

11

★ ★ ★ ★ ★

"WE DONE THINGS ONLY FOOLS'D DO"

Ed King, like everyone else, was helpless to stop Van Zant from these sorts of psychotic episodes, which to King were symptomatic of two things: One was something inside Ronnie that he suppressed but that came out in a Freudian rush when he was drunk. "Ronnie," he said, "was one angry guy. . . . There was something inside him that was eating him up." But for a nonsoutherner like King, it signified something else as well—for him, Van Zant was a metaphor for the best and worst of the South, a region King loved but could never transfuse into his own blood, where it resided by birth for Ronnie and the others. And this, he believed, they held against him.

"Though I was an outsider, I could see the whole picture. And I don't mean to be too critical of the South—I love its charm and I do still live there—but, oh, the stupidity sometimes. It exceeds all ignorance." The worst of it was the "Southern gentlemen" of the band's unstintingly callous treatment of women. "It was unbelievable. You wouldn't even think about doing the kinds of things they did. I was appalled, man. I just thought it was the weirdest thing I'd ever encountered. And to them, it was like nothing."

Al Kooper had the same ambivalence about the band and the region, which hastened his egress from the South. The guns, the misogyny, the routine acceptance of violence and racial stereotypes, all of it got to him eventually; even the sick, drugged-out decadence of L.A.—the place where, as Lawrence Ferlinghetti sagaciously wrote, "the American Dream came too true"—and the rock scene's fatuous acceptance of misogyny on their terms and its embrace of a jive shaman like Carlos Castañeda imparting meaning to essentially meaningless songs seemed harmless by comparison to a wild-eyed badlands with a gun and ammo store on each corner. For Kooper and King, both nonnatives, an impassable cultural chasm always stood between them and the band. The pictures taken of Skynyrd during the time King was in the band almost all contained some sort of underlying if subconscious proof of his alienation. In nearly every one, King is stuck off to the side, seemingly pushed into or situated by choice on the periphery. Still, even if that's how he felt, he suffered the effects of a kind of Stockholm syndrome when it came to Ronnie, feeling a great deal for him on a personal level but unable to tolerate him when he went over the edge of psychopathy. After the debut album came out, Ronnie had told King he hated his bass playing—"Man, you really suck" was how he put it. Indeed, Van Zant had never had much of a relationship with or attachment to the moon-faced Jersey native. Never did King feel he was "one of them" beyond the useful expertise he contributed to the band. Indeed, Ronnie wanted him off the bass and on guitar, creating more "Sweet Home Alabama" riffs. The three-lead-guitar attack that the song had begotten meant King was needed, an invaluable asset on that instrument and a catalyst for the best songs Ronnie ever wrote. Still, King couldn't disregard the nagging, gnawing feeling in his gut that he could take only so much more or risk his own sanity.

★ ★ ★

The Torture Tour was four months in when he came close. The band was ragged and dog tired, and some nights the shows were awful, such as in Ann Arbor on May 25. This was two days after Ronnie had cold-cocked Gary in Cleveland, and the entire band was out of sorts. King, speaking with a reporter the next day, admitted, "We were terrible. We were just horrible; it didn't happen at all. If I'd have been hit in the head with a tomato and a bottle I would have accepted it. Any other time I'd have been raving mad. The audience was real polite and gave us more applause than we'd deserved." He went on, "Our band works on pride. If it doesn't turn out, like that, we're ashamed of it. Our live gigs are what we're really proud of; they're what our reputation is built on. When we go out to promote a record, we can back it up. Tomorrow we're going to spend all day rehearsing. Playing a bad gig like that will bring your spirits up. You're feeling so bad about it, there's no way to go but up."

That same day, King's spirits were broken. Previously a light drinker, he too had become a prisoner of the bottle. He'd start a half-hour before the show to make sure he was high as a kite on stage. "One night somebody forgot to bring the booze," he says, "and it just wasn't the same." After the show the night before, Ronnie and roadie John Butler had gotten into a barroom brawl and spent the night in the local jail for disorderly conduct. Recalls King, "Butler took care of my guitars. It was his job to change my strings every day, and they didn't show up in Pittsburgh for the next show until like five minutes before the show. We didn't know if we'd be able to go on. And that night during 'Free Bird,' I broke two strings, something I never do.

"On the limousine ride back to the hotel Ronnie was pissed, he told me that I didn't amount to a 'pimple on Allen Collins' ass,' which I wasn't going to argue with. But then Ronnie started wanting to fight in the limousine and the driver pulled over and got out of the car and said, 'You guys can drive your own car back.' When I got back to the hotel I said that's it, I just don't need this shit. I mean, if they want to act crazy and fight amongst themselves, that's one thing. But don't steer it my way."

According to Artimus Pyle, Ronnie told Ed to "hit the road," in effect, firing him right there; the irony of such a reaction was that Ronnie had thrown it all on Ed to try to get Rudge to cancel a few shows so that the band could rest, something they were badly in need of. Ronnie, shirking his duties as leader, would not ask for it himself, knowing Rudge would never willingly agree to lose money just so the band could chill. When asked about this, King confirms that a few days before the blowup in the limo, "Ronnie came to me and said, 'Let's cancel some shows.' He said, 'I haven't got the guts to do it, so you do it.'" King would have; however, after Ronnie either fired or simply humiliated him, he says, "I just walked out the next day."

If Ronnie had in fact wimped out rather than make a demand of Rudge, that would have marked him as something of a paper tiger. Still, as arrogant as Ronnie was with the other members of the band, he struck King as a real enigma, more in search of respect by default than by deed, given to terrible insults of his own band as if to convince himself of his own infallibility—a trait that had also become evident by the offense he took when the others indulged heavily in booze and drugs, even as he increased his own capacity to do the same. To Ronnie, his proclivities were no one's business but his—but *theirs* were his business because they threatened the band he'd labored to build. These hypocrisies, mixed with his spontaneous volatility, had become all too much for King, who says, "I had some real problems with Ronnie. I didn't understand why a genius had to act like that."

The pity for him was that he had joined the band because of Ronnie and had only been comfortable with him. "I didn't care for anything about those other guys. I was always a better guitar player than any of them, anyway. I mean, they wrote some good stuff, but Ronnie was the soul of that band." Even as he walked away, it was with mixed feelings. "I was real sorry to give it up, but I didn't have any regrets. I had regrets on how I did it . . . walking out in midtour, but I had to because it was just one of those things that, the longer you stay, the more it has its teeth in you and you can't let it go."

Not bothering to say good-bye, King caught a cab for the airport and flew back to Jacksonville, where he packed his belongings and headed home with his wife to Greenville. He still hoped that Ronnie would call and ask him back and, better still, admit to his faults. And, he admits, "I would have come back. Yeah, absolutely. But I knew he wouldn't do that. Number one, there was his pride. I walked out on him. And number two, Rudge said, 'We don't need him.' I mean, [Ronnie] was really mesmerized by Peter Rudge, who was the only person that I'd ever met that mesmerized Ronnie. Because Ronnie had it all over everybody. But he didn't have it over Pete Rudge."

For King, the portents for the band seemed all bad. "Because it had gotten so violent and it had gotten so mean. I had seen so many mean things. Not necessarily against me but just against people that were close to him, that to me was totally unnecessary. Pretty much every day was traumatic. I just had a bad premonition and felt I should obey the urge to get out when I did. I was from a different mindset from those guys. I was just there to play music. I wasn't in there to get beat up, get spit upon, get dragged around a room, get jagged glass held up to my throat.

"The other guys, they had to put up with all that. It was either that or live the blue-collar life that faced them growing up in Jacksonville. There was no out for anybody, because when you're born on the west side of Jacksonville and you've got this success on your plate right in front of you, what are you going to do, walk away? And I wasn't from there. So I could."

The day King split, Artimus Pyle became enraged at Van Zant for precipitating it. "I had a major fight with Ronnie," he once said. "I was pissed off because I liked Ed and wanted him in the band. So I went to Ronnie's room and me and Ronnie, we went *to it*."

Artimus, who has insisted he was the only one in the band not deathly afraid of confronting Ronnie, didn't say exactly *how* they went to it or the toll it might have taken on someone's teeth. But nothing changed. And while only a few months back they had all been on a high, now, it seemed *nobody* was happy. John Haury, who played in the John Lee Walker Band, Skynyrd's opening act on some dates during the tour, hadn't realized just how much bad blood there was within the band of redneck "brothers." "There were some nights," he said, "everybody would arrive at the show separately and none of them were talking to each other."

* * *

For a band in the middle of a long tour, the timing of Ed King's departure was indeed ominous. Some big dates were coming up, including a few in New York City a week ahead and the fall tour of Europe. Yet Ronnie was hesitant about hiring a permanent replacement; with the way they could overdub in the studio, he believed the two guitarists could create any sort of multiple-instrument sonic effect. And out on the road, Kevin Elson at the board was able to mix the feedback from all those microphones in a way that would *sound* like three guitars or more. This highly technical proficiency was in stark contrast to the continuing beastly behavior within the band. Other incidents on the tour showed Ronnie indeed had cause to wail, "Lord help me, I can't change."

In late June, after a show in Louisville, Ronnie, who had been in a foul mood the whole tour, was awakened at the hotel by a loud argument in the hall between Billy Powell and a road manager. Wrapping a towel around himself, he came out of his room and yelled, "Cool it!" Billy, not appreciating the intrusion, told him, "Fuck you." Ronnie recalled what happened next: "I just walked over and knocked Billy's teeth out, hit the road manager and knocked him down. Then my towel fell off in front of the fuckin' spectators."

After Ronnie went back to his room with no contrition, Billy—for the second time after being a Van Zant target—picked his teeth off the floor, six of them this time. He marched to Ronnie's room and banged on the door and, when Ronnie opened it, screamed, as if with marbles in his mouth, "You're gonna pay for the dentist bill!" Ronnie was so hysterical at the sight and sound of Powell, dripping blood and semitoothless, that he guffawed and got out his checkbook. "I'm sorry, Billy," he said. "Here's the check, man." At least Billy could say he took one for the team by giving Ronnie something to smile at.

The open question was whether Ronnie would alienate *everyone* in the band before he was through. He was still the fighter, but now he was something a good fighter can never afford to be: out of control. He was quite honest about that fact too, and why. "We were doing bottles of Dom Perignon, fifths of whiskey, wine, and beer," he would say. "We couldn't even remember the order of the songs. Some guy crouched behind an amp and shouted them to us. We made the Who look like church boys on Sunday. We done things only fools'd do."

Near the end of the tour, no amount of wreckage or booze or anything else could blow off enough steam to clear their heads or battered bodies. Four days after Ronnie's assault on Powell came a frightening moment in Charlotte. Two shows that week had to be canceled because Ronnie felt under the weather. Then, during the show in Charlotte, he felt faint and nearly blacked out. After making it through, he collapsed backstage and was taken to a hospital where they pumped the *right* kind of fluids into him. Two days later, he was back on his feet on stage in Jackson, Mississippi. Things were near a breaking point. Feeling the strain, Gary would openly start crying for no particular reason. Sometimes one or more of them would be so drunk, they couldn't play a decent lick; at those times, Elson would turn off their mikes from the sound board, which happened more than anyone ever knew.

But none of the wreckage they caused themselves or their habitats caused any damage to the band's marketability—quite the contrary. There seemed to be only new high-water marks. They opened for Eric Clapton in Memphis on April 12, and the June 19 issue of *Rolling Stone* gave them props, if still not fully aware of where they came from, nor how many musicians were onstage: "With three full-time electric guitarists, a piano player and a fireplug of a lead singer who looks like Robert Blake's Baretta in a hippie disguise, Georgia's Lynyrd Skynyrd presents an unusually broad front line . . . [and is] a must see."

* * *

They would not come off the road until July 6, when they played their hometown—for the first time since March 20, 1974—a gig steeped in irony for them since, as Gary would say, "Jacksonville never gave a shit about us until we were famous all over the world." Yet, almost as a taunting reminder of the town's recalcitrance, even that homecoming gig turned ugly. At the Jacksonville Veterans Memorial Coliseum they were introduced by none other than Leonard Skinner, the man whose name they had made synonymous with rock's newest wave. Perhaps feeling he was too big to stay a gym coach or realtor, Skinner had opened a couple of bars. One was the Still, which he renamed Leonard Skinner's on San Juan Avenue, where rock-and-roll bands, with their long hair, played.

After Skinner's name and phone number appeared on the inner sleeve of *Nuthin' Fancy*, his phone, predictably, rang off the hook, yet it said something that he didn't change the number. Sought out for interviews, he would leap at the chance to tell the story that had made him, as the *New York Times* said in its obituary of him in 2010, "arguably the most influential high school gym teacher in American popular culture." Yet as far as he and they had come, Skinner must have wondered that night if he had been right all along about those Shantytown boys. After the Charlie Daniels Band warmed up the sold-out crowd, Skynyrd assembled under the Stars and Bars, but after only a few songs Ronnie became raspy, then began coughing up blood. He stopped in midsong, made a brief announcement that his throat was bleeding, and left the stage. The rest of the band stood around waiting for him to come back, whereupon impatient fans threw bottles onto the stage, which shattered like fragment bombs.

That drove the band offstage, too, where confusion reigned. No further announcement was made, and angry fans in the crowd of fifteen thousand, who had paid a top-shelf six dollars per ticket, stormed onto the stage, kicking at and destroying some of the equipment and instruments. Fights broke out everywhere in the crowd. With a riot erupting, cops brandishing guns were called to the arena. Backstage, Ronnie had again collapsed and was being taken to the emergency room. And Skynyrd, not fighting this time but cutting and running, left the building and ducked into waiting limousines, dodging more bottles thrown by fans who had gathered at the stage door, as roadies salvaged whatever they could on the stage.

The *Jacksonville Journal* headline the next day blared, THE MUSIC STOPPED AND THE FIGHT STARTED. There had been $1,400 in damage done to the building, with sixteen people arrested and one cop injured. The promoters tried to dun Rudge for the refunds they had to make, but they were chasing a shadow—he'd wisely put in all of Skynyrd's booking contracts that any cancellation due to medical reasons, which could conceivably apply to alcohol or any other "medicinal" cause, absolved them of any financial amercement. The easy conclusion to draw from all this was that Skynyrd had gotten what they had wrought: people didn't only come to see the band of brawlin' rednecks; they came to mess with 'em, even *fight* 'em, in a kind of bonding ritual. The mayhem now seemed part and parcel of the Skynyrd experience. During the tour a fan had thrown a package of lit firecrackers onto the stage, sending them scrambling; another time, in Salt Lake City, as Van Zant would recall, "some guy got on stage and had a knife [and] was going for me. One of the security guys got him first, but he cut the security guy all up."

Only a month and a half after the melee in Jacksonville, Skynyrd gulped hard and took another gig opening for Black Sabbath in Jersey City. Leon again wore his holster, but when a 45-rpm plastic record came skimming from the crowd, he couldn't prevent it from lodging in his neck, inches from his carotid artery. At other times, as he said later, "I've had bottles thrown within inches of my head." The band certainly was the subject of great wonderment, incredulity—and danger. And the implication regarding any Skynyrd concert was: come and buy a ticket—you might not only *see* a fight, you might be *in* one. This being so, some of their critics would sense a very discomfiting retrenchment of Old South norms; as Mark Kemp wrote, "Unfortunately, their image merely reinforced stereotypes of the South—not the aw-shucks sentimentalism of Andy Griffith's fictional TV character, but the ass-whupping aggression of the real-life Bull Connor."

In truth, a Skynyrd concert, while a showcase of ass-whupping aggression to be sure, was hardly an homage to Bull Connor. Rather, they were seminally punk, pushing no tangible agenda, spitting in the face of all authority. They were truly scary in one respect—to other, bigger bands for whom they opened. On September 1, the second day of the California swing, they were to open for the Kinks, who decided to cancel at the last minute, not denying rumors that they'd had second thoughts about having to follow Skynyrd—who would want to have to come out and play after "Free Bird"? Skynyrd said they'd go on regardless, sparing the promoters from having to dump the whole show, and few asked for refunds.

Given who and what they were, any publicity was good publicity. Thus a headline such as one in *Circus Raves* in September—LYNYRD SKYNYRD IN TURMOIL—was merely free advertising, furthering the theme of bad boys being bad boys. In the grand scheme of things, at least when it came to their bottom line, if not their mental and physical state of being, a much more significant headline was the one in the October 11 issue of *Billboard*—LYNYRD SKYNYRD: 3 GOLD LPS IN A ROW. *Pronounced* had reached that milestone in September 1974, with *Second Helping* following three months later and *Nuthin' Fancy* in June 1975. Forty years later, with no headlines or advertising needed, the albums go on selling. And nobody still wants to have to come out and play after "Free Bird."

12

★ ★ ★ ★ ★

100 PROOF BLUES

Skynyrd had unearthed something new in popular culture, something distinctly and genuinely *southern*, something that was rising as an antidote to crudely commercial, corporate country rock. The band seemed to have picked up the torch of southern rock heroes who had come before them only to fall before reaching their apogee. The latest to drop was Gram Parsons, the pure country rocker, gifted with perhaps the most emotionally genuine voice in contemporary music, who had died in a motel room near Joshua Tree National Park in September 1973 from an overdose of drugs and alcohol. And the Allman Brothers, imploding by the day, could never really replace Duane Allman or Berry Oakley.

In terms of popularity and sales, the country-rock niche by default was owned by the Eagles, a band whose members—in a perfect allegory of the impersonal, corporate industry rock had become—had to be introduced to each other, formed by managers and producers for quick success. The Eagles also used a skull as a marketing tool, but one of a dead animal in the desert. Their sound was geared around a cowboy rather than redneck ethic with songs like "Tequila Sunrise," "Lyin' Eyes," and "Best of My Love." They sold a massive number of records, and the weepy slide guitars of their brand became a signature of the early Southern California country-rock trend.

There were now a grab bag of southern country-rock units with a new wrinkle—Black Oak Arkansas, for one, combined psychedelia, fifties rock, Hindu spiritualism, and gospel into "psycho-boogie," or "raunch 'n' roll." (Spiritualism with a country twang had been broached by George Harrison with the Beatles, and on the title track of his 1970 *All Things Must Pass* album he added a tart pedal-steel guitar line.) Black Oak—a great but highly underrated influence with Jim "Dandy" Mangrum's sandpaper voice and stage writhing writing the template for heavy metal rock—released their debut album in 1970 and had four through mid-1973, before Skynyrd had even one.

There was also the Outlaws, a veteran country outfit that had broken up in 1971 but reformed with new personnel a year later. Their wrinkle was front man Hughie Thomasson's guitar wizardry and studio innovations, such as having a fuzzy guitar lick on one stereo channel and a clear guitar line on the other, or playing Beatles/Hendrix-style licks in reverse. More and more, the Outlaws, managed by the tall, square-jawed Charlie Brusco, built a following. And Ronnie Van Zant, in a rare show of support for a rival band, urged Alan Walden to move in on them, whereupon Walden and Brusco became comanagers. In 1974 when the Outlaws opened for Lynyrd Skynyrd in Columbia, South Carolina, Ronnie, spying Clive Davis, the veteran music panjandrum who had just created Arista Records, spoke directly to Davis from the stage. "If you don't sign the Outlaws," he told him, "you're the dumbest music person I've ever met—and I know you're not."

Davis did, making the Outlaws the first act signed to Arista and the second Southern-rock band to be taken in by a major label outside the South. Yet once Skynyrd had opened that door, even though they themselves had made their bed using the Confederate flag as their comforter, they began to chafe when the label of "southern rock" was applied to them—not unlike the Eagles when they too were shoehorned into "country rock." It was especially irritating to Ronnie, who had made a real effort to expand the Skynyrd mold with the eclectic buffets of *Second Helping* and *Nuthin' Fancy.*

"Southern Rock's a dead label," he said, "a hype thing for the magazines to blow out of proportion. We don't play like the Allmans did, or like Wet Willie. . . . When I talk about the South and all that I just mean pretty country. Like Tennessee, Kentucky, which is like upstate New York. Really, I can't see no difference between North and South, and I'd like to see this shit about 'southern man' and 'southern this' just thrown away."

This was a truly remarkable stance for a man who had so willingly and unalterably taken up the cudgels for the "Southern Man." Just as remarkably, he said, "We are tired of all this 'southern scene' crap that follows us in newspapers; it's gotten so that a great band from New York has less of a chance now than an average band from the South. People have come in and started to make money, and there are folks now who'll snap you up because you're from Dixie." Of course, it was due to the Allman Brothers and Lynyrd Skynyrd that this was the case at all. Yet now, it seemed as if he was ready to go to war for the *Northern* Man. And some seemed to appreciate it. Music critic Michael Point believed that Skynyrd was "the only Southern band capable of retaining the interest of say, a New Yorker strong on Bad Company."

Van Zant wasn't the only "southern scene" artist who wanted to stretch out—take Barefoot Jerry, for instance, a band composed of Nashville studio musicians who had played on Bob Dylan's sessions in the city and Roy Orbison's "Pretty Woman." In one song they proclaimed, "Proud to be a redneck . . . but I've changed," asserting that "the South's gonna rise again" but "we don't have to be so doggone mean." While satisfied to be just "good ole country hicks," they channeled Marvin Gaye in one song, averring, "Blood is not the answer," condemning the Vietnam War. The burr under Ronnie's saddle *did* have something to do with race—that the image making of Skynyrd had all but precluded non-Caucasians from appreciating them, or caring to. He had read in the rock press numerous times about the white audiences that came to Skynyrd concerts, covered in tattoos and carrying Confederate flags, wearing Skynyrd/Jack Daniel's T-shirts. Such an audience meant that blues songs like "Curtis Loew" and "Call Me the Breeze" would not be recognized for what they were. For many Skynyrd fans, it was still all about "Sweet Home Alabama" and "Free Bird."

Skynyrd had certainly courted the "rowdy bunch of drunks" image that Ronnie also decried—which often seemed to be confirmed by their roadies almost ritualistically getting into fights with audience members and even roadies from other bands. It was a rare night when no one in the Skynyrd retinue came away from a gig without a shiner or broken bone. These effects of the Skynyrd experience might have been quite beneficial in selling them, but for Ronnie they did nothing to reveal that he had broad set of talents and musical palette. What he longed for was to be taken seriously by all demographic metrics and to see some black faces in those crowds. Toward that end, he would make an appeal for that, based on northern hypocrisy: "The difference between blacks and whites, that's changed for sure," he said in 1975. "We don't have any trouble with our brothers. If you want to talk about racial stuff, talk to people from Boston."

So, needing to keep the base growing, he would grit his teeth and say that Skynyrd was "just a little band from Jacksonville," while his eyes were on a bigger prize—a larger mainstream—with every expectation that the new guy pulling strings would make it happen.

* * *

But something else was happening too, something neither Pete Rudge nor anyone in the band could brake. Rossington was right that, as the pressures kept mounting for the band to figuratively get higher, they had to literally get higher. It was little wonder that Bob Burns had snapped on the European tour; all of them barely got through all those weeks under the European magnifying glass in one piece. That Artimus Pyle came in half baked from dropping acid was a sign that Skynyrd was now also in the big leagues of rock self-immolation. The boozing, snorting, popping, and everything else they dabbled in were all part of the time bomb.

"From a manager's perspective," says Charlie Brusco, "you see what's going on with a band—you hate it, you try to tell guys they're killing themselves—but there's not a damn thing you can do about grown men who want to get ripped all the time. There's not a rock band in the history of the world that has ever been able to avoid it, and there never will be. It's why guys drop like flies, die before their time with their livers being rotted away or their hearts giving out. Look at Gregg Allman. That's walking death."

Ronnie's health was already an issue. Two dates on the European tour had been canceled and money refunded when his throat became infected. While always sharp eyed and together while prowling the stage, once off it he would get so falling-down drunk he was incoherent and a danger to all around him, including himself. The courtly southern charmer at those times would become insulting, rude, and threatening—the classic nasty drunk. He'd have run-ins all the time, several with cops outside of clubs that ended with him being thrown in the can until he slept it off and first Walden, then Rudge, paid a fine and got him out. That happened at least six times. Yet he and the others had become proficient at self-denial. Ronnie, in one interview, maintained that he was no longer drinking—that is, except when he did. He said he'd made a $4,000 bet with the others in the band that he could stay off the hard stuff. Instead, he was now drinking only wine. Never mind that he had once sung of "sweet wine" that "it makes a fool of you."

In a profile of the band in the October 1975 issue of *Creem*, Rossington also had some bull to sling. Before, he said, they all drank six fifths of Chivas a night, among other things. "It was like water to us. Then we started getting the shakes and playing so bad we quit drinking." Except of course when they didn't. "Now," he added, "we just drink moderate and have a few to calm down."

Terms like "moderate" and "a few" to Skynyrd entailed a different kind of metric than they did for most civilians. Their capacity seemed infinite, and to other bands they must have looked the way the Who once had to them. But this wasn't all bad from Ronnie's bleary-eyed vantage point. He had wanted to be recognized as a blues singer. And now, as *Creem* observed in its title, he was singing the 100 PROOF BLUES.

* * *

The wonder is that Skynyrd did indeed keep every shred of their base while moving ever forward into new musical avenues. In fact they were permanently affixed to the loam of Tobacco Road. Once, they had opened for some distinctly midlevel acts; now, only an act on the order of Clapton or the Stones could pull rank on them. Their shows in big venues were major rock events. Skynyrd, which once had exactly one roadie, Dean Kilpatrick, now had a mob of roadies. Kilpatrick, who was now called head of security, managed up to twenty roadies, including Gene Odom, Billy McCartney, John Butler, Joe Barnes, Craig Reed, Chuck Flowers, Joe Osborne, and Scott Parsons.

Some fading acts who had been riding high just a few years before were now trying to ride *their* coattails, Ted Nugent and Carlos Santana among them, each of whom took slots as Skynyrd's opening act during their tour. It was a given that, when Skynyrd played on their home turf, they were the attraction, something that applied also at NASCAR speedway concerts at which the biggest country rockers jammed with each other. Bands that had tasted success far sooner than Skynyrd, like the Marshall Tucker and Charlie Daniels bands and Black Oak Arkansas, were now essentially Skynyrd's warm-up acts. On a broader scale, merging a hard-core country sensibility with mainstream rock was a major watershed in pop music, and Skynyrd's pulse-raising impact was more arousing than the superb but medium-cool blues of the now-receding Allman Brothers Band. And with that pulse came a topsy-turvy effect on popular culture. Before, geographical biases had been reflected in literature and art. Even Dennis Hopper's groundbreaking *Easy Rider*, the ultimate parable of 1960s idealism gone sour—with Hopper and Peter Fonda's amoral "free birds" on Harleys descending into the American Hades of the South—ended with a shotgun blast from a redneck in a pickup.

Nor was James Dickey's novel *Deliverance*, immortalized by the squirm-inducing line, delivered in a thick backwoods twang, "Bend over and squeal like a pig, boy," of help to a South in transition and in search of a makeover but still seemingly stuck in hubris and unfocused angst. While Charlie Daniels's 1975 anthem "The South's Gonna Do It Again," a virtual roll call of southern rock acts—Skynyrd, Allman Brothers, Marshall Tucker, ZZ Top, Wet Willie, Barefoot Jerry, Grinderswitch, Elvin Bishop—was intended to defuse that rusty old rubric of defiance by applying it to a new font of southern music, it was annexed in the spirit of the same nativist flag-planting as was "Sweet Home Alabama," more easily done since Daniels had left open what the "it" in the song was supposed to be.

Now, though, in no small part because of the band whose political motives were so hard to decipher, that thirst for freedom and flight had been transmuted to Lynyrd Skynyrd's songs of the great redeeming qualities of the American South. This was more reason why more than a few Yankees witnessing this amazing metamorphosis felt like wheezing *The horror! The horror!*—at least until a closer listening to their records revealed something beneath the cartoon surface that made the South actually seem worth saving, worth *caring* for.

★ ★ ★

With these new parameters being so rewarding, Skynyrd enjoyed an infusion of badly needed cash in their pockets. Ronnie and Judy moved to larger digs, an apartment on the banks of the Cedar River, on—appropriately—Confederate Point Road. Gary Rossington had floated around the area, not settling into a pad he considered home. His drinking had gotten out of hand, and it was almost a relief to those around him when he did cocaine because it meant he wasn't getting so drunk he couldn't see. With those curls and doe-like eyes, he always could reach out and collect any number of women with little effort, and one, a willowy blonde named Martha, became his girlfriend, or so she thought. One morning he rolled over in bed, squinted at her through bloodshot eyes, and asked, "Who are you?" But she stuck with him, and the reward was that in 1977 he would marry her, if not for long.

The cosmetic side of success never overly affected the band. To their credit, they didn't start living lives of wild financial excess. All lived fairly modestly, close to the old neighborhood. They all had either long cars or shiny pickup trucks in their driveways—which they never drove, since all except Artimus had had their licenses suspended for reckless driving, something that would become a graver problem. They could now appreciate how Alan Walden had put money away for their future. Ronnie and Gary had sprung for a fishing boat they named *Bad Company*—for their jukebox hero Paul Rodgers's band but also a term that could describe what they were by then—on which they spent more time reeling in catfish than at home with their wives. Indeed, for Judy, her marriage to Ronnie felt more like a rumor than fact. "I can't even remember the sound of his voice," she lamented. "He really wasn't home all that much."

But he did spend enough time with her to knock her up, another accident he believed might be a blessing. His older daughter, Tammy Michelle, was all but estranged from him, and he wanted to believe that becoming a father again, at the right time, would calm down his primitive instincts and impulses and give him a chance to be a family man for the first time in his life, even if 1976 loomed even more hectic than '75. Then, too, proper fatherhood, as opposed to his experience the first time around, not to mention any little mementos of the road that might have been running around out there, might bring him close to Lacy and Sis, whom he practically brushed past on the way out the door when they would drop in on him and Judy. As it was, his boy's constant run-ins with the law had only made Lacy's hair even grayer, though it didn't prevent him from bragging around town about his son's success or sometimes coming out on the road with them. But in Ronnie's mind, it was easier to avoid Lacy than to promise he would clean up his act. Thus, he erected yet another barrier to their relationship without even knowing it.

As Artimus Pyle came to recognize, "Ronnie's biggest disappointment was that he couldn't please his father. I found that so bizarre because all his father ever did was sing his praises. Yet he felt that way. I could never figure out why because Lacy adored Ronnie. Maybe he never told Ronnie."

Even now, as accomplished as Van Zant was, he felt inadequate about dropping out. Counseling a roadie to stay in school, he told him, "You're getting something I never had a chance to get, an education. I'd give anything if I could have that now." Seen through that prism, writing lyrics to a song didn't mean a damn thing. As if to unburden himself, Ronnie himself would brag on Lacy and admit to his failure to live up to his father's expectations. In 1975 he told an interviewer, "I learned everything I know from him. He always wanted me to be something I could never be—and I'm sorry to disappoint him. He wanted me to be just like him. But I couldn't be."

13

★ ★ ★ ★ ★

SOUNDMAN GOD

By age twenty-seven, it was about time Ronnie Van Zant grew up. As it was, with his thinning hair and expanding waistline, he looked around forty, and was also a touch more well appointed. Rudge forbade the leader of the "American Stones" from coming onstage barefoot—something Van Zant had never let on was the result of his old football ankle injury, which made it hard to stand a long time in shoes, instead saying that he just liked to "feel the burn" of the stage boards. Now he would need to grin and bear the pain. Now, too, he could chuck his old sweat-stained hats and don replacements made specially for him by the Texas Hatters company.

His material and paternal yearnings seemed to be taken care of, but his thirst for world conquest was only going to become more demanding, which was a recognition that, while Lynyrd Skynyrd were the last people in the world who would have ever expected such status for themselves, in 1976 they were the new thing in rock. In moving the ball down the field more than any other group of southern rock polecats ever could have, they had broken down too many old barriers to count. Al Kooper put his finger on the pulse of what they were, saying of them years later, "When I found them they were a great heavy metal band. I just tried to give them a recording identity." Not *rock* or *country*, but *heavy metal.*

Accordingly, the Skynyrd fold of country rock *was* a heavy-metal identity. Soon, the Skynyrd "look"—not really a look at all but rather an *antifashion* statement: denim, sometimes torn, with T-shirts, cut-off vests, and longer than long hair—would become the uniform of heavy-metal bands, and remains so even to this day. The stark minimalism of the visual part of the equation stood in raging contrast to the growling passion and decibel level of the performance; nothing else—no mincing about, no glittery outfits, no fireworks—was there to distract attention from the music. It was all a product of Shantytown, which had finally found a context. Even any principled wariness about the Confederate flag was now passé. Artimus Pyle, behind whom the flag was draped like a Damoclean sword every night, said years later that he "hated" it and that it was "offensive to some people [who] think we hate black people."

Pyle nonetheless added some punch to the stage act. He was more animated and played with more finesse than Burns. He and Wilkeson would quickly find a rhythm groove in which the backbeat was tighter and more coordinated. Leon had come a long way on bass. He was so nimble fingered now that he was playing lead notes and rhythm notes in split-second intervals, a technique mastered by only a few elite bass players like Motown's immortal James Jamerson and John Entwistle, whom Leon had of course been able to observe at close range on the Who tour and who could make ungodly sounds come from four strings. Still, Leon was by choice the least noticed member of Skynyrd, usually hanging back near the rear of the stage, to the right of the drums, so he could always hear the beat being banged out and to keep his bone-rattling bass notes in perfect coordination. He still attracted notice by wearing all manner of bargain basement haberdashery, including vintage policemen's suits and hats, his favorites being an oversized porkpie and an English bobby's cap. For this reason, he was sometimes taken to be the token Brit in a group that by then was fully in the hands of a Brit calling the shots.

* * *

Peter Rudge, who kept a hand in every pot of the band's affairs, found them a new producer, a tricky matter given their quirks, egos, and methods, not to mention their propensity for fighting like drunks in a barroom. Rudge, who had to have an album in hand for an early February release, could not afford to inject a novice into this mulligan stew. So he went straight to the top, to the A-list of producers, to arguably the most respected of them all—Tom Dowd, who at fifty-two had done studio work that had been heard by virtually everyone who listened to music, though doing so was actually a step down for him. During World War II, as a physicist, he had been on the Manhattan Project team that had developed the atom bomb. Moving into music, he engineered and produced for Atlantic Records the likes of Ray Charles, Ruth Brown, Bobby Darin's "Mack the Knife," John Coltrane, Charlie Parker, and Thelonious Monk. A pioneer of multitrack and stereo recording, he produced hits for the Rascals, Aretha Franklin, Otis Redding, Cream, Eric Clapton, and the Allman Brothers, proving no idiom was beyond him. Not for nothing was he known as "Soundman God."

There were other, typically connived industry considerations attached to the decision. Dowd's contract with Warner Communications, Atlantic's parent company, forbade him to produce noncompany acts. But Ahmet Ertegun was very interested in signing Skynyrd to Atlantic when their MCA contract would expire with the album that came after this one, and thought Dowd would be the conduit. Dowd had worked at the Stax studio in Memphis, at Muscle Shoals, and established the Criteria Studios in Miami where he produced Clapton's *461 Ocean Boulevard* and *Layla and Other Assorted Love Songs*, the title track of the latter being a cornucopia of slide guitar madness with Duane Allman stoking Clapton. Dowd knew all about southern rock—hell, *all* rock, all *music*. Most of all, he could work fast, which was necessary since the band had to squeeze the recording into the seams between their perpetual tour dates. After a short layover at home, they were off on another touring jag in mid-August, bouncing from Tampa to Charleston to Jersey City to San Diego.

There would then be nine gigs out west through September before they took a *long* boozy flight to Europe for a fourteen-date tour in October and four more shows in November. Dowd would need to somehow get eight songs done during a week set aside in L.A. for that purpose in September at the Record Plant. There would be no chance to get them back for any overdubs or retakes until Thanksgiving when they would get back home to Jacksonville for a few weeks.

Before agreeing to Dowd, Ronnie had gone around looking for producers, flattering them all. Paul Hornsby, Marshall Tucker's producer, said Ronnie told him he wanted to hire him but that "it's a democracy in the band. Unfortunately, I'm always outvoted." Said Hornsby, "If he had his way, we would have worked together." But that was likely what other producers believed too. In reality Ronnie's word was law—or else; the Skynyrd "democracy" was more like a banana republic. As Pyle says, "It was his show, his dream—we were just renting space." And Ronnie was smitten with Dowd, whom he called "a master."

Thus, the ruddy-faced, bearded Dowd—who was inducted into the Rock and Roll Hall of Fame in 2012, a decade after his death—came with Rudge to Skynyrd's concert in Santa Monica, was introduced to the band, and within days was in the studio with them, facing perhaps the biggest challenge of his career. Dowd actually had a double challenge; he would also produce the long-delayed live album, which would need to be released first, in the fall, for the European tour. Happily for Dowd, while the band still had rough-edged ways about them, they were now on a level of songwriting expertise and studio musicianship that, as it had for Al Kooper, made such shoestring recording possible. Although writing songs was never easy, the simple foundation of their songs had been refined to a science.

Gary Rossington explained the alchemic process years later: "We used a lot of D-C-G progressions. There's only seven chords, so you got to use the same ones over and over. It's all in what you do with them. I could write a dozen different songs with the same three or four chords but they'd all be entirely different."

Of course, it wasn't *quite* that easy in practice, but in a nutshell, this was the essence of Skynyrd's infectious sound—though Van Zant's lyrics were from a whole other place, a spontaneous combustion that defied formula. And as if any time frame would be enough to accommodate it, they ripped out six tracks in two days. It was a remarkable feat, inasmuch as they were also their usual snarling, arguing selves, agreeing on little until Dowd settled the issues with his expertise. The first to be cut, on September 7, was the Van Zant–Collins track "Cry for the Bad Man," the title of which suggested perhaps self-pity for the bad men of Skynyrd, but which was aimed squarely between Alan Walden's eyes. Subtle as a two-by-four, Ronnie steamed, "I'd rather quit and go back home / Than to deal with the money miser"—the term Walden sarcastically uses to describe the way Ronnie came to regard him. Nor was Ronnie coy about it, saying it was about "a gentleman we did business with at one time, and he really messed us over, cost us a lot of money . . . treated us real bad, and finally we got out from under these contracts with him."

Clearly autobiographical was the next in line, "Double Trouble." "Eleven times I been busted, eleven times I been to jail," Ronnie trilled of an arrest record that had grown a long way since Rossington had first stuck that phrase on him. He also recycled his favorite metaphor: the "black cat" that "crosses your trail." With a smirk, he admitted, "Double Trouble, is what my friends all call me." Soon, when he would perform it in concert, fans would scream back at him each letter as he spelled out "T-R-O-U-B-L-E." The third track was another bow to J.J. Cale, a cover of his "(I Got the) Same Old Blues," a stripped-down, blues-bar piece with a superb slide guitar by Rossington. Then, on the eighth, they cut Van Zant and Collins's "Every Mother's Son," a crisp, down-home ballad with some sparking Billy Powell piano runs and Ronnie in a higher, Neil Young–like register delivering the very fatalistic line "Well, I've been ridin' a winning horse for a long, long time / Sometimes I wonder is this the end of the line."

In retrospect one can find apparent or construed references like this to impending death lurking in Ronnie's lyrics, even going back to "Free Bird." One music chronicler believed that "the man's departure *appears* to be from his lover but ultimately must be from life itself"; in this view, "Lord knows I can't change" really means *Lord knows I can't change it*—not if life is predestined otherwise. It was easy to retroactively dedicate the song to Duane Allman, who lived and died as Ronnie believed he himself was fated to, and according to other Skynyrd members Van Zant frequently struck the theme of not living past his thirtieth birthday. If he had such depressing thoughts in mind, however, he left them in the ellipses of the lyrics. Still, the mood of *Nuthin' Fancy* was contemplative, even regretful, true to the country tradition. The broadening that Van Zant wanted would have to wait until they would get back into the studio in November to complete the album. There would be a lot to do in the meantime, on a journey Jerry Garcia might define in terms that Ronnie could appreciate—trouble ahead, trouble behind.

* * *

Tom Dowd, with half the album in the can, pivoted to the live album (which would be released just as the band finished off the studio album in November), the highlight of which would of course be "Free Bird," the song that made every live concert a group catharsis. The song's evolution had indeed made it into a ritual exercise. Early on, hardcore

Skynyrd fans began screaming "Free Bird!" throughout concerts. This grew into a ritual similar to that of Allman Brothers' concert crowds shouting "Whipping Post!" For years, Ronnie had been coyly asking the crowd before the song's accustomed slot as the second encore, "What song is it you wanna hear?," which was followed by requisite shouts of "Free Bird!" The track on the live album would capture every ounce of the delirious, dizzying escalation from swaying, cigarette-lighter-clutching mellowness to the pandemonium of sonic madness when the girls, many half dressed and riding atop their boyfriends' shoulders, would especially lose all control. It would also be something it was not when it was written and recorded—an homage to Duane Allman.

Ronnie hadn't known Duane well, but now he believed the man deserved commemoration from the band that was running the Allman Brothers off the field. And Ronnie wasn't above milking it either; in concert, he would offer a brief soliloquy about Duane, leading to the canard that the song was in itself a tribute and had been written as such. Other times he would also include Berry Oakley in these preludes, calling Duane and Berry "free birds." If only they had known. Yet the truth was that Ronnie had said when they were alive, "They're a part of my crowd, but I don't really know those guys." No matter. Ronnie, no dummy, knew that epoxying his band to the Allman Brothers was a proven selling point, and this new version of history only made "Free Bird" more contextual and more popular. Even how the title appeared on the jacket of the single release—"Freebird"—caused hard-core Skynyrd fans to take note; that jacket would become a collector's item as a Skynyrd anomaly.

If their signature song was now something on the order of a Ronnie conceit, this was just part of a deepening chasm between actual reality and Ronnie's reality, the best of which could be seen on a stage or on a vinyl record and the worst of which could be seen most everywhere else. If he had learned he had little to fear from the American justice system, being able to "get loose" on foreign soil led him and the others in his trail to think they had even less to worry about. Skynyrd's second European tour would be perhaps the single most concentrated period of havoc they ever created. It was a wonder that Rossington, Van Zant's fishing mate and punching bag, made it back home intact.

It took only eight shows on the tour for all hell to break loose. In

Portsmouth, England, before a show on October 25, again with Black Sabbath, a drunken Ronnie got into an argument with Gary over, of all things, how to pronounce "schnapps"—as much as was ever needed for him to start something. He broke a bottle of whiskey over John Butler's head, just like in a movie, leaving him bleeding profusely, and then grabbed a shard of broken glass and began slashing at Gary's wrists, leaving a deep cut on Gary's hand—his *left* hand, providentially, not the one he played his guitar with. Gary, defending himself, grabbed Ronnie's neck, choking him. But Ronnie, the fighter, broke free and continued his slashing, cutting both of Rossington's hands and breaking his own right hand in the process.

The melee, like a hockey fight, seemed to peter out by mutual consent, just another day in Skynyrdville. Ronnie and Gary made the usual trip to the hospital for their hands to be bandaged, and then were taken back to the arena; the bandages added to the Skynyrd schtick, but Rossington's hands were damaged enough that he had to play guitar with two fingers for a while. While both men had forgotten about the ugly scene, it left Ozzy Osbourne and his own prototypical band of mental cases baffled. Sabbath guitarist Zakk Wylde said, "All I remember was that the guitar player came out with a bandage on his hand and the singer came out with a bandage on his head, and they were hugging each other, saying, 'I'm sorry, brother—I love you, man.'"

It was too much for Artimus Pyle, who recalls the broken-glass incident as "really scary." As he had after Ed King's departure, Pyle said, he had "a major confrontation" with Ronnie the next day. "I busted his door down [and] I was ready to whip his ass. . . . I said, 'How can you do that to people you love?' And he says, 'I was drunk, I was drunk.'" Hearing that old dodge again, Artimus told him, "That's bullshit. That's no excuse." Even so, if any bobbies came looking for Mr. Van Zant, it wasn't with an arrest warrant for attempted homicide but for an autograph. No wonder Leon always donned a bobby hat when he played in London, and the band would write on its next album cover, "Thanks to the people of Europe." What's more, the incident was played in the rock press as just another story of Skynyrd making mayhem, even as parody; in *New Musical Express,* the writer gleefully called the tussle a "bloodbath" and chortled, "When a band start slashing each other's wrists before gigs you know they're confident."

The lunacy wasn't done yet. Once again having escaped a criminal situation with impunity, Ronnie decided on the flight from Germany to Belgium that he would throw another roadie, Joe Barnes, *off the plane*, which happened to be thirty thousand feet in the air at the time. This was, he determined, the price Barnes had to pay for failing to bring a cart stocked with booze onto the plane. Apparently quite serious and already too drunk for any more booze to have mattered, he tried to pry open a cabin door so he could heave Barnes out. Unable to, he simply punched Barnes hard in the stomach, doubling him over in intense pain. Barnes, later claiming he had sustained a serious injury, filed a personal injury lawsuit against Van Zant for $250,000, which was settled out of court.

During the band's booze- and drug-saturated heyday, these psychotic episodes seemed no more than a manifestation of the rock lifestyle. Besides, Ronnie could have made the claim, reasonably enough for him, that he had been taken to the woodshed for it in the many fistfights he'd had with his own confreres in the band, though no one could remember getting the best of him in these clashes; usually a split lip or black eye was the toll he had to pay, upon which, as Wylde noted, they were the best of friends again. It was crazy. It was sick. And it was dangerous to everyone's health—but in those times, it could seem normal, even amusing, to behold. Decades of reflection, though, led Pyle to say, "Looking back, it wasn't funny. It wasn't funny at all."

* * *

Still, there was always the filthy lucre to soothe—and gauze over—the ills and consequences of intoxication, even if, once it was common knowledge that they were all rolling in dough, certain perks vanished. At Hell House, for example, they had never paid an electric bill of more than around twelve dollars a month, despite sending hundreds of volts running through a mass of wires to high-powered guitars and amplifiers and keeping the lights on all night. Now, with no warning or explanation, the power company began to bill them for a hundred bucks a month. Also, a sheriff who lived down the road, who had never given them any trouble, came around one day with an "offer" when the music got loud. As Rossington recalled, "He said, 'We've been known to overlook these things, if you know what I mean.' He looked at us and we said, 'Yeah, we know what you mean, but forget it.'"

It wasn't the last time such generous offers were made by men in uniform. In Jacksonville, where delinquents from Shantytown were never tolerated easily, cops seemingly were itching to drum up some kudos by busting the glorified hoodlums for something, anything. The easiest and by far most frequent means was to spy one of them behind the wheel of a car, liable as they were they to break some traffic law, get into an accident, or drive without a license—or perhaps the officers might extort some graft out of them. And although they were in a stratum now where they could buy their way out of trouble, which happened all the time, it was a relief that they would only be home for a few weeks at a time before heading back out on the long road. Clearly, they had grown far too big for Jacksonville and too easy to target. Yet something in the blood and the soil kept bringing them back.

14

★ ★ ★ ★ ★

BETTER GET OUTTA MY WAY

Not only had Skynyrd now caught up to and passed the Allman Brothers, but they had become, to much of the rock intelligentsia—if not to the Yankee holdouts who refused to believe they were more subtle than the "Sweet Home Alabama" lyrics and Confederate flag—the certified *equal* of the biggest-selling American band of the 1970s, the Eagles. This thesis would only grow stronger in retrospect; to one pop culture and country music historian, Barbara Ching, "the Eagles were country rock, and their country was America; Skynyrd was country rock in a country ruled by the Eagles." The difference, she wrote, could be boiled down to the reality that the southern rockers engaged in a "struggle over the role and meaning of white southern manhood," their music something like a numbing agent for the "defeat and anger" felt by the "marginalized southern male" and giving license to rebellious Southern youth to break the stereotype of "unsophisticated dullards and backward bigots." Most of the newer country-rock acts, pretenders or otherwise, had to choose between the two models. L.A.'s version was the peaceful, easy kind—Poco, Linda Ronstadt, the second incarnation of Neil Young's Crazy Horse, the transplanted Texans England Dan and John Ford Coley—while Dixie had the sweatier, boozier blasts of Foghat and Texas blues rockers Edgar and Johnny Winter.

As the leader of that rat pack, Lynyrd Skynyrd turned to completing their fourth studio album, booking Phil Walden's Capricorn Studio in Macon for a week commencing November 25. Weeks before then, Tom Dowd flew to Jacksonville to spend some time with the band and go over the songs they had. He stayed at Ronnie's house, where he could study the band in their element. On Dowd's first day there, Ronnie, who, like the others at some time or other, had had his license revoked for repeated infractions, asked the producer to drive him to a rehearsal. Dowd got behind the wheel of the vintage canary-yellow Mercedes-Benz convertible. Even though Dowd was driving slowly, a cop almost immediately pulled the car over.

"The cop looks in the car," Dowd once recalled, "and Ronnie leans across and says, 'Hi, officer!' and he waves to him." A few minutes later, another cop pulled them over. Seeing Ronnie smirking, Tom knew what the ride was all about. "They all figured they were busting him for driving. He wanted me to drive his car into town so he could make fun of all these police officers."

The band had by then gone to great lengths to keep the cops at bay, one way being to play, as Ronnie noted to Dowd, "six to ten free concerts [in Jacksonville] because nobody wants to go to jail." Laughing because this was one of the periods in which he had no license, he said, "Now I don't have to do them no concerts no more," which Dowd thought was "his sweet revenge," such victories being taken in small doses. Other times, Ronnie would take Dowd fishing, bringing along his two Chihuahuas and a sawed-off billy club—"for gators," he explained. In Van Zant's backyard was a shed with a broken door engraved with HOLIDAY INN. Dowd asked what that was about. "All the hotels we trash they keep on charging us for the goddamn stuff we trash," Ronnie said, "so I make them send it to me." Other such mementos were all over the house, too, not as material possessions but punching bags of a sort. "If he was mad," Dowd learned, "he'd go down and he'd start throwing broken TV sets out the window. [He'd say] 'I paid for it once, I can do anything I want with it.' This was his way of working off some of his animosity and some of his frustration."

* * *

After the sessions got underway, Gary got into *his* car and, with yawning predictability, had an accident—one can only imagine what these Skynyrd boys were paying for repairs and insurance. His injuries were minor but delayed the sessions, just one more hurdle for Dowd in finishing the project. Trying to stitch together a tone and texture from songs with no connection, he thought the tired band lacked some zip; so as Kooper had, he brought in a trio of female backup singers—Leslie Hawkins, JoJo Billingsley, and Cassie Gaines—who were billed on the album as the "Honnicutts," and would henceforth be Skynyrd's permanent trio of "Honkettes." But he also ran into many of the same obstacles that had plagued Kooper and would later call the sessions "laborious." Dowd's manner was more rigid than Kooper's, and the band would chafe when he'd break in and yell through his microphone, "You're playing like dog-meat today!" or a brusque "Cut!" when they would change chords and parts on the fly, their normal way since they almost never came in with a complete arrangement for a song.

For Dowd, Van Zant was impossible. Ronnie would sing a few notes, take off his headphones, say, "I ain't singing for shit today," and walk out the door for the day. As Dowd would recall, "The man *knew* when he could sing. I couldn't say, 'Come on, Ronnie, you can finish this song.' I couldn't coax him to do diddly-squat." With the limited time they had, patience wore thin on both sides. But Dowd did lay down a helpful law—no drinking before or during sessions. He also forbid the usual coterie of groupies, dope dealers, and other leeches to hang out in the studio and get in the way.

Somehow the tracks fell in line. The first was the Van Zant–Collins–Rossington song "Roll Gypsy Roll," another of their chugging "road" songs, with a Collins twelve-string guitar that sounded like a banjo, a lilting Powell organ line, and some "Whipping Post"-style lyrics—"Ridin' on a greyhound, countin' those white lines / Destination I don't know and I'm feelin' like I'm dyin.'" Next was Van Zant and Collins's mournful "All I Can Do Is Write About It," the "it" being the destruction of the South's natural resources, its land and its air, by corporate commercialization. One of the few acoustic pieces in the Skynyrd catalog, with a piano solo by Billy and mandolin and dobro parts by Muscle Shoals' Barry Harwood, Ronnie's heartfelt lament cries, "I can see the concrete slowly creepin' / Lord take me and mine before that comes."

Now, with one day left before they would have to prepare for their next tour, to begin in Sudbury, Canada, on December 10, and needing some rock-out material, they had to go back to an old cut from their Muscle Shoals tapes, "Trust," with Ronnie wailing another sexist creed: "Don't tell your woman that you love her / Because that's when your trouble begins." The last track would give the work its identity. "Gimme Back My Bullets" was a song that, like "Saturday Night Special," was not what the title suggested, a make-good sequel to "Special" and a recommitment to the gun culture they had never really renounced. Rather, it was a bit of industryspeak that Ronnie and Gary had made into a song after "Sweet Home Alabama" peaked, equating "hard times" and "pressures" with the loss of those precious "bullets" that accompany hits up the chart at the whim of record critics—"pencil pushers," as he sang, who had "better get outta my way," because "I'm leavin' this game one step ahead of you / And you will not hear me cry 'cause I do not sing the blues." The problem with these protestations was that they were now tiresome and tendentious, not to mention hardly credible, considering how well they'd done, even without any singles coming near the Top 10 since. But Van Zant would flog the theme until his dying day.

With nine tracks in all (three future CD reissues would also include live tracks of the songs), the hard blues-rock tone, sneering vocal, and sure-to-be misconstrued meaning of "Gimme Back My Bullets" made for a trenchant theme and title for the album, even if only a couple of songs were in that vein. (The band had given some thought to calling the album *Ain't No Dowd About It*, though it was agreed no one would get what that meant.) An appropriately dark cover was created by their art designer George Osaki, half in black and white, half in sepia tone, with each of the dour-faced Skynyrd members looking bleary eyed or drunk or stoned, and posing in a photo by Moshe Brakha like they were taking a group mug shot. Only Billy, at the far right, smiled. Ronnie, Leon, and Billy each cradled a can of beer.

The back cover, also shot by Brakha, was unnerving, showing the band in dim light on a dark street in front of a honky-tonk bar, whiskey bottles and beer cans in hand, sizing up a mysterious stranger seen from the rear, with something like the handle of a gun on his hip. The logo chosen for the LP—a baseball with an eerie, skeletal hand gripping a gun, bony finger on the trigger, tongue sticking out of the barrel—left no doubt that the band and MCA had no intention of clarifying the bullet theme. Acknowledgments were strewn all over the back cover, which called Pete Rudge "a gentleman" and credited Tom Dowd *twice*, once in recognition for "putting up with us"—something Al Kooper could surely relate to, though he might also have wondered why they'd never credited *him* for that.

When the album was released on February 2, Kooper, after hearing it, was in no mood to be magnanimous, and pronounced it "flat as a pancake," mainly, he said, because "I knew how to record them—that vision I had [and] to make that salable." Self-serving or not, this slam—and his feeling that Ed King's loss hurt badly—was actually an accurate analysis. Much of the incoming flak would sound similar and burst mainly around the producer Skynyrd had lavished all that praise on. For all Dowd's efforts, he had failed to gun the Skynyrd engine. And apparently the band secretly agreed, with consequences that would soon land Dowd into the same perdition as Kooper.

* * *

Although Skynyrd went into hype mode—"This was the most pleasant album we ever did," Ronnie said, with Allen calling it "material-wise, our best album"—their market sensed a disconnect. While much of what they heard on the mixes kicked ass in the usual fashion, the album would stumble out of the gate, and the dangers inherent in pushing a metal/redneck agenda would be evident when the band broke into "Gimme Back My Bullets," Ronnie's recital of the title phrase prompting fans already familiar with the tune to do just that—throw *real* bullets onto the stage. Tom Dowd was astonished. "Here'd come .22s, .22 longs, .38s, .45s, coming up on stage like an arsenal." Fearing that some of those cartridges might explode if they hit a hot light or a wall with too much force, the band decided to stop playing it live, even if it was the title track of the album. Of course, that only created another urban legend attached to Skynyrd and made an industry song a *pro-gun* song.

However, although most reviews were favorable, even a rave such as one in *Hit Parader* was apt to opine that, although Van Zant sang with "a rich measure of personal conviction . . . about contemporary southern livin'" and "more maturity," overall "the fire and anger is somewhat channeled." And the *Rolling Stone* notice was brutal, scolding them for "inertia" and "poor material, fully half of which I couldn't have imagined Lynyrd Skynyrd recording two years ago." Skynyrd, it said, "is a good band in limbo," a verdict shared by Robert Christgau's real-time review in the *Village Voice*, which read: "Unfortunately, the music could use some Yankee calculation—from Al Kooper of Forest Hills, who I figure was good for two hooks per album, and Ed King of New Jersey . . . whose guitar fills carried a lot more zing than three doodooing

Honnicutts." While such tut-tutting from the Yankee literati might have made Ronnie react by saying *See what I mean?*, lagging sales had a more tangible effect. This would be Skynyrd's worst-selling album, going no higher than number twenty on the chart and needing twenty years to be certified gold; the only singles that would come from it, "Double Trouble" and "Roll Gypsy Roll," stiffed, only the former making the chart at all, at number eighty—proving Ronnie's lament that it sucked to lose those magic bullets. Rossington's explanation was almost helpless. "We were kind of lost," he said.

Ronnie now had to reconsider getting back to the formula that had gotten Skynyrd to the dance. He put out the word for a guitar man, and the first to answer the call was no ordinary one. Leslie West, a man with a resume nearly as long as anyone's in rock, had recently disbanded the power trio Mountain, which he had created in 1969, with the Rascals' producer Felix Pappalardi, to be what was called a "louder version of Cream." Because of the hit "Mississippi Queen," Mountain, for whom Skynyrd had opened a show in 1970, was sometimes mistaken for a country-rock unit, but West, a Jewish native New Yorker, had played the underground Greenwich Village circuit in the 1960s, played on sessions for the Who with Al Kooper, and produced and played on an album with Jack Bruce.

Although Ronnie couldn't have given a hang about hiring a so-called country musician, he was taken with West, a massive man with a gregarious stage presence, and for West the proposed pairing was tantalizing. He auditioned for Ronnie in a New York hotel bar when Skynyrd was in town, and then waited . . . and waited for the invitation that never came. There never was any reason given, but Ronnie was perhaps unwilling to do what the Eagles had done when they brought in Joe Walsh: make way for a known figure with a resume and better personality. The same may have applied when they also dabbled with hiring Wayne Perkins, a former Muscle Shoals Swamper who had played on scores of sessions—including Jimmy Johnson's sessions with Skynyrd—before forming the band Smith Perkins Smith, touring Europe, and then playing sessions with Bob Marley and the Wailers, Leon Russell, and Eric Clapton. Perkins sat in on a few concerts with Skynyrd but was let go. He couldn't have been too upset, though; the same year, the Rolling Stones hired him to play lead guitar on their *Black and Blue* album, and he later cowrote the soundtrack albums for *Back to School* and *The Karate Kid, Part II.*

It was only as a favor to one of the Skynyrd brood that the right man for the job came along. Seeing these auditions going on, Honkette Cassie Gaines touted her younger brother Steve, an itinerant guitar player born and living in Oklahoma and struggling along on the lounge circuit with a band of his own, Crawdad, which had recorded without success at the Capricorn Studios and Leon Russell's studio in Tulsa. (MCA put the Russell session tapes out in 1988 in an album called *One in the Sun.*) He'd also played with the redoubtable white-soul master Mitch Ryder in Detroit, but now he was going nowhere and was a tough sell. Cassie, a bright and determined woman, met resistance when she suggested they let him jam with them. "Fuck no," Gary told her. "Nobody jams with us!"

She persisted, though, and when they got to Kansas City on May 11, they relented. Steve Gaines came straight from a club his band was playing nearby, and without hearing them play one note or ever having played any of their songs, he was thrown into the frying pan, joining them onstage for the show they were playing. The first song he had to somehow keep up with was one of the band's staples, the great old Jimmie Rodgers country yodel "T for Texas." They told Kevin Elson to be ready to cut Gaines's microphone if he fell behind, but as soon as he began, Rossington would recall, "Allen and I looked at each other and our jaws dropped. . . . He could play anything, chicken' pickin', country blues, hard rock."

After the show, Gaines shook their hands and left, not expecting to hear from them again. But later the band was assured by Kevin Elson, who had heard Gaines's parts clearly through his headset, "This guy can play." They did audition a few other guitarists, not only for talent but, as Ronnie said, "to check out their heads, y'know, see if they can put up with our shit." Apparently none of them made either or both grades, and within a week they called Gaines and told him to get his rear end to another gig, in Myrtle Beach, South Carolina, on May 31. After giving Gaines one more chance to shine or wash out, the band agreed to offer him a contract. Gaines, wasting no time, dumped his own band and signed. For the next month, they would be preparing for the live album, playing a gig here and there, but mainly holed up in Jacksonville rehearsing, and Gaines would become a hugely valuable asset.

Boyish and handsome, as lean and lanky as Rossington and Collins, Gaines was by appearance as innocent as they were grizzled. Born coincidentally on the same day as Ed King, September 14, 1949, he was married but far more committed to the concept than the rest of the band, being nothing like the ritual philanderers he was now among—and this trait, they seemed to know, would be a welcome change from their usual demented behavior. For a while, he merely kept up, playing quiet rhythm parts. Audiences did not yet know who he was and were a little baffled when Ronnie would call him out by name. But gradually he began to let loose and provide the same depth, fullness, fire—and idiomatic "bluesiness," as Tom Dowd called it—to their raging guitar assaults. Soon he was playing on those long solo interchanges with Gary and Allen as if he had been there all along, and Ronnie had already decided to push him far more out front than those two, asking him for song material for the next album and telling Steve he would be singing lead on them.

* * *

As Ronnie perceived, the timing of Gaines's entry was perfect for such a widening of the Skynyrd borders. Indeed, it seemed that Fate had intervened when the live album had to be scrapped from its original record date, which was to be during their two-day engagement at the Beacon Theatre on April 10 and 11. Before they even got there, there arose, as Dowd once said, "a comedic set of circumstances," beginning with the issue of Ronnie's throat. He had never cut back on his cigarettes and booze consumption and was paying for it, big time, now that cocaine was also in the equation. He would normally cough up so much bloody phlegm that it was alarming. It was touch and go whether he would be able to sing at all or whether he'd be ordered to rest his savaged vocal cords for a few months. Indeed, at a major gig that year at New Orleans' Sugar Bowl his voice was gone. The band was to share the bill with ZZ Top that night, but when the show began, Skynyrd's roadies were there but not Skynyrd. This happened again at a May 23 concert in Charlotte when Ronnie walked off the stage midshow. By the time of the Beacon shows Ronnie could only sing in a rasp.

But another problem developed when Artimus Pyle, during a stopover in South Carolina, decided to do some hang-gliding off a cliff and promptly broke his leg. The rest of the band was in New York for the Beacon shows, but for three days no one heard from him. When he finally showed up, he was on crutches. That might have sufficed, but by then Gary had somehow slammed a door on his left hand, breaking his ring finger. Though the live album was shelved, the Beacon shows limped on, with rabid audiences close to seeing a Skynyrd crack-up. During the final show, Allen and Leon blew fuses on their guitars and then their own fuses; in a fit of pique, aping the Who, they smashed their instruments to bits on the stage floor and threw broken pieces into the audience—one piece caused a bloody cut on a girl's face, another expense Pete Rudge had to pay for. Then, during the wrap party, Ronnie punctuated the freak show engagement by "creepin'" Charlie Brusco, right in the jaw.

Dowd and the band hopefully rescheduled the live album recording for July 7–9 during a three-night run at Atlanta's Fox Theater. It was during this interval that Gaines came aboard, and in a real break he would have a place on the very important live double LP. For Gaines, who followed Cassie and their father Bud in moving to Jacksonville with his wife Teresa and their young daughter Corrina, it was a relief to be out of the club grind and playing in an A-list band; and his sense of boyish optimism was a rare departure in a cesspool of fatalism and dark obsessions. "This is the beginning," he bubbled after his hiring. "I hope to be playing for the rest of my life in some way. My head's cleared out and I can just think about music more." In many ways, Steve Gaines, who was not a heavy drinker or drug user, seemed like a metaphor for renewal, even rebirth. Ronnie would begin to elucidate some of these same thoughts, seeing in the fresh-faced Gaines something he himself would like to be, if only he could allow himself to give it a try.

15

★ ★ ★ ★ ★

T-R-O-U-B-L-E

In 1976 Lynyrd Skynyrd was in full throttle, and so was southern rock. In an ever-lengthening chain, along came analogs like Foghat, Wet Willie, White Witch, Jonathan Edwards, Grinderswitch, Itchy Brother, the Ozark Mountain Daredevils, and Molly Hatchet. The last, a direct descendant of Skynyrd, had formed in Jacksonville (its name taken from a prostitute who had murdered her clients) and was being managed by Alan Walden's former partner Pat Armstrong, their recordings made in Skynyrd's newly built Riverside Studios, which Donnie Van Zant's .38 Special also used and helped finance. The parallel arc of L.A.-based country rock was evolving, too, its chain made longer by highly talented acts such as the post–Richie Furay incarnation of Poco, Rick Nelson in his post–Stone Canyon Band phase, Little Feat, Firefall, Elvin Bishop, and the bluegrass-rooted New Riders of the Purple Sage. But the kings of the hill were the Eagles and that prickly band of rednecks from Jacksonville whose name had once been unpronounceable but by now had elevated even former gym teacher Leonard Skinner into a lowercase, incidental icon.

Phil Walden, on the other hand, was not enjoying himself as much as Leonard Skinner was thanks in part to the success of the band named after him. With Capricorn Records' meal ticket, the Allman Brothers Band, in decline, Gregg Allman and Dickey Betts began solo careers while Allman's checkered life became a gossip-page favorite during his short-lived marriage to Cher, the chanteuse of cheesy pop. Allman's drug abuse escalated, as did that of the rest of the Allman band, and their

1975 album *Win, Lose or Draw* was a critical and commercial bomb, a prime example of how fickle success can be. A year later, Allman, busted on federal drug charges, turned state's evidence against the band's tour manager Scooter Herring, prompting four Allman bandmates to vow never to work with Allman again—a vow that was easily discarded, given the perpetual touring proceeds brought in by the epochal group long after their prime and even to this day.

There would be no new Allman Brothers product for two years, a period during which it was assumed they had broken up. In the meantime, the hard upward thrust of the band the elder Walden brother had turned down, which his little brother had ushered to success, was the death knell of Capricorn Records. Once, Walden's operational battle cry was that no southern band could possibly burgeon outside of his arc. Now they *had* to. Riding the idiom Phil Walden had foreseen, southern rock was making a fortune for bands scattered on labels mainly outside the South. Foghat, for example, was on the Bearsville label founded by Bob Dylan's former manager Albert Grossman and based near Woodstock, New York. The Ozark Mountain Daredevils were on A&M. The Outlaws, still comanaged by Charlie Brusco and Alan Walden, were going strong at Arista. The way to the promised land for southern rockers was to follow not Phil Walden but the money, the kind handed to them in advances from the big national record houses that dwarfed Capricorn.

Walden was still a highly respected music apparatchik, however. When the South laid on hands for Jimmy Carter during the '76 presidential campaign, country music—country *rock*, not the Nashville brand, which was staunchly Republican—followed Walden's lead and united behind the smiling Georgia peanut farmer. Walden even brought the Allmans together for fund-raising concerts and enlisted the redneck band that had bragged about not being bothered by matters such as Watergate. For Skynyrd, joining this crusade was a half-hearted endeavor at best. What tipped it was their sense of southern pride. While Carter was a former naval officer, engineer, and thriving businessman, his less intellectually gifted, beer-guzzling brother and his silver-haired matriarch with the honeyed drawl were being parodied as typical of a Deep South gooberocracy. And so southern rockers far and wide came to play at a gigantic fund-raiser for Carter on May 1 at Jacksonville's cavernous

Gator Bowl, calling the event the Southern Jam. One by one they laid on hands for *this* far more enlightened "Gov'nor," first the Allmans, followed by Charlie Daniels, Marshall Tucker, the Outlaws, and .38 Special.

And Skynyrd? As hopeless as their addictions were and as uninterested as they were in political huckstering, their leader didn't make it onto the stage. After snorting cocaine in his trailer, Ronnie again began coughing up blood and begged off. When Skynyrd came on, Charlie Daniels announced that he was going to stand in for Van Zant, who was "indisposed." That was one way of putting it. When Carter narrowly defeated placeholder president Gerald Ford, Walden was accorded a place of honor at the inauguration, and the Daniels and Tucker bands played at the ball and were invited to the White House for periodic events. But the invitations for Skynyrd, who might have been a tad too red in the neck for the born-again Christian president, must have gotten lost in the mail.

★ ★ ★

By then nothing seemed to go smoothly for Skynyrd. On April 30 Ronnie had become angry at the usually mild-mannered Leon Wilkeson during a set in Lakeland, Florida, and the two had a brief pushing and grabbing match. As the live album again drew near, the bandmates again weren't talking to each other, not a good thing with the pressure on to finally get the live album done. After arriving in Atlanta, they made it through three days of tense rehearsals. Then it was show time at the Fox Theater, a venue they had chosen for an engagement as part of a fund-raising drive to keep the old theater from being razed. For their efforts, Skynyrd would be honored by Atlanta mayor Maynard Jackson, whom they presented with a gold record of the work. At the opening show on July 7, Tom Dowd monitored the sound in a mobile sound studio outside the hall and was delighted to hear Skynyrd playing with tremendous energy before a stoked-up audience, such that the *Atlanta Constitution* called the show "hypnotic." Ronnie indeed would give it all he had, bloody discharges notwithstanding. He would be so drained and his voice so ragged after the third show that an ensuing gig on the tenth would have to be scrubbed.

From these three shows would be taken fourteen songs for the double LP (reduced to twelve on the first CD reissue in 1986, then bumped back up to twelve with three bonus tracks on the second CD reissue a decade later, and then finally expanded to twenty-four tracks on the extensively remixed 2001 CD reissue, on which the tracks were presented in their original order on the set list). The "Free Bird" encore ran thirteen and a half minutes (nearly fifteen minutes on the second reissue). The song list included "Workin' for MCA," "I Ain't the One," "Searching," "Tuesday's Gone"—which they hadn't performed in two years—"Saturday Night Special," "Sweet Home Alabama," "Gimme Three Steps," "Call Me the Breeze," "The Needle and the Spoon," and "Crossroads"—the last a remarkable cover of the Robert Johnson blues classic with Ronnie's gritty vocal as convincing as Clapton's cover with Cream.

One new original, "Travellin' Man," from a rare collaboration with Leon, was Ronnie's psalm for Lacy—"My father was a trucker for the years of 23 / And on the day that I was born his truck was left to me," and ever since, "I am just a mover, movin' fast as sound / Always free, sometimes lonely, always movin' around." The last song to get a place was "T for Texas," with those Jimmie Rodgers lyrics about being treated like "dirty dogs" and having "had more pretty women than a passenger train could haul" a Skynyrd epitaph of sorts. It also was an introduction to the skills of Steve Gaines, whom fans would learn was a new member of the band when the album came out.

The set, *One More from the Road*, was an extraordinary work, the single best and purest example—at least until the 2001 remaster with Dowd's liberal overdubbing scrubbed—of how Lynyrd Skynyrd sounded before a live audience. Of particular note were the extended arrangements of some songs, which Stephen Thomas Erlewine notes were "as long as those of the Allmans, but always much rawer, nearly dangerous." Dowd's praise for the album was effusive, even if he said so himself. "The energy's really there. Like *Otis and Booker T Live in Europe*!" he said, apparently meaning the 1967 Stax album *Otis Redding: Live in Europe*, on which the soul legend was backed by Booker T. and the MG's, high praise indeed as this was the only live album by Redding released during his lifetime. "That record represented every record they had made but they played it better and it was recorded better than the ones that were hits."

Clearly, it was a barometer of its time. Released on September 13, 1976, with an initial run of four hundred thousand copies, within weeks that was kicked up to six hundred thousand. Just as excited as Dowd were the critics, with *Rolling Stone*'s John Milward hailing the band's "Southern blues-rock diced with the sharp blade of British hard rock" as "a prime cut of guitar rock" and Ronnie's "world-weary" vocals "barroom-tough on rockers, properly vulnerable on . . . 'Searching' and 'The Needle and the Spoon.'" By year's end, it had reached number nineteen, and within a year it would go gold, then platinum by the end of '76, and triple platinum in 1987, the biggest seller of any Skynyrd album, with over three million units sold to date. If "Sweet Home Alabama" was their "Ramblin' Man," *One More from the Road* was their *Eat a Peach*, the Allmans' 1972 million-selling double album. Meanwhile, caught in the jet stream, *Gimme Back My Bullets* picked up more sales, as did the older albums. Skynyrd, it seemed, had become quite nearly a turnkey operation.

★ ★ ★

One More from the Road was an appropriate rallying cry for the band. With no delay, they were back out on it, one more time. Through July, they played gigs in their home state, one at Miami's baseball stadium, and then in Nashville and Chicago. On August 1 at a sold-out Macon Coliseum, they broke the Allman Brothers' attendance record there. The long road was so winding now that it took Skynyrd off to England again for exactly two shows, a trip made necessary because Pete Rudge had the leverage to put them onto the same stage as the Rolling Stones, whom he had booked as the headliner at the Knebworth Festival in Hertfordshire county, north of London. This open-air site had hosted the big summer music event in England since 1974, when sixty thousand people attended a show that included the Allman Brothers, the Doobie Brothers, and Van Morrison. The next edition drew one hundred thousand for Pink Floyd, the Steve Miller Band, and Captain Beefheart. In '76, ticket sales zoomed for the August 21 concert there when some idle musings by the Stones about performing for the "last time" were taken to mean they were about to disband. Actually, all they had said was that it would be their first and last time playing Knebworth. Rudge, seeing the numbers build, gave Skynyrd marching orders to get on a plane.

Ronnie, who was awaiting the birth of his second child, gritted his teeth and went. But since he was homesick away from the States, he took Lacy with him. The two of them had come a ways since Ronnie had dropped out of school, and were constantly trying to mend old wounds; Ronnie hoped the trip would help Lacy see the respect his boy was getting all over the world. The old dog, for his part, needed little convincing; he had long accepted the role of the "Father of Southern Rock," words he had embroidered on his stationery and handkerchiefs. Making the rounds of Skynyrd concerts close to home, he was instantly recognizable because of his long white Santa Claus beard and sometimes full Confederate Army uniform and hat, entertaining whomever he saw with yarns told through a mouth with progressively fewer teeth.

Skynyrd's appearance at Knebworth was eagerly awaited. Posters for the event, at Rudge's directive, featured their image above that of the Stones, with the headline KNEBWORTH FESTIVAL '76 WELCOMES AMERICA'S CONFEDERATE ROCKERS LYNYRD SKYNYRD. They warmed up the day before with a show in nearby Hemel Hempstead. On a stifling hot, brilliant day the next afternoon, the massive crowd at Knebworth grew by the hour. The official attendance that day was 120,000, but there were probably twice that on the grounds under a blistering sun. Not that big crowds were a big deal for Skynyrd; in Chicago they'd recently played before one hundred thousand in Soldier Field. And back in '74 at the Ozark Music Festival at the Missouri State Fairgrounds in Sedalia, around 350,000 had crammed into the quaint venue. Ronnie liked saying that beyond the first few rows everything seemed a blur anyway. And Artimus added that a crowd like that created a feeling of such enormous power that he could, with one word, incite either a riot or a mass cleanup of the grounds.

They were on the undercard that day with 10cc, Todd Rundgren, the Don Harrison Band led by former Creedence Clearwater Revival's Stu Cook and Doug Clifford, and the Jefferson Airplane spinoff Hot Tuna. They were scheduled to appear at 3:15 PM as an early act leading up to the Stones' evening set. However, with all the Confederate flags in the massive crowd, it was clear that interest in the band was higher than previously believed, so promoter Freddy Bannister shifted them into the spot immediately before the Stones. This was also a fallback since there was doubt the Stones were in any condition to play, having come in so wrecked that they barely knew where they were. With so many watching—including the Royal Family and Paul and Linda McCartney—a bad gig by the Stones might leave a stain on the event; in this scenario, Bannister would bank on the rednecks from the colonies to save the day.

This reality hardly fazed Skynyrd. Before the show, as Pyle recalled, Ronnie and Gary sat under a tent behind the stage calmly smoking hash with Mick Jagger. "They were tapping a pipe . . . passing this thing around," laughed Pyle, who had his own celebrity smoke-in. When he walked into the band's trailer before the show, he saw Leon and Billy passing joints around with a familiar-looking fellow wearing wrap-around sunglasses.

"Hey, you'd never guess who's here smoking a joint with us," Leon said through the fog. Artimus squinted through the smoke and instantly recognized the guest toker as Jack Nicholson, who had come from L.A. to view the Stones.

For the next hour, they all got stoned. Then at around five o'clock, as twilight crept in, Skynyrd entered the long, canopied, orange-colored stage to their usual play-on music, "Dixie." Clad in a black T-shirt reading MUSCLE SHOALS SOUND, Ronnie checked out the mass of humanity in front of him. With little fanfare, he called out, "Hello, how are you?" Skynyrd then kicked into "Workin' for MCA." The normal Skynyrd set was around an hour. Now, wanting badly to upstage the Stones, they went on for ninety minutes, holding that gigantic crowd in their palms. Observers had only seen them play as well and with as much sting just once, when they were recording the live album.

As people waved the Stars and Bars and American flags along with the Union Jack, the band blasted through a dozen songs, ending with a mesmerizing fourteen-minute rendition of "Free Bird." Freely trespassing on the tongue-shaped ramp at the foot of the stage built for Mick Jagger to preen and strut on, Skynyrd stomped the floorboards as the guitar solos escalated in intensity, with Alan, clad all in red and looking like a big stick of licorice sprouting unruly hair, manically leaping up and down, and a bare-chested Artimus hammering out wild drum fills and cymbal crashes. The electrifying set indeed turned out to be the high point of the festival, in contrast to the Stones' sloppy, heavy-lidded performance, which came after midnight and a four-hour delay. The Brit rock press vilified their poor showing, some calling it a "fiasco" and "a shambling parody."

During the day, when there were air shows and clowns to entertain the crowd, the vibe had been felicitous; Pyle felt he had to note that "there were no drug overdoses." And Skynyrd basked in the afterglow of this victorious stage of their ascendance. Artimus would habitually speak of having "blown away" the Stones, who Billy Powell said were strung out on Quaaludes—"I know this for a fact." Skynyrd felt the timing was right to strike a new theme: that of maturing, sobering up, and reaching a real crossroads of personal reformation. "It's the first time we've seen our audience in eight years," Ronnie told the press. It sounded good, anyway—no matter that he had been seen downing shots of straight bourbon before and even during the show, when he periodically grabbed a bottle of whiskey and took a swig; nor that after the show, Gene Odom saw him go shot-for-shot after being challenged to a drinking contest by J. Paul Getty III, the billionaire's playboy son. Several years before the young man had been infamously kidnapped and held for ransom, an episode during which the kidnappers had cut off his ear and sent it to his grandfather with a ransom note—to Skynyrd that made the young Getty about the coolest guy they'd ever met.

* * *

The reforming of Skynyrd was a *very* hard sell, given that their image was so intertwined with their excesses. Indeed, one British reviewer wrote that "tasting Lynyrd Skynyrd live feels like having a bottle of Jack Daniel's shoved down your throat." To be sure, the bandmates were threats to themselves and anyone around them, particularly when one of them turned the key in a car. It had become a joke to them that they lost their licenses so much yet kept on driving, openly cackling about the fake licenses they got, and even with police laying in wait, still avoiding prosecution when they cracked up. Once when Al Kooper asked Wilkeson for his address, Leon handed him a license. Kooper asked, "Don't you need this?"

"Nah, keep it," Wilkeson told him. "I got a few of those."

Not long after the band had gotten home, Gary, the world's worst driver, went out in his Ford Torino on Labor Day, drunk and high on Quaaludes, and passed out with his foot on the accelerator. The car careened off Mandarin Road, crashed into a telephone pole, then a tree, and then finally careened into someone's home. Once more cheating death and the likelihood of injuring or killing others, he bruised some ribs and spent a week in the hospital. Amazingly, this still didn't seem enough cause for Jacksonville's finest to charge him with any crime or revoke his license—an absolute crime in itself—instead allowing Pete Rudge to merely pay fines and restitution to the owner of the home that was damaged. Rossington, as usual, could cover the bandages with his frilly jackets and go on playing guitar, for a while in a neck brace. When Ronnie heard of this latest mishap, he was not amused. Visiting Gary in the hospital, he let him have it.

"I told him he was stupid," he later told Gene Odom, apparently not appreciating the irony, "'cause what he was doing was only gonna hurt the band and everything we've worked for."

Van Zant, with the same lack of irony, for years had insisted he wanted to clean up and broaden the image of the band into something more than a bunch of barroom bruisers who could also play music. And now he resolved to prove Skynyrd could give up the booze, the one-night stands, and the crazy-ass driving, and settle down in some quiet little town—even if he knew it really didn't have a chance in hell of happening. His own habits and deceits aside, for Ronnie, life as a magnum rock star was no more than a dizzying, kaleidoscopic blot, senseless and unrequiting, a life whizzing by through bus and airplane windows, seen through the eyes of men who were almost always eight miles high. In his newly adopted phase, he began dropping hints that he might give up music for a while, dry out, and become a homebody at last.

This seemed plausible when on September 19 Judy gave birth to a daughter they named Melody. The next five shows were canceled, and Ronnie flew home, seeing visions of redemption for a life lived for varying reasons in confusion, anger, and regret. He moved his family to a new home on a quiet lane in a woody area off Brickyard Road in Orange Park, again just off the Saint Johns River, with a guitar-shaped swimming pool in back. To all who saw him, he took vows of sobriety he knew he wouldn't keep, as if the vows themselves marked a kind of turning point in his life, to be reserved at that moment and then chased sometime in the future. He could even get philosophical about it. "For the first time I'm really thinking about the future," he said at the time. "I'm twenty-seven now [he was twenty-eight] and I've got a baby girl and I plan to stick around and watch her grow up. I also plan to collect for the last ten years of self-abuse."

It sounded convincing. Tom Dowd for one believed he saw in Ronnie "a more serious person." Pulling rank as the leader he was, in the wake of Gary's latest misadventure on the road, he began openly turning on the others in the band, regarding them as immature snot-nosed kids who just didn't get it. "These boys are still boys, and they're never gonna stop on their own. . . . If this keeps up, somebody's gonna get killed," he said. And he wasn't just whistlin' Dixie. Rossington wasn't the only one who'd had a near miss. In recent months Powell had almost killed himself in a motorcycle accident, Collins had fractured his skull driving a jeep over an embankment, and Pyle had broken his leg in a car crash. Dean Kilpatrick, who was always on the periphery of Skynyrd madness, had crashed the band's van, without them in it, into the back of a Trailways bus on the off-ramp of the interstate, putting him in the hospital with injuries so severe he needed his spleen removed.

Despite the fact that he saw himself as the sole grown-up of the bunch, Ronnie was obviously the last to lecture anyone else about this sort of thing, least of all the men he had influenced so heavily by his own ongoing erratic, inebriated behavior. Still, he would try hard to play the sanctification and sympathy cards. The problem was, as good as he made it sound, the road called, as it always did, one more time. And that was when he would make a liar and a fool of himself.

16

★ ★ ★ ★ ★

LOOK WHAT'S GOING ON INSIDE YOU

With two Skynyrd albums climbing the charts on almost concurrent paths, MCA's ads and band-licensed items such as Skynyrd T-shirts and everything from Skynyrd belts to Skynyrd necklace pendants, Skynyrd photos, and Skynyrd underwear—all of which were now hawked as collectibles under the corporate banner of Broken Arrow Productions, run out of Peter Rudge's office suite—were now full-frontal everything. The Confederate flag was paired with the old skull motif, now updated with wings spreading on either side of a flying skull, *and* the Jack Daniel's logo, which was beneficial to both the band and the booze maker. Ronnie, meanwhile, was strutting hard. After getting home from Knebworth, he began wearing a T-shirt that definitely was *not* for sale. It read, WHO THE FUCK ARE THE ROLLING STONES ANYWAY?

That cocky attitude was as salable a quality as any band apparel. As it stood now, the hippies loved Skynyrd. The bikers loved 'em. The drunks loved 'em. The potheads and coke sniffers loved 'em. The metalheads loved 'em. The "Free Bird"-grooving, mellowed-out yuppie crowd loved 'em. The right-wing nuts loved 'em. Only Lester Bangs still seemed to hate 'em. They cut across all cultural and musical fault lines, upscale, low scale, any scale. This was especially timely, as it erected a buffer zone against the malefaction of disco, and the way they transformed their aversion to snobbery into a kind of reverse snobbery portended the breakout of punk. It was all extremely profitable too. Rudge, as crassly commercial as he was, would enclose in the next album a form for the "Lynyrd Skynyrd Survival Kit," a collection of items with the reminder to "send check or money order" plus a dollar in postage.

The cash streams were deep and rich, and the Shantytown boys were doing all right, if not ostentatiously so. They were still close to home—no L.A. migration for these boys. Gary had bought a home across the river in the chic Mandarin section of Jacksonville, where some of his best car crashes had occurred. Allen and Kathy had a home built on two acres a few miles to the east on Julington Creek, surrounded by a high fence. Steve, Billy, Leon, and Artimus lived in comfort, if not splendor. They had it all, it seemed, if one didn't count sobriety or industry power, which they likely believed they would never have.

With the release of the live album, Skynyrd believed they had fulfilled their commitment to MCA. Pete Rudge had planned to negotiate with Ahmet Ertegun, signing the band to Atlantic Records, the first step of which had been to hire Dowd to produce them. However, complications arose when MCA pointed out that they needed to record one more *studio* album before they could field offers from other labels. What's more, MCA was prepared to better any other offer, so tied was the label to its top act, and Rudge advised the band to forget about going elsewhere. They would still be workin' for MCA, ball and chain and all.

That being the assumption, the company had a directive for Skynyrd—get out some hit singles. Mike Maitland had been bugging Rudge about this for some time, as none of the singles that had been released had done much, save for "Sweet Home Alabama." Maitland himself called Ronnie with his ukase. "We've got you back in this market," he said, meaning the sales mainstream. "Now you're going to go pop. I want three hit singles on the next album."

"What's a hit single?" Ronnie wanted to know.

"A record that's not more than three minutes long."

This was a touchy subject with the group, who had become somewhat defensive about their lack of hit-single material; it seemed irrelevant given their massive album sales. What's more, it could even be said that Skynyrd had helped render the single 45-rpm record obsolete; in the new age of album rock, if a fan liked a particular song on an album, he'd simply buy the album, which seemed to put each song into a context. Indeed, suggestive of "Free Bird," the Eagles' *Desperado* was so popular that the title track, which was never released as a single, was their most requested song, while the two singles from that double-platinum album tanked. Nor was "Stairway to Heaven"—a song that now vies with "Free Bird" for the top spot on classic radio all-time lists—ever a single. Led Zeppelin, which only had two Top 10 hits in the United States, owns the biggest-selling album in history, the nine-time platinum *Led Zeppelin IV*, and the third-biggest-selling double album, *Physical Graffiti*. Pink Floyd, whose album *The Wall* has still sold the most double LPs in history, 23 million, only notched one Top 10 hit, the title track. Deep Purple also had just one Top 10 song.

The difference was that, in America, the album-rock gods the Eagles, Fleetwood Mac, Stevie Wonder, and Chicago had consistent and *big* hits, not to mention Grammy awards. And so Skynyrd, reluctantly, accepted the challenge of making hits without compromising their integrity—and certainly not going too pop, a notion that made their skin crawl. They seemed to have the ideal guy to move them into wider mainstream territory. But Skynyrd being Skynyrd, even God—Soundman God—was about to fall out of their favor.

* * *

There was no way Skynyrd could create such new material utilizing the old system of waiting until they got into the studio and hoping for lightning. Now, they would come to arenas early to hash out songs for the next album, sessions for which were scheduled at Dowd's Criteria Studios in Miami in the early spring of 1977. And there was no dearth of arenas at which to do this. Rudge had not cut back their touring, nor his propensity for booking them on a whim thousands of miles across the sea. They went back again to London twice—each time for *one* show—first on October 9 at the Capital Theatre in Cardiff, Wales, and then on December 20 at London's Odeon (bootlegs of both shows would surface years later on the Oh Boy and Flying Horse labels). And as if all that travel wasn't crazy enough, Rudge booked them on their first trip to the Far East, with five shows in Tokyo in mid-January 1977; from there they'd go right back to England for three weeks.

While Cameron Crowe, who accompanied them for a *Rolling*

Stone article, saw that trip as "the beginning of a real new way of handling themselves," once they were in Japan the sake flowed right along with the Kentucky bourbon. A day after they arrived, Ronnie turned twenty-nine, and the promoter threw a birthday party for him and took the entire troupe to a nightclub. Plied with champagne all night, the band was quickly in a fighting mood. Before long, two German tourists accosted a couple of Honkettes and Mary Beth Medley—Peter Rudge's assistant and Crowe's girlfriend—outside the ladies' room and then followed the girls back to their table. Recognizing Ronnie, they began to taunt him, yet another occasion when some nimrod thought it would be fun to pick a fight with Lynyrd Skynyrd.

Ronnie kept his cool initially. But then one of the Germans pinched Mary Beth on the behind, and another knocked Ronnie's hat off; and before anyone knew it, a brawl had erupted. Champagne bottles were being thrown back and forth, sending people in the club running for cover. The Skynyrd boys were pummeling the jokers when the cops rushed in, requiring the promoter to do a lot of talking, and perhaps grease a few palms, for the group to be let go. The German pair was arrested and, so the story went, deported.

Ronnie did take some measures to at least limit the booze. He put Gene Odom in charge of keeping the stuff away from the band's trailers and dressing rooms. The ever-obedient bulldog, Odom had taken some punishment himself as a Skynyrd roadie; one night in Salt Lake City, a nut wielding a knife had attempted to scale the stage before being subdued by Odom, whose arm was slashed perilously close to an artery. But that was child's play compared to the wrath of Skynyrd when they discovered that Odom had poured the contents of whatever booze was around down the john and intercepted record company leeches before they could leave the guys those telltale envelopes of white powder. The only concession Odom made was allowing a single six-pack of beer in, not for each member of Skynyrd but for *all* of them. As Odom recalled, "I'm not saying there weren't serious lapses. . . . They'd get around the roadblock by [drinking] at the hotel bar before the show [but] they expressed their appreciation." He recalled Alan telling him, "We never thought we could play in front of fifteen thousand people sober," and then being ecstatic that they indeed could.

To be sure, their shows in Japan might have been the first ones in a long while that they played mostly clean and sober, allowing them to actually grasp the satisfaction of being mobbed from the time they stepped off the plane and thousands of Japanese fans welcomed them "just like the Beatles," as Honkette Leslie Hawkins put it. During shows, their lyrics were sung back at them by people whose only knowledge of English was limited to that in rock-and-roll songs. The trip was by all measures a tremendous success, another Skynyrd triumph, and one that they could see through mainly clear eyes. Even they had to admit that was almost as good as a belt of Irish whiskey.

⋆ ⋆ ⋆

When they returned from the mini world tour in April, they picked right back up with shows across the South. Then Ronnie finally got to see Melody, if only for fleeting moments between rehearsals at Riverside Studio, while the band prepared for the new album sessions at Tom Dowd's Criteria Studios in Miami. However, despite Mike Maitland's hit-singles directive, Ronnie was having trouble wrapping his mind around the concept. "We're not experts on 45s," he told one interviewer. "I don't know anyone who is except Elton John. We're not in the business to put out 45s, just to make albums." Even if album sales flagged, he said, "that's fine, too." And since no one at MCA ever thought "Free Bird" would fly because of its length, Rossington's take was "What do they know?"

Tom Dowd figured Ronnie would only be able to go so far trying to give MCA what it wanted. "Ronnie wasn't inclined to make Top Ten records or be a formula writer," he said. "Ronnie was an observer and a storyteller. He didn't want to write 'Leader of the Pack.'" Consequently, when the sessions got underway, each time a track was completed Ronnie asked how long it was, something he had never done. If it was longer than three and a half minutes, Dowd would say he'd speed up the tape or shorten the intro, again, something that never would have been tolerated in the past. Dowd would later recall that "it was like handcuffs. Absolutely limiting and debilitating to him. It was embarrassing."

Worse, the songs they cut at Criteria were lacking in their usual gut-kicking impact, something no one was willing to say except, of all people, Steve Gaines and Kevin Elson. As the soundman remembered, "I told them if they released it their career was over, and Steve Gaines was the only one who agreed with me." If there was a reason for any drop in energy, Ronnie was convinced, it had to be Dowd's fault; the producer was recording Rod Stewart's *Foot Loose and Fancy Free* album in his own studio at the same time, crimping his focus on Skynyrd. Thus, mercurial as always, Ronnie suddenly had a revelation: the fault lay not with the band but with the studio. He told Dowd they were through with sessions there and would head to Doraville—*their* home, not Dowd's—to resume work at Studio One.

This would present a hardship for Dowd since he would need to commute back and forth, but he didn't begrudge them; it was their album, their call. And so they packed up and left, looking for an environment more conducive to their art. Yet before a single note was recorded in Doraville, the newly "clean and sober" Skynyrd slid backward yet again. The band, Dowd, the roadies, and various Skynyrd leeches were all quartered in a hotel in Atlanta. There, four days before the sessions were to begin, Leon dropped some acid in his room and decided he really *did* want to be a free bird. Dowd, in the room directly below, glanced out his fourth-floor window and was startled to see two skinny legs dangling from the room above. In a panic, he raced upstairs to Wilkeson's room, where he saw him hanging, each hand being held desperately by a roadie, and screaming, "Let me go! I want to fly!"

They were able to pull him back into the room, but by then hotel attendants had already called the Georgia state police. Now Dowd had to explain to the troopers that "somebody drugged this man and this is not his normal state of conduct," though just whom that conduct *would* be normal for was a mystery. After Dowd promised it would not happen again, the cops let it slide, another bullet dodged by the band, and two roadies were assigned to keep a vigil with Leon. "You sit on top of this son of a bitch and don't let him loose," Dowd ordered them.

It did no good. Shortly after, a still-addled Leon grabbed hold of a television and tossed it out the window. It landed on a car in the parking lot, the crash jolting people awake and sending security guards running upstairs looking for him. Like a chase scene in a movie, Leon bolted past them and through the hallways—waving his gun. Soon the cops were back, joining in the chase. They caught up to him, cuffed him, and called for an ambulance to take him to a hospital, and a possible arraignment. Dowd, having to think quickly, reached an amenable local doctor he knew who rushed over and vouched that Wilkeson was his patient and he would take responsibility for him.

Farcical as it was, it kept Leon free. And Ronnie, who had impulsively told Artimus during the craziness that Leon was out of the band, quickly relented. Life went on for Skynyrd. But Dowd, who hadn't signed on to save psychos from themselves and jail, was a nervous wreck. He insisted later that he'd had enough of the band: "I checked out the next morning and that's where I broke off with them."

* * *

Actually, he didn't do that, not then, maybe not ever. After a few days' delay for Leon to get his addled head together, Dowd conducted a few sessions at Studio One, which were mainly devoted to rerecording all but one of the tracks cut at Criteria. Ronnie then told him that it might help the project if another producer was called in to collaborate. That had to really hurt Dowd. He hadn't been fired but, highly offended, he *now* broke off. The next day when the session was supposed to begin, people milled about the studio asking, "Where's Tom?" The answer was, back in Miami, not having said a word to anyone that he was going.

Now, needing just one producer, Ronnie called Rodney Mills, the Doraville engineer who had crowded Al Kooper out on *Nuthin' Fancy*. Mills had an easygoing manner that the band preferred over the autocratic styles of Kooper and Dowd. And Mills, who had been working as road manager for the Atlanta Rhythm Section, jumped at the chance, quitting his work on tour with the Section to take the job, which had him working hand in hand with Kevin Elson, who now knew how to reproduce the Skynyrd sound in concert better than anyone.

Dowd did eventually send an emissary to Doraville, engineer Barry Rudolph, a studio veteran who had just helped produce a Waylon Jennings album. When he got there, Rudolph was stunned to find that the entire album had been unofficially completed. "I didn't know exactly what I was doing there," he says. Rudolph, who considered Mills and Elson to be no more than engineers, thought some of the songs needed a lot of work and wanted to rerecord them, for a *third* time, fourth in all. These included "That Smell" and "What's Your Name." But getting anything done was a strain. Although the sessions did run clean and sober, Rudolph says, "a couple of their buddies would come in and get 'em going, like Robert Nix, he'd do things like hold up a joint in the middle of the control room. They would be in the middle of the best take and would stop playing and go ahead and smoke it. They nearly killed me. We would work 'til about two or three in the morning, and then they would want to go out and party. Being local heroes, it was pretty much carte blanche everywhere they went: anything they wanted, as much as they wanted. . . . We'd get back to the hotel at ten in the morning. By the end of the week I was fried."

Whether Dowd fully intended to work with them again was unclear. But Skynyrd couldn't worry about that now. With Dowd physically gone, and believing he was holding them back anyway, they went to work with Rudolph, the priority being the most commercially oriented song, "What's Your Name," which was Ronnie's most overt attempt at a three-minute hit. Recycling the beat of "Gimme Three Steps," the Van Zant–Rossington composition—which Dowd and Steve Cropper, the fabled Stax/Volt guitarist, helped develop during the Criteria sessions, though they were stiffed of writing credits—told a semifable of a night "in Boise, Idaho," when Ronnie had picked up a "little queen" in a bar before the band was evicted from the room for making "a mess," and then not quite being able to remember her name during and after a strenuous night with her. As with many Van Zant songs, though, in the underbrush lay a trace of guilt about living such an amoral life and betraying his wife for the carnal conquests of the rock ethos. True to form, this Van Zant lyric was more than met the ear and more than he probably realized.

Those clues to the man's humanity, so often buried within a hard crust of conceit and redneck smugness, were even harder to decipher in the song's delirious blues-bar, horn-heavy arrangement and hip, redneck chic—"What's your name, little girl? What's your name? / Shootin' you straight, little girl? Won't you do the same?"—that made the song irresistible from the first note. The best to come from the album, however, was a song Ronnie never expected would be a single, given his determination that, if other tracks were to be compromised, he would compensate with a song that would push the boundaries of pop music. He had been wanting to get off his chest what he thought of Gary's self-induced brushes with death, and the other guys' misadventures with drugs and booze; and he didn't plan to spare himself from the warning none of them would obey. The result, "That Smell," moved the earth in a way no Skynyrd song ever did.

Indeed, oblique references to George Wallace and Watergate and pointed blandishments about senseless gun violence seemed tame beside Ronnie's magnifying glass into drug culture. Before then, drug references begat in pop songs were usually metaphorical ("Lucy in the Sky with Diamonds," "Got to Get You into My Life," "Eight Miles High"). Few rock lyrics spoke of actual drugs or used street terms for them; among those that did, "One Toke Over the Line" was an *endorsement* of harmless "sweet Jesus" drug escapism. The more cautionary songs—"Life in the Fast Lane," "Witchy Woman," "Gold Dust Woman"—weaved unmistakable but still a bit hazy quatrains about silver spoons and lines on mirrors.

Ronnie had waded deeply into this same metaphorical pool with "The Needle and the Spoon," in the more starkly admonitory tone of John Lennon's "Cold Turkey." But now he left nothing to imagination. He dropped in curdling caveats about "too much coke and too much smoke" and having "another blow for your nose." The message was in the hook: "the smell of death surrounds you." Each line was more harrowing and delicious than the one before it, though it was hard to top the opening line, with Rossington's squealing guitar and trail-away feedback prefacing a reference meant squarely for him—"Whiskey bottles and brand new cars / Oak tree, you're in my way." At one point Van Zant tauntingly sang of "Prince Charming," using Gary's nickname. But while such taunts were aimed at the prince, admonitions like "one hell of a price for you to get your kicks" and "look what's going on inside you" were aimed just as squarely at himself, the biggest fool of all.

With its tightly integrated solo guitar tradeoffs, foot-tapping beat, and gospel-like harmonies by the Honkettes—their wail of "Yeah, you!" after the hook was priceless—the song was dark hearted and completely infectious. Indeed, if "Sweet Home Alabama" was Skynyrd's "Ramblin' Man," one could call "That Smell" their "Hotel California," a connection Barry Rudolph was thinking about when he engineered the song, saying later, "I was going for that sort of production." But it was more, more too than Eric Clapton's cover the same year of J.J. Cale's grim "Cocaine," equating the white powder with a seductress who "don't lie." Skynyrd had concocted the first, and still the coolest, drug-*and*-death song ever.

* * *

As cutting-edge as "The Smell" was, Skynyrd refrained from making it so dark that it would be turbid rather than entertaining. And as it turned out, in the midst of disco's ascent, the song's upbeat, Diesel-powered beat could even pass as a *dance* record. And everyone knew it *would* be heard, that it *was* hit material, and would have to be put out as a single for all these reasons, even though it was the longest cut on the album, over five and a half minutes—and that, says Rudolph, was after MCA cut the original two-minute guitar intro. Even with a harrowing theme, Skynyrd's formula remained the same; "simple man" lyrics—as Ronnie once said, "I think if you write it really simple, then you can reach more people that way because people are going to understand what you're talking about"—combined with ear-splitting levels of aural escapism and open-wound emotion.

"A lot of the songs that Ronnie wrote," said Artimus Pyle, "had to do, directly or indirectly, with family, you know, and about the environment, about gun control, about the abuse of drugs. It wasn't like trying to cram it down, but it was about the real world." In the case of "That Smell," it was an all-too-real world. But Ronnie wasn't through. He had written perhaps his best collection of songs for the album, which was why he had been so puzzled about why they didn't fly as recorded by Dowd.

What was most welcome was the entrée of Steve Gaines as a valuable collaborator. He and Van Zant wrote "You Got That Right," another fatalistic "live fast, die young" avowal, attesting, "I tried everything in my life / Things I like I try 'em twice" and "When my time's up, I'll hold my own / You won't find me in an old folks' home." The twist was that it was sung as a duet between the two, Gaines's melodic blues burr cranking up Ronnie's prickly conviction, making for a whole new, and endearing, Skynyrd mode.

Gaines, in fact, was given tremendous rein on the album, which featured one more song cowritten by him and Ronnie—"I Never Dreamed," with Ronnie projecting about death again, this time with dread: "I never dreamed that you would leave me / But now you're gone," leaving him "empty" and "lonely" and desperately pleading, "I never dreamed that I would beg you / Woman I need you now." This was projection writing from the pit of Ronnie's tortured soul, and it had never before been brought out the way it was by Steve, whose slide guitar country funk and quiet harmony vocals were especially pungent on those tunes and the two others he had written alone. On those two, "I Know a Little," an old-time jazz/swing riff, and "Ain't No Good Life," Ronnie allowed their newest member that rare privilege of singing lead, something he had not done since Rickey Medlocke.

Gaines's guttural blues timber was more Joe Cocker than Ronnie Van Zant, but not at all against the Skynyrd grain, and his sinewy guitar and Powell's Ray Manzarek–like organ line brought the band exactly to where Ronnie had wanted to be for years: into the realm of *real* blues, not just a countrified version. Indeed, the level of sophistication on the album was revelatory; if songs had been trenchant before, now they had more depth and introspection, even if they were despondent. The guitars were still front and center, and they knocked down walls at times; but they did so within a quieter, even holistic sort of entirety. Gaines even had a hand in making "That Smell" so satisfying, by arranging the Doraville redo.

Ronnie completed the album with a convincing cover of Merle Haggard's "Honky Tonk Night Time Man" and a track from the unreleased Muscle Shoals tapes produced by Jimmy Johnson that he always liked, the Van Zant–Rossington song "One More Time." Because the song had Ed King and Rickey Medlocke on it, both would be given credits on the album jacket—a jacket that foretold just how little time Lynyrd Skynyrd had left before Lucifer came to the door.

17

★ ★ ★ ★ ★

STRIKING FIRE AND DRAWING BLOOD

Even now, despite not showing up to the band's sessions, Tom Dowd had still not officially quit as Skynyrd's producer. Whether he ever considered working with them again seemed a moot point since his time was monopolized by the Rod Stewart album, sessions for which were held in Miami, Canada, and L.A. Dowd was also newly wed and trying to find time for his new wife. He hadn't heard a thing more about Skynyrd until he was in L.A. mixing down the Stewart LP and was told the Skynyrd album was being mixed at Capitol Records, Rodney Mills and Kevin Elson having taken the tapes out to that state-of-the-art facility.

"They're what?!" he asked, clearly shocked at the news. He got in his car, drove to Capitol, and burst into the studio where Mills and Elson were going about their work.

"Man, you left us!" said Elson.

Dowd had kept in touch enough with Doraville to know that whatever had been accomplished, several songs still needed horns added to them. "We didn't finish making the album, how can you be mastering? We have to put horns on."

They told him they'd already put horns on one cut but that the brass didn't sound right.

"Give me the goddamn tape and I'll put horns on it for you in about an hour and a half."

Dowd made some calls, carted the tapes to the Wally Heider mobile studio and overdubbed the horns. Two hours later, he delivered the tapes to Ronnie, who'd come west with Mills.

"That's it! You're right!" Dowd quotes Ronnie as saying.

At that point, according to Dowd's take, the band wanted him to continue mixing the entire album, but he was too busy with Rod Stewart. By then, too, a bizarre situation had developed concerning the album jacket. The liner notes, which had already been written, omitted any mention of Dowd, even though the band recognized his engineer at Criteria, Dennis Herkendorfer. The glaring omission would spark rumors that they were either being vindictive or that Dowd, in a fit of pique, had asked that his name be left out of the credits because he hadn't produced the entire LP. Ronnie didn't make things any clearer when he later said of the matter, "We love Tom Dowd . . . but we [didn't] want him to mix this record," which sounded a lot like what Skynyrd had said about Al Kooper when *his* end came. In any event, the band directed that future releases of the album credit Dowd, as well as Mills and Jimmy Johnson, a retro shout-out to the old Muscle Shoals duo, who never got to see their own Skynyrd tapes released as a complete album—ten of the twenty-seven tracks would trickle onto two retrospective albums in 1978 and 1991—until 1998, when Bruce Eder, on AllMusic.com, ventured that the work, called *Skynyrd's First: The Complete Muscle Shoals Album*, "may be the greatest unissued first album ever to surface from a major band."

Skynyrd had always felt constrained by producers, and although Mills was a major factor in keeping the album on track, the band now believed they were the best producers for their music. And having done what MCA asked, Ronnie saw no further need to be a pop songwriter.

"That's the last time I ever write a three-minute song, as long as I fuckin' live," he swore. "If I want to write a book, I'm going to write a book and not a piece of toilet paper."

* * *

Of course, the album was nothing of the kind. Nor was it close to playing it safe. They called it *Street Survivors*, but rather than this being merely metaphorical, they explained to designer George Osaki that they wanted to be seen, looking weathered and wiser, as literally threatened by some force closing in on them, as if they were the sole survivors of apocalyptic doom—a premise that could be extrapolated from the impending doom of "That Smell" but which Ronnie saw in a thousand different ways. Osaki hired photographer David Alexander, who had designed the cover of the Eagles' *Desperado* and *Hotel California* and albums by Linda Ronstadt, the Marshall Tucker Band, and the Sex Pistols.

Alexander took the most visually striking route. Posing them on a movie set on the back lot at MCA/Universal studios between facades of baroque buildings, their faces dour, Artimus in a VEGETARIAN T-shirt, Leon in one reading MY GRASS IS BLUE—a reference not to weed but to bluegrass music—Alexander detonated flames from gasoline-filled troughs in front of and behind them. The motif was supposed to be Skynyrd coming into town and setting it on fire. However, a more disturbing scene emerged—Skynyrd being consumed by flames, particularly Gaines, clad in a devilish red shirt, arms at his sides, eyes closed, in some kind of ritualistic satanic immolation. It was jarring, unnerving, even shocking, and portended something awful, though one could also have seen it as symbolic of the three-guitar Skynyrd attack that the astute rock critic Greil Marcus had once described as "striking fire and drawing blood."

In truth, the album would have had no trouble gaining attention, no matter the cover. It was long awaited and would not disappoint. Robert Christgau analyzed it as a sum of more than its parts: "As with too many LPs by good road bands, each side here begins with two strong cuts and then winds down. The difference is that the two strong cuts are very strong and the weak ones gain presence with each listen." Yet it was that cover with those engulfing flames that would turn the album into a prophecy, all too soon and all too horribly fulfilled.

* * *

Though it was largely a sham, Skynyrd kept up the public pretense of being "reformed" rednecks. Kicking off another of their seamless tours, they did their usual round of media interviews, this time pushing the party line of reformation. Not everyone, or even most, bought it. Headlines in the rock press still read more like those in the supermarket tabloids—ROUGH, ROWDY, RIBALD ROCK, ONE MO' BRAWL FROM THE ROAD, HANGING OUT WITH LYNYRD SKYNYRD CAN GET YOU SHOT, SLEAZY RIDERS, LYNYRD SKYNYRD: DOES THER CONSCIENCE BOTHER THEM? When

Time got around to noticing them in October 1976, the headline they ran was THE ROTGUT LIFE. And as late as September 1977 there was a Skynyrd article with the not altogether exaggerated title A BLOOD BATH EVERY NIGHT. All this being the case, it stood to reason that, as *Crawdaddy*'s Mitch Glazer posited, a dose of Skynyrd "goes down better if you're a little wrecked."

Pressing on through the summer, the band rolled into Philadelphia's massive JFK Stadium on June 11, agreeing to open for Peter Frampton, the British teen-idol guitarist whose 1976 live double album *Frampton Comes Alive!* sold six million copies just that year, humbling even the exemplary sales of *One More from the Road.* Yet after three Top 20 singles Frampton was losing some sheen. That day in Philly was not kind to him, in large part due to Skynyrd. It was another of those all-day affairs with hundred-thousand-plus crowds, and another chance for Skynyrd to eat the headliner's lunch. And after their set a good half of the crowd walked out as Frampton played what Pete Rudge assistant Chris Charlesworth recalled as a "very limp closing set."

Skynyrd, he said, hadn't even needed to exert themselves very much to steal the show. "They'd played an hour-long set—short for them—and restricted themselves to their best-known songs with a minimum of fuss and a maximum of swagger. 'Free Bird' brought that huge crowd to their feet and as I watched from the side of the stage, just behind their amplifiers, it seemed to me that all 100,000 of them were stomping and cheering as the band played faster and faster to the song's stupendous finale."

Four days later, they headlined at the Summer Festival in Springfield, Massachusetts, with .38 Special and Foreigner opening for them. As the tour went west, they had top billing at Bill Graham's Days on the Green on July 3 at the Oakland Coliseum and on the same night were in Tulsa, before flying right back to Oakland a day later for the finale of the three-day Graham event. At times like that, it was helpful that they now had their own charter plane, a Convair CV-300, which Rudge had first leased in April. But these backbreaking tours, combined with years of punishing their internal organs every way they could, clearly had taken a toll. They looked older now. Ronnie's waistline jiggled from years of being filled with booze and corn pone. Leon and Steve had bushy beards like Artimus, giving them the look of the three wise men. Collins had remained clean-shaven and still had the look of a crazy-eyed teenager;

but those eyes had dark circles under them, and he was sometimes unable to speak coherently. Rossington still had his curls and good looks, but his nose was red, bulbous, and frequently bloody from all the cocaine forced through his nostrils. With guitars in their hands, they were even now wiry tarantulas on stage, but Collins's frenetic leaping around and Pyle's rabid drumming were about the only thing approaching high-voltage activity that Skynyrd could muster.

Ronnie Van Zant for his part was still the fighter, albeit tempered by age, weariness, and the wisdom to pick his spots. Pyle saw the difference after Gaines had arrived. At one time or another, he said, "I pulled off [of Ronnie] Billy, Leon, Gary, and Allen. Ronnie didn't mess with me and Steve because he knew he couldn't whip my ass and he had a great amount of respect for Steve. He'd leave the stage in front of 200,000 people and let Steve sing a song. That tells you something."

Although Pyle later claimed he had threatened to quit the band unless it cleaned itself up, clearly most of them were back on the sauce by then—the weed, the powder, the pills—and cared not who knew it. Ronnie playfully bantered between songs on the tour that "these intermissions are brought to you by the Budweiser king of beer"—a statement that, unlike in today's commercialized rock orbit, had no connection to any corporate endorsement deal, that crude rock reality still being a few years away. After taking a swig from a can of Bud, he would slyly apply the kicker: "not to mention Acapulco gold." At a concert in Charleston, Ronnie took out a joint and blew marijuana smoke in the faces of Rossington, Collins, and Gaines, saying to the crowd, "And you don't think they ain't fucked up?"

Pete Rudge apparently was of little use in Skynyrd's half-hearted reformation. Those cocaine-covered meetings in his New York office went on unabated, and whenever the band came into the general vicinity Rudge would be there with some familiar blandishments. Before the band's July 13 gig in Asbury Park, New Jersey, Rod Stewart and Ten Years After, Mick and Bianca Jagger happened by the band's trailer. "We're talking, and the next thing I knew," Pyle recalled, "Mick goes into the bathroom. Ronnie's in the bathroom, too, with Pete Rudge. And guess what they were doing in there." Awkwardly, Artimus tried to make small talk with Bianca amid loud snorting noises emanating from the john. Also during that swing through the New York area, Dean Kilpatrick was said to have been extremely close with sixteen-year-old *Exorcist* actress Linda Blair, who developed a wild crush on him after they met. As things now stood, such behavior was horrifyingly normal.

* * *

Street Survivors was released October 17, along with the single "That Smell," which quickly toppled cultural barriers about what a pop song could say. When the album went out it shipped gold, selling half a million on preorder alone. They were on another endless tour by then, this one scheduled to keep them occupied for four more months with major appearances that included the band's first gig at Madison Square Garden on November 10 and in virtually every other big market arena until the tour's end in Honolulu in February 1978. Four days before the album came out, on October 13, they finally headed toward home, landing in Statesboro, Georgia, for a concert at Georgia Southern College, and then went on to the Hollywood Sportatorium in Miami, the Bayfront Center in Saint Petersburg, the Lakeland Civic Center, and Greenville, South Carolina's Memorial Auditorium on the nineteenth.

In Greenville, Gene Odom recalled, he saw "an obviously inebriated" Van Zant "ranting and cursing," another indication, among many, that "Ronnie never should have been around alcohol." Pyle would have his own takeaway from that concert. After the show, he said, a longtime Skynyrd fan had told him, "I was totally sober and I enjoyed myself more than I had ever enjoyed myself at any concert." It seemed that some Skynyrd adherents, at least, weren't getting quite as wrecked anymore, a rite of maturation that Skynyrd could not quite bring themselves to practice.

The next stop was two days later, October 21, at the LSU Assembly Center in Baton Rouge, 669 miles to the southwest. Once more they wearily hauled their tired bones into their leased Convair. The capacity of the plane was twenty-four, not including two pilots, and every seat was taken, though one that had been reserved for Honkette JoJo Billingsley had been given to someone else because she had gone home feeling ill, and in any case was petrified of getting on the plane. Indeed, she wasn't the only member of the troupe to believe that; others considered getting to Baton Rouge through other means. The Convair had become a matter of grave concern lately for ample reason.

* * *

The decision to lease a private plane wasn't only a matter of status or comfort but rather a necessity once the overage delinquents of Skynyrd had caused too many disturbances on their charter flights. Ronnie's attempt to throw John Butler out of a plane over Europe was not an isolated incident. Tom Dowd had flown with them and couldn't believe how rowdy they'd get, behavior that often prompted flight crews to threaten them with arrest when they got on the ground. Word had gotten out, and the airlines were loath to book them. Thus Rudge, that April, leased the Convair from a small aviation firm, the L&J Company of Addison.

The plane was a relic, a converted CV-240, the type of craft John F. Kennedy had used during his 1960 campaign, a two-propeller aircraft dating back to 1947, the third of its kind ever built. Rock being a small world, the plane had recently been used by Aerosmith, who had flown in it to several shows at which they opened for Skynyrd. When Aerosmith was about to tour again that spring, their pilot and assistant chief of flight operations, Zunk Buker, inspected the plane. To his amazement, the two pilots who would be flying it, Captain Walter W. McCreary and First Officer William J. Gray Jr., both of whom were in the early thirties and had limited flight experience, were "smoking and passing around an open bottle of Jack Daniel's in the cockpit," according to Buker, who called the band's manager David Krebs.

"No way we are going to fly this airplane," he said.

Krebs said, yes, they would, as it would save the band $30,000 on that leg of their tour.

"The plane isn't safe," Buker reiterated. "We're not doing it."

Again rebuffed, Buker gave an ultimatum: "If you're flying them in this airplane, I'm resigning—effective immediately."

Only then did management give in, buying Aerosmith a Cessna 310 for $200,000. The fact that Rudge saved a few dollars of Skynyrd's money by leasing at bargain basement rates—three payments of $5,000—Aerosmith's old, discarded bucket of bolts could not have pleased Skynyrd, though it seemed like a typical Rudge business decision; according to Chris Charlesworth, Rudge was always looking for ways to scrimp and save. Paul Welch, a new soundman hired by Skynyrd, who was manning the board with Kevin Elson on the tour, says the band actually had for some time been after Rudge to buy them a spiffy new status-symbol jet too but that, like Aerosmith's management, Rudge had wanted to squeeze one more tour out of the old tomato can to save money.

Perhaps tellingly, Rudge himself would not set foot on the plane. Instead, he flew first class to Skynyrd gigs on commercial airline flights while, as Pyle said, "we were flying in a plane that looked like it belonged to the Clampett family."

★ ★ ★

By October the plane had over twenty-nine thousand flight hours and seemed rickety. During its first use on Skynyrd tours, McCreary was again the copilot, under a seasoned pilot named Les Long, who had since quit the company that hired the pilots, Falcon Aviation of Lawrenceville, Georgia. For this tour, the pilot would be McCreary himself; his joint-passing partner, Bill Gary, would be the copilot. The plane had not seen any problems until, on the way in from Miami to Greenville, Ken Peden, a sound technician, reported seeing a six-foot flame shooting from one of the engines en route. Though the plane landed safely, the incident scared him to no end and kept everyone in the Skynyrd party on edge about the aircraft.

The band themselves preferred riding their tour bus, which had snazzy, flashing blue lights and the Skynyrd logo painted onto each side. But it had to be a relief that they would be able to drink or smoke what they wanted and throw punches at whom they wanted in blissful peace. And even Pyle, who has been known to contradict himself, said once that "when we flew into town in that plane it was wonderful because it was just such a cool, old airplane." Still, just hours before the plane would depart for the next gig, the band was so concerned about a repeat of that flaming engine that they sent Dean Kilpatrick and the tour manager Ron Eckerman, whom Pete Rudge had expressly told to get some answers from the pilots, to find McCreary and Gray. They went to the pair's hotel room, but the two had already departed, leaving a message at the desk that they had gone to Greenville Downtown Airport early to work on the troublesome engine. Gene Odom, also looking for answers, found them on the tarmac tinkering around with the engine.

"What's wrong with the plane?" Odom demanded to know. "That was a helluva trip comin' up here."

Gray said something about the magneto, a magnet-operated generator, and that they'd called ahead to Baton Rouge to have a mechanic ready to repair it when they arrived.

"*Baton Rouge*?!" Odom said. "That's crazy. Why don't you have him fly here?"

"No reason to," Gray said. "It's just something we need to fix so the engine will run better." The fire Peden had seen, McCreary added, "wasn't as bad as it looked. Besides, we can fly the plane on one engine if we had to."

These explanations themselves were reason enough for alarm. One word from Ronnie and the whole flight would have been bagged. And, according to Alex Hodges, the plane issue had become the fulcrum of a broader range of discontent by the band as it approached this fateful flight.

"I spoke with Ronnie a day before, and he had definitely soured on Rudge, for a lot of things, but the plane was one of 'em. It sort of symbolized to the band that Rudge was doing things on the cheap, and here they were one of the biggest bands in the world. They had fired Alan Walden because they wanted to be like the Rolling Stones, but here they were still being treated like dirty rednecks. And Ronnie told me, 'We're not happy with Premier Talent.' He said he wanted me to book their next tour. I don't know if he wanted to go back to Alan—probably not, that was a dead issue. But he always thought I was much more on his wavelength and had a better understanding of what Skynyrd was, and he wanted me to go back to booking them—which would have been the first step toward firing Rudge.

"That conversation left me with a very uneasy feeling. They were not a happy bunch, and the plane was like a metaphor for them being trapped in a bad situation. I'm not gonna lie and say I sensed the plane was gonna go down, but I was very uneasy about them gettin' on it, I'll tell you that."

But if Ronnie ever had a moment of hesitation about getting on, he opted to go ahead, as he always did despite the fact that, as Odom says, "he hated snakes and always hated to fly."

Van Zant believed in superstitions—witness his frantic overreaction when the Confederate flag hit the floor. Odom recalled when Ronnie once saw an actual black cat creepin' in front of his car and then licked his index finger and left three Xs on the window. Now, fears aside, he was either putting up a brave front or was too drunk to care when he boarded. Encountering a worried-looking Odom at the door, he told him, "C'mon, let's go. If it's your time to go, it's your time to go."

After JoJo Billingsley had gone home, she called Allen and said she'd had a dream the plane had crashed, and had woken up "screaming and crying." Allen, typically, was fearless. But Cassie Gaines almost bailed. She made reservations to take a commercial flight to Baton Rouge before she was eventually persuaded to travel with the band. Dean Kilpatrick, for his part, never had a doubt he would go with them. Ever the good soldier, he had grown like the rest of them into his late twenties. To them he was more than a roadie. One time in Paris, after Artimus was detained by the gendarmes for riding a motorcycle without a helmet, Dean passed himself off as Pyle for a photo shoot, with no one in the French press the wiser. Not completely recovered from his own injuries from crashing the band's van into a Greyhound bus, he was back, boldly leading the roadies onto the plane with not a moment of hesitation.

And so, despite the grumbling about the plane, they filed on one by one: the band, Cassie Gaines and Leslie Hawkins, the roadies, sound and lighting men including Kevin Elson and their new concert sound engineer Paul Welch, Odom, and cameraman Bill Sykes, who was making a documentary of the tour. Always protective of Ronnie, Pyle would say later that Van Zant was "the healthiest, strongest he'd been in a long time" on the day of that flight, though Ronnie was so hung over he could barely see straight.

The plane was overloaded, crammed full of luggage and equipment and sundry mementos the band had gotten in Japan. Again, the pilots saw no problem. For two hours the flight was delayed as they attempted to get the dodgy engine to fire up. Then, at 4:02 PM, they took off. As they reached twelve thousand feet, below them panned out the landscape that had bred and sustained them, the South of old and new cultures, big cities and backwoods, old plantations and new superhighways.

This land had been built by men like Lacy Van Zant, one look at whom brought to mind Pat Conroy's description, "as Southern as black-eyed peas, scuppernong wine, she-crab soup, Crimson Tide tailgating and a dog with ticks," people "so relentlessly Southern [they] make me feel that I was born in Minnesota!" Lacy Van Zant's oldest son was relentlessly a Southern Man, right to the end, but one with some cracks in the veneer of toughness and invincibility. Odom remembers a conversation he'd had with Ronnie a day before, when, letting down his fighter's stance, he'd admitted he had a fear of being booed off the stage.

"He said, 'I don't know what they see in me, and one day they're gonna wake up.'"

Ronnie had taken his accustomed seat in row one, with Dean seated between him and Rossington. Across the aisle, Leon sat between Steve and Cassie. The skies were, just as they had sung, so blue. The soil and kith and kin of the South lay below them, reassuring as always. It was a good day. Any day in the bank was always a good day.

18

★ ★ ★ ★ ★

"PLANE CRASH!"

Two hours into the flight, with a half hour until the destination, Ronnie was fast asleep, his face buried in a pillow. A little while later, the band felt they had to address the issue of the plane. Without waiting to get to Baton Rouge, they decided that they would junk the Convair and buy a Learjet like the other big rock acts. That decision made, they felt relief they wouldn't have to go through all this agita again. One more landing and the Convair was gone for good. Feeling better, they began messing around, playing poker and doing some terrible white-boy disco dancing in the aisle. Pyle said there was no booze on board, no pot. "Everybody was basically straight and having a good time"—not that they weren't still feeling the effects of the drinking they had done at the hotel before the flight.

Unbeknownst to the passengers, though, the plane was in trouble. Fuel had been leaking for some time, and the engines now began to sputter. Paul Welch maintained later that he saw the engine trailing fire as on the previous flight. At the time, Pyle happened to be in the cockpit with Allen, watching the sun set against a brilliant orange twilight sky. The pilots didn't seem disturbed but, hearing the engine wheeze, Artimus, whose father had died in a plane crash, knew something was wrong. So did Billy Powell, who soon joined them in the cockpit. Billy would say he heard a no-longer-confident Gray mutter, "Oh my God!" as the right engine cut out. Both pilots, Powell said, "were young and they panicked, so they jettisoned the fuel by accident."

They may also have pumped too much into the crippled engine, the one with the excess sparking, explaining what Welch saw. In any case, if the pilots were unfazed, they themselves couldn't determine how much was being wasted because the fuel gauge was broken. The only way to estimate what they had left was the highly unreliable, Stone Age way: dropping a dipstick into the tank. After McCreary had done so, Powell said, the pilot seemed to be "clearly in shock. His eyes were bugged out."

The pilots tried siphoning fuel from the left to the right engine, but apparently they accidentally dumped critical fuel from the plane, leading the left engine to quit. Only moments before, Gray had told Odom, "Everything is under control." Now, at 6:39 PM, the pilots radioed the Houston Air Route Traffic Control Center and were cleared to descend to six thousand feet. Three minutes later, Gray told the controller, "We need to get to a airport, the closest airport you've got, sir." The controller asked the crew if they were in an emergency status.

"Yes, sir," Gray said, "we're low on fuel and we're just about out of it, we want vectors to McComb, post haste please, sir."

That meant McComb–Pike County Airport in McComb, Mississippi, eighty miles from Jackson in the southwest quadrant of the state. Given a path there, a few minutes later Gray told the controller, "We are not declaring an emergency, but we do need to get close to McComb as straight and good as [we] can get, sir." Then, at 6:45, "Center, five victor Mike we're out of fuel."

Houston replied, "Roger, understand you're out of fuel?"

"I am sorry," Gray clarified, "it's just an indication of it," not explaining what, in lieu of a working gauge, that indication was. Seconds later, the controller requested what the plane's altitude was.

"We're at four point five," said Gray, meaning 4,500 feet. That was the last time anyone on the ground heard from the pilots. Several attempts were made to contact them, and located a weak transmission from an emergency locator transmitter, but there was no response.

In the plane, William Gray finally came into the cabin and made an announcement to the passengers. "We're out of gas—put your heads between your legs and buckle up tight."

As Rossington later said, "We were just freaked out." Ashen, the passengers began sitting down and buckling up. But Ronnie was out of it, spread out in the aisle, either unable to sleep in his seat or so hung over that he had collapsed, or because, as Odom says, he had given him two sleeping pills to help him sleep. Odom would tell later of trying to lift him bodily and dump him in his seat, but that might not have happened. Chris Charlesworth recalled that people on the flight told him Ronnie was "flat out drunk" and lying immobile "in the aisle when the plane went down. No one could move him to a seat, let alone strap him in."

It seemed everyone on the plane had a different story about what Ronnie was or was not doing as the plane was going down. Pyle even said that, rather than being out cold on the floor, Van Zant had at the first sign of danger walked toward the back of the plane. "[H]e stood right beside me and we shook hands, the old hippie handshake, and I looked into his eyes and he smiled a beautiful smile . . . and he rolled his eyes like, 'Oh, shit, here we go.' He had a crimson velour pillow, and he was walking back to the front of the plane, and I thought, 'Bad idea . . . the front of the plane's not a good place to be.'"

* * *

Regardless of the confusion about Van Zant's actions, there evidently was little panic as the drama unfolded. In an eerie silence, people began softly weeping and saying prayers. Some sat as if catatonic. Most hoped that the peaceful fall through the sky meant the landing would be as smooth. As nightfall descended, they could see lights in the distance, and then the dark outline of swampland and forests, and then trees. For all their failures, McCreary and Gray were bringing the plane in level and true at a slight angle. Had there been a clearing, it might have landed on its belly and remained upright, perhaps limiting the damage. But, losing power and coming to a near crawl, it couldn't clear those damn trees.

Odom, in another claim, said that moments before, he had raced to the cockpit again and told McCreary and Gray, "I hope you two sons of bitches live through this, so I can kill both of you." The most common hope among the passengers, though, was simply to live through the coming disaster. The silence was interrupted by treetop branches tickling the bottom of the plane. Then came thumping. Now the trees were visible in the murky light outside the windows. Odom insists that as this happened, he was still trying to get Ronnie into his seat. As he struggled to lift him, Ronnie, he said, could only mutter, "Man, just let me sleep." Odom, who never would buckle himself in, says he slapped Van Zant hard across the face and yelled, "Ronnie, man, the fuckin' plane is crashin'!"

Indeed, the plane could not get through the trees and hit an eighty-foot pine, shearing off a wing and sharply changing the angle of the landing. Then it hit a second one, tearing off the entire front section, which became mangled in a grotesque L shape as it slid through a thicket of brush and swamp, strewing debris and wreckage 150 feet. As soon as the nose hit the turf, McCreary and Gray died on impact from massive injuries. The passengers, no matter where they were sitting, were tossed about like rag dolls. Cabin walls were ripped apart. Seatbelts broke away, and cushions, luggage, books, trays, food, and pieces of fuselage flew wildly, becoming deadly projectiles. Some people were ejected from the twisted cabin, while others, mainly in the rear section that came to rest fairly intact, were still upright in their seats, in shock. Everywhere, bones were broken, flesh punctured.

Only feet behind the cockpit, Steve and Cassie Gaines and Dean Kilpatrick had also been killed on impact, suffering massive injuries from head to toe. Somehow, Gary, Kevin, and Ronnie seemed to have lucked out. As the front of the plane had crumpled like an accordion they'd been thrown bodily atop Steve Gaines and Kilpatrick. Both of Gary's arms and his pelvis were broken—"I broke just about every bone in my body," he would later say—and Kevin's legs, right arm, and right ankle were broken in addition to a collapsed lung. For a few precious seconds, amid all this carnage, Ronnie seemed to have escaped serious injury. He had some lower-body fractures and contusions, but nothing life threatening, until the plane skidded into another tree and a limb that penetrated the plane struck him squarely in the forehead, dealing one single blow. A lethal blow.

At twenty-nine, Ronald Wayne Van Zant couldn't get by that one creepin' black cat and had ridden that last horse. His complicated life, carved in nearly equal measures of self-confidence and self-doubt, was over in a split second of chaos, broken and lifeless in the Mississippi swampland. It was terrain he knew and had even sung about in "Mississippi Kid," but in the end it was terrain he couldn't fight his way free of.

★ ★ ★

Bunched in the mangled front section was Allen Collins, his spine badly injured and his right arm so badly cut that he would almost die of blood loss and his arm would nearly need to be amputated. Leon Wilkeson's chest was injured, and in addition to his severe internal injuries, his left arm and leg were broken; later, at the hospital, his heart would stop beating twice on the operating table before surgeons were able to revive a steady heartbeat. Billy Powell's right knee was broken, and his face was left in a bloody pulp. Gene Odom, who was thrown fifty feet from the plane, his neck broken, and was seriously burned even though the plane never caught on fire, crawled back toward the plane. When he got to Billy, he said, "he pushed me away. His nose was almost torn from his face, and he was afraid he might lose it in the mud and the dark."

Artimus Pyle, meanwhile, the only one of the band members fortunate enough to have been sitting in the back, still had broken ribs and bruises all over his body. In shock and pain, not knowing who was dead or alive or where he was, with his clothes nearly torn off, he made his way through the bodies of moaning, terrified people and began to trudge through the pitch blackness outside, wading through swampland, unsure if there were alligators in there.

In one of his many narratives of survival told in the years since, he said, "We hit the ground. I forced myself out from under the wreckage. My chest was crushed. . . . My breastplate was cracked on impact. All of the cartilage was ripped from the impact. . . . But I started walking to get help. . . . I remember looking up from the swamp, and help was so close but so far away. And then I heard this snake slither up to me in the darkness and I remember saying, out loud, 'Snake, I will bite your fucking head off.' Nothing was going to stop me from getting help. I'm a Marine. We don't leave anyone behind."

In all his renderings of this heroic effort, Pyle has always seemed to forget that he didn't make that expedition himself. When he set out, he was with Ken Peden and another roadie, Mark Frank, both of whom were also covered in blood and braving their own injuries. Peden, a Mississippi native, was familiar with the kind of woods they had to traverse, and led them through to a cow pasture and then a dirt road. When they tried to flag down a passing pickup truck, the driver sped past them—with legitimate cause. News reports that day said three convicts had escaped from jail and were suspected of being somewhere in the swamps. The few people who lived in the area were on edge.

* * *

At 6:55 PM, another plane had reported to a controller at McComb Airport that an aircraft had crashed in heavily wooded terrain near Gillsburg, Mississippi, a good twenty miles beyond McComb, almost right on the southern border with Louisiana, and sixty miles short of Baton Rouge—in the proverbial middle of nowhere, the closest incorporated town being Liverpool, Louisiana, ten miles to the south. It was sixty-two degrees, the wind calm, so weather had nothing to do with the plane having overshot its coordinates so much. The plane had no flight data recorder (it was not required to), so the mystery of what had happened would never be definitively known. However, the only plausible explanation is that the pilots had miscalculated and mishandled the crisis in every possible way, costing them their own and others' lives and altering the course of music and culture in those frightful minutes over Mississippi.

Now bodies were scattered through the woods and in need of help before still others died as well. Pyle, Peden, and Frank meanwhile found a clearing, a plowed field behind a farmhouse (actually, a mobile home). After climbing over a barbed wire fence into a barnyard, they were met by a man with a shotgun, the owner of the home, Johnny Mote, a twenty-two-year-old farmer. Seeing the bedraggled, mud-and-blood-covered trio—and with the news of the escaped convicts in mind—*he* freaked. As Pyle recalled, "I've got long hair and I look like Charles Manson and I'm covered with blood. He thought I was an escaped convict. He raised his shotgun and pointed it over my head and pulled off a round and the residual buckshot caught me in my left shoulder and spun me around and I fell to the ground." Pyle could only call out "Plane crash!" as he went down.

"Is that what that was?" asked Mote, who had heard the rumble of the plane.

He apologized for shooting Pyle and helped him to his feet. While the three men told of the plane going down, Peden would later say, Mote's wife was "hugging me around the neck and telling me, 'We've got to get them out!'" Pyle would say he got into Mote's pickup and the two of them careened down dirt roads getting help. However, Peden said Pyle remained outside Mote's house nursing his shoulder and waiting for help. In any case, within a few minutes—remarkably, given the conditions—medics were already at the crash scene. So were dozens of gawkers trying to get a glimpse of the plane. Floodlights bathed the area like a movie set. The Red Cross, having just had a blood drive, was able to give transfusions at the site. Most of those who remained conscious were so disoriented and in shock that they couldn't identify themselves or anyone else; many would never remember exactly what happened when the plane hit. Some would be in comas for days or weeks.

The dead were taken to a temporary morgue in a high school gym. Nineteen of the surviving victims were taken to Southwest Regional Medical Center in McComb, and one was transported to Beachman Memorial Hospital in Magnolia. Gary recalled lying on the cold, wet ground for an hour waiting to be lifted into an ambulance; the carnage around him, he said, looked "like Vietnam or something." The band members were taken to McComb, where all thirty-one people on staff were called in. The first floor was turned into an emergency room. The injured all were conscious and wailing hysterically in pain. Allen's arm, nearly severed, hung limply as he was carried in on a stretcher. He and many others would require delicate neurosurgery, not a common procedure at the time. Most of the victims would not leave the hospital for weeks. Miraculously, though, all would come out alive.

* * *

Among those waiting at the airport in Baton Rouge was George Osaki, the band's album designer. He had been at his hotel when a bellboy told him about the crash. Osaki then flew to McComb and was brought to Southwest Regional. He was given a list of rooms that the surviving members of the band were in. Not seeing all the bandmates listed, he asked, "Where's Ronnie and Steve?"

"Come with us to the morgue," he was told.

This was before there had been a confirmation of anyone's death, and Osaki remembers the sick feeling he had after walking through the morgue door. "I'd never seen a dead person before. They pulled the sheets back. . . . I saw Cassie, she was mangled, Steve was mangled, Ronnie, it was like he was sleeping. I wanted to go shake him up and say,

'Ronnie, wake up!' My legs just went and a cop held me up. . . . They didn't know Lynyrd Skynyrd, I was the only guy there who knew who the people were. . . . I told them who everybody was and they took me out of there."

An early report on a local Mississippi TV station said there had been no survivors. Some radio and TV stations across the country ran with the erroneous report. That night, the actual toll was revealed in McComb's *Enterprise-Journal*, the front-page blaring the news that GILLSBURG PLANE CRASH KILLS SIX, HURTS 20 INCLUDING ROCK SINGERS. The paper also ran a photo of the twisted wreckage, an image that would be seen all across the world in the next twenty-four hours. Back in Jacksonville, the Skynyrd wives didn't hear about the plane going down for hours. Charlesworth, who was to fly to Baton Rouge the next day, was in Peter Rudge's office with the staffers celebrating *Street Survivors* going gold. When he got home, he heard the stunning news on TV.

"I tried to call Rudge at home," he said. "Peter had just heard too. He was on his way to the office. I grabbed a cab and went straight there. I was the first to arrive, and the phones were all ringing at once. Then Rudge arrived. He'd been to pick up a carton of cigarettes because he knew it would be a long night. He looked distraught and opened a bottle of red wine but he somehow maintained his composure until, eventually, around 1 AM, we heard that Ronnie was dead. Then he went alone into the office kitchen and wept. The girls who worked at Sir manned the phones all night, crying as they did. The various wives and girlfriends of the guys in the band and the road crew were on the lines wanting to know the latest. Eventually they all gathered at Ronnie and Judy's house and what dreadful scenes of hysteria and grief that house must have witnessed that night I can barely imagine. The job of telling Judy that Ronnie was dead fell to Rudge."

* * *

For Rudge, it was a day of excruciating drama and trauma. Not only had he lost the guts of his top American act, but it had been his decision to use the Convair. Some within the Skynyrd extended family would hold him to account for that; and some survivors would sue him and the band for having put them in a flying death trap. But for now, Rudge could only try to make things easier for the families. He sent private planes that industry people put at his disposal to pick up the wives and take them to McComb. When Rudge himself got there he went straight to the hospital. Clay Johnson, one of the roadies, says he asked him "why he put a million-dollar band in a dollar-ninety-eight airplane." Says Johnson: "He didn't have much to say . . . but, you know, he was in shock."

Judy arrived early the next morning to claim Ronnie's body at the morgue, and then take his remains home. Meanwhile at the crash site, some strange things were happening. The gawkers had increased in number, and security was lax. It would be learned that the victims' belongings, when cleared from the woods, had been looted, and items such as cameras, wallets, and jewelry were stolen. A briefcase with the band's proceeds from the tour, which was carried by Ron Eckerman, was found, forced open, with $1,100 in cash missing. "Souvenir" hunters had to be chased away by the cops. Eventually, around $6,900 in cash and almost $88,000 in checks were somehow recovered.

Months after the crash, the National Transportation Safety Board (NTSB) completed its investigation and determined that the probable cause of the crash was fuel exhaustion and "total loss of power from both engines due to crew inattention to fuel supply." The board blamed "inadequate flight planning and engine malfunction of undetermined nature" in the right engine, which had resulted in "higher than normal fuel consumption." Although Odom raised the possibility that Gray had been using cocaine before the flight, pharmacological tests indicated no traces of drugs or alcohol in either pilot's blood. McCreary's flight bag did contain a prescription drug, Librax, an anxiety reliever, but it was said not to be a factor. The bottom line was that McCreary and Gray were "either negligent or ignorant" of the available fuel supply.

Ronnie Van Zant, Steve and Cassie Gaines, and Dean Kilpatrick had lost their lives due to the worst possible and least acceptable reason: incompetence. It was, as Ronnie had sung about the way he thought he might actually die, "one hell of a price" to pay for putting a million-dollar band in a dollar-ninety-eight airplane. That price was quantified by a headline two days later in the *Dallas Morning News*: LYNYRD SKYNYRD IS DECEASED.

EPILOGUE

★ ★ ★ ★ ★

A SORT OF HEREDITARY OBLIGATION

> *I'm bad and I'm going to hell, and I don't care. I'd rather be in hell than anywhere where you are.*
>
> —William Faulkner, *The Sound and the Fury*

Although even the NTSB report called it a miracle that more had not perished in the swamps of Gillsburg, the death of Lynyrd Skynyrd's beating heart and three others who were perhaps the most innocent and well-liked among the inner circle made the tragedy almost unspeakably sad. Ed King once recalled, "I was making dinner [and] my mother called me. . . . She had heard the news first. And I flipped on the TV, saw a little bit, then got in the car and went straight to Mississippi. I went to visit everybody in the hospital. And then I went to Ronnie's funeral after that, then I just drove home, all in a daze." He says now: "When those guys told me about what happened on the plane, I couldn't imagine going through that. You can survive something like that, but you'll never be the same. I knew, and they knew, that they'd live with it every day of their lives."

Alex Hodges, who had booked every Skynyrd tour except that last, fatal one, heard about the crash on the radio and thought of the conversation he'd had with Ronnie about the plane. "I was devastated of course, but I couldn't help but wonder why he had gotten on that flight.

I was angry at him for doing it. Then I blamed myself for not telling him, 'Don't do it!,' because Ronnie listened to me. He respected me. He relied on me to be straight with him. And in that case, I failed him. I did.

"Like Alan Walden, I had worked for two giants of music who both died the same way, Otis Redding and Ronnie Van Zant. And I had spoken with Otis, too, a day before that doomed flight. I was supposed to go with him, but I had other business. The last thing he said to me was, 'See you Monday,' when he was going to come home to Macon, Georgia. Those words stay with you, they haunt you, and when Ronnie told me they were gonna junk that plane I should have said, 'Don't push your luck any further. Take a commercial flight.' If I had, I would still have Ronnie Van Zant as my friend."

Charlie Brusco was in New York on business, staying at the Sherry-Netherland hotel. "Someone told me there'd been a crash, that Lynyrd Skynyrd was on the plane. The extent of it wasn't yet known, but as soon as I heard it, I knew, I just knew, that Ronnie was dead. I always saw Ronnie in a longer lens, as a tragic figure running on borrowed time. When you look back, it seems foreordained that he'd die when he did."

Aerosmith could have fainted when they heard the news. David Krebs, the accountant who had insisted they keep flying in that plane, immediately called Zunk Bunker and said, "I owe you an apology."

All across the rock meridians they laid hands on, but in the South the reaction was so grieved, and the sense of loss so great that everyone who mourned sounded as if a family member had been lost. Charlie Daniels heard when he was in Saint Louis on tour. He about fell to the floor but decided he'd perform the show. "If it were us," he said, "I wouldn't want them to blow off a show. So we went onstage that night and we played a lot and we played hard." Weeks later, it hit him hard. "It was just . . . depressing," he said. "It was like a weight mashing down on my head."

* * *

Steve and Cassie Gaines were laid to rest first, on October 23, at Jacksonville Memory Gardens in Orange Park. Dean Kilpatrick was buried at Arlington Park Cemetery in Jacksonville. On October 25 a private ceremony was held for Ronnie at the Memory Gardens. With the public outside the gate straining to get a look, the 150 guests arrived at the chapel. Ed King and Bob Burns were there, but of the crash survivors only Billy Powell was able to leave his hospital bed and attend. Charlie

Daniels of course was there, as was Dickey Betts. Al Kooper came in from L.A., Tom Dowd from Miami. Merle Haggard's "I Take a Lot of Pride in What I Am" and David Allan Coe's "Another Pretty Country Song" were played through loudspeakers. The service was hosted by David Evans, the engineer on *Nuthin' Fancy*, who was a part-time pastor and had grown close to Ronnie. Giving the eulogy, Daniels read a poem that had been inscribed on a cement bench near the headstone, about "a brief candle, both ends burning, an endless mile, a bus wheel turning," ending with the line "Fly on proud bird, you're free at last."

As Donnie Van Zant sang "Amazing Grace," Ronnie was lowered into his grave, just to the left of Steve Gaines and in front of Cassie Gaines, his black Texas Hatters gambler's hat and his fishing pole placed beside him in the casket. Lacy and Sis Van Zant were so distraught they needed to be steadied as they walked to their seats. Lacy seemed as if he had been kicked in the solar plexus, and his moods swung between grief and anger. As JoJo Billingsley remembered, "he came up to me, scooped down and got a handful of sandy dirt and wiped it across my mouth and said, 'Girl, kiss this ground you're walking on' and left me standing there." She had felt awful enough without being reminded that she had made the decision Ronnie hadn't, but Lacy was feeling no sympathy for the living and couldn't soothe himself with incantations of faith. Years later, he recalled of his son, "He said to me many times, 'Daddy, I'll never be 30 years old.' I said, 'Why are you talking this gunk?' and he said, 'Daddy, that's my limit.'" But when the end did come, Lacy had his fall guy.

"God," he seethed, "was a jealous God, taking him for reasons I don't know."

The Skynyrd men shared some of that biliousness, with more destructive consequences. Billy Powell once said the remaining members of the group came away "bitter" and "blaming God for everything." That, he said, soon led to "probably the heaviest drug use of our lives. We were just all getting drunk all the time, doing downers and stuff, just being real bitter."

* * *

On a purely commercial level, the tragedy, as it normally does in rock, meant there would be a short-term spike in sales. *Street Survivors*, no doubt a Top 10 album in any case, peaked at number five. "What's Your

Name" was hurriedly released in November as a more pleasant, upbeat alternative to the now-too-prophetic "That Smell" and rose to number thirteen. However, only days after the crash, the album had a new look. Out of deference to the Van Zant and Gaines families, MCA called back George Osaki to redesign the cover. Now, with a prosaic shot of the band in the same outfits as the original on the cover, hundreds of thousands of "flame" albums were recalled, though just in the United States, quickly providing another reason for the original to become a collector's item. In Baton Rouge, when promoters offered ticket holders refunds for the concert that never happened, only a handful of people turned their tickets in.

Money in fact seemed to be heavy on people's minds. Rudge had included in his leasing agreement with L&J a $2 million insurance policy with a liability of $100,000 per seat. If Pyle is correct that the flight was a sober one, there was good reason for it: the last clause of the lease agreement read, "Lessee shall hold Lessor harmless in any event that drugs or narcotics of any kind should be brought aboard this aircraft for any purpose." Regardless, L&J claimed it was not liable since the lease had given the band responsibility for the flight. This was so outrageous a claim that the Federal Aviation Administration sued L&J for having used such vague contract language. It took months for the families to recover a cent, and some survivors sued Rudge and the Lynyrd Skynyrd corporation for placing them in mortal danger. Those suits would drag on for years, without success but draining much of the band's coffers and Rudge's blood.

* * *

Remembering the day the music died in the South, the Charlie Daniels Band's 1978 song "Reflections" referred to "Ronnie, my buddy, above all the rest," telling him, "I miss you the most." Other bands who had soldiered with Skynyrd composed their own elegies. Atlanta Rhythm Section's "Large Time" is dedicated "to the survivors: Allen, Gary, Leon, Billy, Artimus . . . In loving memory of Ronnie Van Zant, Steve Gaines, Cassie Gaines & Dean Kilpatrick." Journey, on its *Infinity* album, commemorated Van Zant with the line "Fly on Freebird." Molly Hatchet's tribute was, "Here's to you Ronnie, you're gone, but your song remains." The Outlaws' *Bring It Back Alive* album read, "The Lynyrd Skynyrd Band

and Crew—You're with us every night." The Henry Paul Band's 1979 song "Grey Ghost" lamented, "A free bird falling from the sky brings a bitter end to another Southern man." The Allman Brothers Band's 1981 *Brothers of the Road* was a tribute to those who "fell along the way."

That Van Zant died falling from the sky—during what was called the Tour of the Survivors—was one of those eerily sardonic rock-and-roll ironies, in hindsight a portent of something truly dreadful, in the manner of Marvin Gaye's vain plea, "Father, father, we don't need to escalate." For Skynyrd, it was particularly cruel and mocking. Yet if Ronnie could have possibly written a lyric about that mordancy he surely would have testified it was better to have flown high and crashed than never to have flown at all. Robert Christgau wrote in his *Street Survivor* review that "some rock deaths are irrelevant, while others make a kind of sense because the artists involved so obviously long to transcend (or escape) their own mortality. But for Ronnie Van Zant, life and mortality were the same thing—there was no way to embrace one without at least keeping company with the other. So it makes sense that 'That Smell' is the smell of death, or that in 'You Got That Right' Van Zant boasts that he'll never be found in an old folks' home."

The pity was that long before he would have reached old age, he surely would have prospered further. Adds Christgau: "I'm not just being sentimental. . . . I know Van Zant had his limits. But I mourn him not least because I suspect that he had more good music left in him than Bing and Elvis put together."

Of the crash victims, Rossington and Collins had the hardest time becoming whole again. Once the wounds healed, Allen became even more reckless, self-medicating with an endless chain of booze and Quaaludes, and Rossington's cocaine intake escalated. Neither was able to sleep, and nightmares often jolted them out of their slumbers in a cold sweat. The biggest psychological block was trying to live with the fact that they had made it out of the plane alive but Ronnie, Steve, Cassie, and Dean hadn't. And one need not have even been on that plane to be consumed by the same guilt. Chuck Flowers, the longtime roadie who had once roomed with Ronnie, had been fired only days before the last flight over some hotel bill expenses. After the crash, Flowers, unable to accept his good fortune, reached for a rifle that Ronnie had once given him as a gift and fatally shot himself in the head.

* * *

The redneck-blues/hard-rock formula that had swept the country in the mid-1970s burned on without them for a while, with the movie *Urban Cowboy* codifying the coolness of New South norms. Yet the film's soundtrack included the Eagles, Bob Seger, and Linda Ronstadt—but not Lynyrd Skynyrd. Three years in death, their stamp on the culture was already dimming, part of an overall recession of a South that had been so ascendant in their wake.

There were other victims too. Phil Walden didn't survive long as an industry titan. At its peak his Capricorn roster owned Southern rock. But when record companies across the country caught up to Capricorn in signing country-rock acts, Walden's kingdom atrophied. After Dickey Betts sued Capricorn for back royalties and won an $870,000 judgment, Walden folded Capricorn in 1979 and filed for bankruptcy. Walden, who had drug and alcohol issues himself and went into seclusion for most of the 1980s, resurfaced as a talent manager, and in 1992 briefly reformed Capricorn, basing it in Nashville. But by 2000 he had to sell off most of his priceless record catalog and shortly after closed Capricorn for good. Six years later, he died of cancer at age sixty-six.

Meanwhile, Alan Walden's career pretty much evaporated, leaving him to be his own cheerleader about his nurturing of Skynyrd. "I got the Who tour when all others failed!" he likes to claim, speciously. "I got the best dates for the band and built a foundation the current band lives on! Take away 'Free Bird,' 'Gimme Three Steps,' 'Sweet Home Alabama,' 'Simple Man,' 'I Ain't the One' and what do you have left? If these songs were dropped from the set, would you pay to see them?" As much as he would profit from his old copyrights—such as selling "Sweet Home Alabama" and "Free Bird" to movies like *Forrest Gump* and TV commercials—the "other" Walden was just a pale ghost of rock-and-roll past.

The endless return on "Sweet Home Alabama" benefited Ed King as well. "It's been paying the rent" ever since it was released, he says now. King, who lives in Nashville, has inevitably wondered if he's still alive to collect his writing royalties only because of the unpleasantness that led him to quit the band. Rather being relieved, he has struggled with the same inner guilt that led Chuck Flowers to put a bullet in his head.

The all-but-forgotten Bob Burns didn't make out so well. Unlike King, when Burns left the band he had no writing royalties, and his one-sixth share of sales of the three albums he'd played on slowed and then stopped. Burns hired a lawyer who went to see Pete Rudge and was told Bob was owed a mere $10,000. Burns, who was living in southern Florida and struggling, knew he was being lied to but would have taken it. Instead, when he dropped in on Rossington and Collins a few years after the crash, they said they'd pay him but only if he relinquished all future royalties on albums that would go on to sell in the millions. Offended, he filed a lawsuit against the band and MCA and wound up with a $500,000 settlement.

Meanwhile it seemed Pete Rudge just couldn't win. He filed suit against MCA for a greater share of back royalties, and when he didn't prevail, the band sued *him*. Although Rudge had signed to manage other acts, including .38 Special, he had banked almost everything on Skynyrd, and his obsessive focus on them had led the Who to hire a new management company in 1976. The Stones left soon after. "Nothing was ever the same again at Sir Productions," recalls Chris Charlesworth. "All the plans we'd had for Skynyrd were dashed. They were bringing in plenty of money and without them the funds dried up, so it was obvious Sir wouldn't last. Later, the grief turned to anger, and there were terrible recriminations: lawsuits, bad vibes, fights with Rudge, deep shit. At least one surviving roadie committed suicide and another went mad and was institutionalized."

Rudge himself went into a tailspin, almost killing himself with booze and coke. "When I walked out of Sir Productions I didn't see him again for 22 years," Charlesworth said of the years Rudge hit bottom and battled cancer. He survived, but Skynyrd's demise was his own. Once, he'd had under his wing the Stones, the Who, and Lynyrd Skynyrd. When he resurfaced years later, it was as a producer of low-budget films in England, a long, long way down.

* * *

Skynyrd as a living, breathing entity seemed by mutual consent to be over. All of them had pledged never to reunite under the Lynyrd Skynyrd name, there being no point, without Ronnie, other than cheap commercial manipulation. "We wanted to be America's Rolling Stones," Rossington said by way of a valediction, "to be the biggest band over here. And I believe we were on our way." All one needed to add was "amen." They made it an official denouement while they were, as Billy Powell said, "doing a bunch of drugs one night. They got this piece of paper saying they'd never use the name Lynyrd Skynyrd again." Whatever royalties would still accrue would be divvied among Rossington, Collins, Judy Van Zant, and Teresa Gaines, each of whom had a one-quarter split.

However, the survivors would informally unite, alone or a few at a time, at gigs such as a January 1979 Charlie Daniels's Volunteer Jam in Nashville and in February 1980 at Orlando's Great Southern Music Hall. By then, with big money on the table from MCA, Rossington and Collins had taken steps to form a Skynyrd spinoff band, enlisting Powell and Wilkeson as well. The group, the Rossington-Collins Band (RCB), made a conscious effort *not* to invite comparisons with Skynyrd, and employed a female lead singer, Dale Krantz, a tough, pretty blonde who had sung backup with .38 Special. Rossington defined the band's sound as "not Skynyrd but good-as-shit music." Wilkeson, who said he'd had "haunting premonitions" about the crash, admitted, "I wouldn't care if we were called Sammy Hamburger and the Buns. Just to be working is a blessing."

Krantz and Rossington cowrote much of the material, with Collins and guitarist Barry Harwood pairing off for other songs. They recorded two albums, *Anytime, Anyplace, Anywhere* and *This Is the Way*, both of which were reviewed and sold fairly well, the former reaching number fifteen and going gold, the latter number fifty-five. However, Collins was sinking. Irrationally, he began to resent Krantz, perhaps because, as Pyle says, both men had fallen head over heels for her, it being merely incidental to Collins that he had a pregnant wife back home, and Gary had won her.

At an RCB gig in Lubbock, the two old friends argued beforehand, nothing unusual for them, but then on stage Allen lost it, kicking Dale's microphone over and walking off, leaving the band to play without him. Backstage, he and Dale got in each other's faces, and she made plans to go home. The next night's show was canceled; but the problem was smoothed over, and the tour continued, though with constant tension.

Then came the nadir of Collins's life. In Jacksonville, Kathy Collins was in a movie theater with their two young daughters when she collapsed and died of a massive brain hemorrhage. Not only had the two girls seen their mother die, the child inside her had also died. Billy Powell said it "destroyed Allen. He dove into a bottle and never came out."

Collins tried going on. But the old deliriously leaping beanpole was now a sullen, depressing figure. "He became real bitter, even with me," Rossington said. One reason was that both men were still after Dale Krantz. As this love triangle escalated, the tour became unbearable, the two either avoiding or bickering with each other. They managed to cut the second RCB album in 1982; but during the tour for it Gary broke his leg in an accident, and the tour ended. By year's end, Gary had a victory, however, convincing Krantz to marry him. But when sales of the album lagged, MCA dropped RCB, and the band folded.

Collins subsequently formed the Allen Collins Band with Leon, Billy, Harwood, and guitarist Randall Hall. MCA took a shot on them, and they cut a 1983 album, *Here, There and Back.* It sold fairly well, but not only was the Skynyrd spinoff thing—which also included two albums by the Artimus Pyle Band—played out, so was Collins. He was arrested no less than eighteen times for drunk driving, but only after a DUI conviction in 1983 did he do any hard time, two months in a Duval County jail. Then, in January 1986, he was out in his new jet-black Thunderbird with his girlfriend Debra Jean Watts and lost control. The car flipped over on Plummer Grant Road and, not belted in, both were thrown from the car. Debra died of head injuries en route to the hospital. Allen lived, but his neck was broken, just centimeters from where it had been broken in the plane crash. He had gotten lucky then, but now he was left paralyzed from the chest down. After another long hospital stay, he was charged with DUI manslaughter, pleaded no contest, and served no time—a result that was, no doubt, out of pity, as he was confined to a wheelchair and barely able to speak.

His daughters had been living with Eva Collins, and now his home was sold. He moved in with Larkin, who played the role he never had when Allen was young, feeding and cleaning him; incidentally, Larkin also was given power of attorney for his son, and made executor of his estate. Allen was a pathetic and heartbreaking sight, the irony of which was that, in this condition, relieved of having to live the high life, he actually seemed more at ease with himself. When people visited him, they could not help but be overcome with emotion, yet there he would be in his wheelchair, the least upset of everyone. The pressure was finally off, though there had indeed been one hell of a price to pay for peace.

* * *

MCA first broached a Skynyrd nostalgia wave only a year after the crash, releasing *Skynyrd's First and . . . Last* out of the old unreleased Muscle Shoals tapes. The label and the band enjoyed a huge profit when the LP climbed to number fifteen and went platinum. They did even better in 1979 with the double album *Gold & Platinum*, which hit number twelve and went triple platinum. Marking a decade since the crash, MCA released *Legend*, drawn from unreleased demos, which nonetheless rose to number forty-one and went gold. Now seemed the right time for the surviving band members to amend the injunction against ever playing as Lynyrd Skynyrd anymore. With enormous moneymaking potential staring at them, most readily agreed to reunite the band.

The holdout was Rossington. After his marriage to Dale, they settled down and had two daughters. In '86 they had formed the Rossington Band, and Gary hired Charlie Brusco as his manager. An album for MCA was put out entitled *Returned to the Scene of the Crime.* He wanted to believe he was well beyond Skynyrd. What's more, Dale saw a Skynyrd reunion as a threat to her. "Dale just really bitched me out," Powell recalled. "She told me, 'Why are you trying to take my career away from me and take my husband away from me?' Of course to this day she thanks me for it all the time."

Brusco, who favored the reunion, says, "It was very, very difficult for Gary. He knew how great the appeal of Skynyrd was, but at the same time he could barely think of Skynyrd. Gary knew the weight of Lynyrd Skynyrd would be all on him. So he needed all the assurances he could get."

After being promised that his own band would open for Skynyrd, Gary signed up. Now, all that was needed was to amend the old agreement, now stipulating that the Skynyrd name could only be used provided three Van Zant–era members were on stage. A new corporate entity, The Tribute Inc., was created for the reunion tour and concurrent album project. By then Judy had remarried, to Jack Grondin, a drummer for .38 Special, with whom she had a son, and as she said, "For ten years I didn't even want to deal with the tragedy." But now she did, mainly she said to safeguard Ronnie's name and legacy, to the point where she sometimes annoyed Gary, who was the new band's leader. Ed King also signed up, making for an impressive cast—not to mention a spooky one; when Johnny Van Zant, whose albums were being produced by Al Kooper, agreed to moonlight from his band to sing lead, people would do double-takes because of his eerie resemblance to Ronnie. And so Skynyrd was back, for better or worse.

* * *

After a few months of shaking off the cobwebs performing periodic one-nighters across the country, the Skynyrd reunion tour was ready for a fall kickoff. On September 6, they made their first official appearance at Charlie Daniels's Volunteer Jam at Nashville's Starwood Amphitheatre, on a bill with William Lee Golden, Stevie Ray Vaughan, Gary Chapman, and Great White, the Skynyrd connection breaking attendance records for the annual event. The group had added guitarist Randall Hall to solo with Rossington and Ed King. They broke out the old Confederate flag imagery, but the rebel-redneck context was ameliorated by a teary sentimentality. When "Free Bird" again played, with no vocal, the arena would be dimmed save for a single spotlight illuminating Ronnie's old black Stetson sitting atop a central mike stand.

Artimus, his long hair and beard shaven, giving him a preppy look, acted as spokesman for the tour, introducing each member before each concert began. He would bring a bottle of beer on stage, not whiskey, and wore a T-shirt with a Confederate flag—perhaps brushing aside his stated loathing of the symbol—in the name of solidarity with the band, their fallen leader, and the South. Allen, who was billed now as the band's musical director, looked genuinely happy to be alive. He would pump a fist in his wheelchair when introduced at each venue, before wheeling himself off stage to thunderous cheers. Pyle introduced each band member, longtime roadies, Brusco, Bill Graham, Odom, Lacy, and various Skynyrd adjutants. He called for a moment of silence for Ronnie, Steve, Dean, and Cassie, and then handed the microphone to Allen. "Hello, Nashville!" he brayed. "I gotta introduce one of the best bands in the world—the best band in the world." Then, before the opening bars of "Free Bird," Johnny Van Zant would tell the crowd, "We want you to keep Lynyrd Skynyrd music alive forever. . . . You gotta let 'em hear you in heaven tonight."

The vibes were all good, and they rode a convoy of sympathy, nostalgia, and raves in the press that were reflected in the headlines: LYNYRD SKYNYRD'S HAPPY ENDING and FREEBIRD RISES FROM THE ASHES. The always smarmy *New York Post*'s headline was SMASHED & CRASHED BUT STILL RAISIN' HELL. Sales of new, improved Skynyrd skull-and-bones T-shirts were brisk. And the money came pouring in—$8 million in profits. This made it obvious that one reunion tour wouldn't suffice; it would have to be extended, into an ongoing franchise, beginning with the Tribute Tour in 1988, dates for which Brusco began busily booking. That, however, sounded a sour note with Judy. She had not been consulted on these new proceedings, nor had the recently remarried Teresa Gaines Rapp. Apparently the Rossington faction had believed they could scare both women off by taking a vote ousting both as officers and shareholders. Not one to scare easily, Judy countersued, asking for sole control of the Skynyrd name.

This put the second tour on hold, and lawyers for the band and Judy battled it out for months. As it turned out, Judy was much more like the fighter she had married than anyone thought. She was resolute, calm under pressure, and ultimately she gained the upper hand. Indeed, both Pyle and Powell became so frantic that Judy would win and cut *them* out that they almost begged for mercy, Powell saying in a deposition that the IRS had already placed a $179,000 lien on his house. Powell would later say, Judy "sued our pants off. And I was mad at her like you wouldn't believe. I thought she was screwing us. Then I realized later, she had to do that to protect Ronnie's estate from Gary and them."

The band in its defense claimed Judy was not a director at all since she had not actually signed the 1978 agreement; but that failed to resonate, and seeing the sympathy she generated, they settled, giving Judy and Teresa several hundred thousand dollars and a combined 30 percent of all future Skynyrd profits. As if out of spite, though, Gary refused to allow Judy and Larkin Collins, who believed he now had a say in such matters, to release any old Skynyrd recordings, including a session recorded at a Memphis radio station and a live concert recorded right before the plane crash. Skynyrd was a profitable enough concern now for these squabbles to be fought over big money. Where it had once been all about the music and attitude, the business of Lynyrd Skynyrd was now all about business.

★ ★ ★

Allen Collins had become an effective, cheerful spokesman for antidrug and antidrinking public service campaigns, able to speak only a few words on the topic after being brought to the stage at Skynyrd concerts. By September 1989, however, he had deteriorated and had to be hospitalized with pneumonia. He lapsed into a coma, and on January 23, 1990, he died of respiratory failure, finally at peace after thirty-seven years of hell. He was buried in a grave beside Kathy in Riverside Memorial Park. His funeral had none of the fanfare or curiosity of Ronnie's—and none of his old bandmates, most glaringly Rossington. Even though Gary was forever to be linked with Allen for giving the band its metal credentials, their falling-out was an especially ugly footnote, and Pyle for one believes it was caused by the strong-willed woman who seemed to control Gary's thinking and never cut Collins any slack for breaking up RCB.

"Dale drove a wedge between Gary and Allen like you wouldn't believe," Pyle told writer Marley Brant in the early 2000s. "I had to beg Gary to go see Allen the day he died in the hospital. I had to beg the whole band to go over and see Allen a couple of days before he died. . . . I shamed them into going to see Allen. He loved it, and it meant a lot to him."

★ ★ ★

Charlie Brusco landed Skynyrd with Atlantic Records for a 1991 album. There would be another album two years later, also produced by Tom Dowd at Criteria. Seeking the old voodoo, Rossington and Ed King cowrote six of the tracks, with help from both Johnny and Donnie Van Zant, and the work had the old swagger but could fairly be called Skynyrd lite. Billy Altman in *Rolling Stone* ventured that Skynyrd could "cook up enough noisy raunch to please most of the noncoms in the invisible guitar army that's always on red alert out there in the hinterlands. Marshall Tucker—call your office."

Those albums were the end of the line for Pyle. He split by mutual agreement, given what he called a "settlement" from Skynyrd. The next anyone heard about him was something so depraved it was outrageous even by Skynyrd standards. In 1993 he was accused by his live-in girlfriend of having sex with *his own two daughters, aged four and eight.* Thrown in jail and charged with sexual battery and lewd assault against minors, he strenuously denied the charges, which he called "worse than murder," though rape or penetration was never alleged, and said he was set up by the girlfriend. He claimed he did nothing worse than bathe the children. But facing a maximum sentence of life in prison, he pleaded guilty to attempted sexual battery and "touching his children" and was given eight years' probation. Having spent $500,000 in legal bills, he came back home to find all his possessions had been taken by the now ex-girlfriend.

"Three days after I was thrown in jail, not one, but two of her boyfriends moved into my house," he said. "She gave them all of my cars. I had four beautiful automobiles. She gave them ten sets of drums that I had collected all over the world. And my home."

Pyle badly wanted back in the band, but likely knew better. After his arrest, the remaining members turned their backs on him. "I went down and tried to talk to Gary and Johnny one day," he recalled. "I told them I need to go out with the band a play a couple of shows. [They] were so far out on cocaine, neither of them could look me in the eye. I told them, 'Fellas, this is not a joke. This is a life-threatening situation.'" Pyle said he looked straight at Gary and said, "You told me that I saved your life in the plane crash. You say there'd be no band if it wasn't for me, that you owe your lives to me. I would ask a simple favor of this."

Instead, Pyle said, "Every one of them, the management, Brusco, they all turned their backs on me."

Brusco has no problem owning up to that. "Artimus could never be taken back into the band after copping that plea. It was an impossibility, and anything else he says to fudge that is bullshit."

★ ★ ★

The rites of mourning long over, "Free Bird" was just another arm-swaying, fist-pumping memory rush, no longer performed solemnly with the empty chair. Johnny now sang his brother's immortal vocal, something that Judy regarded as blasphemous, saying sadly, "It makes me miss Ronnie even more." There were dates at some big venues—they were booked, for example, by Bill Graham to play the Cow Palace on New Year's Eve 1989 and 1990 and Willie Nelson's Farm Aid event in 1992—but the bulk of their appearances were of a lowercase variety: a racetrack, a county fair, a country club wedding.

Judy by now had assumed a lead role in the band's affairs. In the mid-1990s she divorced and married a third time, to a country singer named "Big Jim" Jenness, and opened a recording facility in Jacksonville Beach called Made in the Shade Studios, named after Ronnie's long-ago, swaggering pet phrase as a teenager about the sure stardom waiting for him in the future, and later Skynyrd song of the same name. Judy and Melody also paid $1 million for a Jacksonville Beach restaurant they called Freebird Live. She hired an agent to negotiate book and movie deals about the band; Brad Pitt, she thought, would be ideal for the role of Ronnie. But those ventures, too, produced static from Rossington and Larkin Collins, who refused to sign off on them without equal compensation and control. "I'm all for a new movie, if it's done right," said Larkin. "If it's not, they'll have a fight on their hands."

In 1997, after one album for Phil Walden's briefly restored Capricorn label, the band put much effort into honoring—or cashing in on—the twentieth anniversary of the crash, with the double album *Twenty*, cutting it at Muscle Shoals for the CMC label, part of the giant BMG music publishing conglomerate, but not before they had made some changes, some voluntary, some not. First, Randall Hall, who had been made a partner in the Skynyrd corporation, had refused to go on tour with them in '93, bringing about his firing. Hall sued the band for $500,000 and eventually won an out-of-court settlement.

Then there was Ed King. Soldiering on with the group despite mounting health problems, he became weaker until one day he collapsed on stage. He was diagnosed with congestive heart failure that necessitated, at forty-six, a transplant. King left the band, began treatment, and went on a waiting list for a transplant. Facing an avalanche of medical bills, he asked the band for some financial aid and even offered to participate in studio work.

"They promised to take care of me," King recalls, "and I had agreed to work on the anniversary album. Next thing I knew, the management is telling me I won't be needed, and Gary isn't returning my calls."

Clearly, Rossington was making these decisions, and things like sentimentality and gratitude did not factor in. If King couldn't tour, he was of no value. King went on, for a time, believing that when he was well enough he could return. In the meantime, almost every cent he had went to keeping him alive and paying for heart surgery. Brusco brought on Hughie Thomasson, the quirky guitarist from the Outlaws, to replace him. Hall was replaced by Mike Estes from Blackfoot, which had disbanded in 1993. Estes was then replaced by former Blackfoot bandmate and old Skynyrd confrere Rickey Medlocke, whom Gary had wanted to join the band for years. Medlocke hadn't cared to be a spare part, but when the *Freebird* documentary was being made with the approval of all Skynyrd factions, he agreed to participate in the movie. Invited to jam with them, the charismatic "rattlesnake rocker" caught the old fever and joined full time.

* * *

Twenty, produced at Muscle Shoals by Josh Leo, a major player in soft country rock, really was nuthin' fancy, save for a gimmicky "duet" between Johnny and Ronnie, using the latter's old vocal track on "Travellin' Man." But the heavily hyped album peaked at number ninety-seven, which was still better than the 1999 *Edge of Forever*, which dodged the charts altogether. Still, Brusco had a lot be proud of, having taken the band from a reunion tour to multialbum deals with big labels. Feeling good, he told an interviewer in 1999 that the group had sold out its hundred-city tour, and box office receipts ranged from $70,000 to $150,000 per show. Yet no sooner had he made that glowing assessment than he too was axed along with comanager Joe Boyland.

Brusco recalls, carefully, "I was fired because of some differences of opinions," the kernel of which was that Skynyrd, as he saw it, had—mistakenly, he believed—veered from being a tribute band to one that seemed to want to recast itself as a contemporary country act. Both he and Boyland went on to manage Bad Company, and Skynyrd cast its lot with Nashville-based Vector Management, which represented Lyle Lovett and Hank Williams Jr. Signed by its president Ken Levitan, Skynyrd would be handled by an ambitious publicist named Ross Schilling.

If the band sniffed money and acclaim, however, the most pungent aroma around them was indeed that of death. After the turn of the millennium, it surrounded Leon Wilkeson. By far the most likable and gentle souled of all those who ever soldiered with Skynyrd, the Thumper—so known for both his bass lines and the bible he always carried—had once defecated in a pillowcase rather than bother the band's driver to stop the tour bus. Never completely stable psychologically and a poor candidate for booze and drug abuse given his frailty, he had married and divorced four times and now spent most of his time alone, abandoning all family and most of his friends. Despite annual royalties totaling over $100,000, he had squandered almost all his money and had been checked into drug rehab several times. But it seemed nothing could head off trouble.

In 1995 Ed King was startled to find Wilkeson one day with his throat cut and bleeding on the empty bus. Wilkeson was taken to the hospital and recovered; no one ever knew who had tried to kill him, and he was too drunk to know himself. At decade's end he was battling lung and liver disease and living in the basement of his manager Dale Bowman, whose home he was paying for though he himself had no home. Then on July 27, 2001, he was found dead at forty-nine in his room at the Sawgrass Marriott Hotel in Ponte Vedra Beach. He had ingested a number of prescription drugs, fallen asleep facedown on the pillow, and with his breathing problems, smothered himself to death.

Skynyrd, who had fairly ignored Leon's crumbling condition, moved on after this latest loss in the family, dedicating a song to him called "Mad Hatter" on their 2003 *Vicious Cycle* album—a title that could not have been more apt for them.

That album was their fourth in six years for CMC, following a double-CD live album, *Lyve from Steel Town*, recorded in Pittsburgh in 1997, and 1999's *Edge of Forever*, produced by Ron Nevison, who had produced Ozzy Osbourne, Kiss, and Meat Loaf. Both albums did little; neither did *Vicious Cycle*, which was shifted to the Sanctuary Records label, another BMG subsidiary and at the time the largest independent music publisher and distributor in the world. It didn't matter. The LP, overseen by Ocean Way Nashville's engineer Ben Fowler, never charted; another ambitious project, the 2004 double-CD/DVD live set, *Lynyrd Skynyrd Live: The Vicious Cycle Tour*, also went nearly unnoticed.

Worse still, from the start of their second incarnation they had dusted off the skull-and-bones logo and the Stars and Bars and rekindled old memories and political debates. Now that decision caused more static than it had in 1975, and Rossington in his role as sole survivor–cum–corporate soldier, had to defend it. He regurgitated the sophism that the flag was "unfairly being used as a symbol by various hate groups, which is something that we don't support. . . . The Confederate flag means something more to us, heritage not hate." Back in the glory days, tortuous explanations like that had sufficed. But now "Sweet Home Alabama" had been adopted by the spawn of the devil—in 1988, a lamentable punk rock outfit called Skrewdriver, self-described as a "white power skinhead rock band," covered the song. Little wonder that Skynyrd made a grudging but necessary concession. They unveiled a new hybrid flag—half Stars and Bars, half Stars and Stripes. The real wonder is that no one had thought to do that way back when it really mattered, though it likely would have been shot down as a wussy compromise, something Skynyrd didn't do then, but had to now.

* * *

Rossington and Jenness, each of whom were said to have a net worth estimated at around $40 million, were able to shelve their petty sniping long enough for Skynyrd's induction into the Rock and Roll Hall of Fame in March 2006 at the Waldorf Astoria Hotel ballroom. But Judy again prevailed on band protocol. When they would be called up from the audience to receive statuettes and say a few words, only those who had played in the band up until the time of the crash would be permitted onstage. Also on stage would be Ronnie's two daughters and granddaughter, Larkin Collins, Allen's daughter, Leon's son, Teresa Gaines Rapp, the two surviving Honkettes, Johnny Van Zant, and Rickey Medlocke. In a move seemingly calculated to tap the band into the consciousness of the modern music market, the induction speech was given not by any contemporary such as Charlie Daniels but, irrationally, by the Detroit hip-hop/country star Kid Rock—who nonetheless would provide a handsome new source of royalties two years later with a song called "All Summer Long," conjoining "Sweet Home Alabama" and Warren Zevon's "Werewolves of London," with Billy Powell on piano.

Judy was the first to speak. "No one deserves to be here tonight any more than Ronnie Van Zant," she said, setting an emotional tone. When the band performed "Sweet Home Alabama"—with Kid Rock inexplicably doing a duet with Johnny—and "Free Bird," Bob Burns and Ed King took their places, no doubt with a flood of mixed feelings.

But while King enjoyed the evening and the recognition he had never gotten before, this was yet another tease. He had finally gotten word that a heart donor had been found and that he would have the transplant soon after. The surgery went well, and before long King was up and about, playing his guitar with a new energy. Remembering that Rossington had told him he'd be taken back when he was healthy, Ed tried to punch that ticket. But he was told there was no room for him and that he should enjoy his retirement. Crushed, he sued the band for going back on a vow that had never been put in writing, something Gary Rossington was too smart, or cunning, to have done.

* * *

The bright side of the Skynyrd legacy has lived on in the music, but the dark side pops up in unfortunate ways. When a drug smuggler was arrested in Miami 2002, the warrant said that among his physical characteristics were a tattoo on his left arm ("face Ronnie van Zant") and one on his right arm ("flag confederate w/dead soldier"). In 2008 a fifty-year-old man with a familiar surname and a job as leader of a rock band in Jacksonville was busted on cocaine possession charges. The local paper reported, with no real proof, VAN ZANT ARRESTED ON DRUG CHARGES. HE IS RELATED TO FORMER LYNYRD SKYNYRD LEADER, RONNIE VAN ZANT.

To be certain, Skynyrd wears its many-edged legacy fitfully—and tenuously. After they were dropped by BMG, their 2009 album *God & Guns* was released on a sublabel of Roadrunner Records, a subsidiary of Warner Music Group, with a specialty label for them, Loud & Proud Records. The album, recorded in Nashville, was produced by Bob Marlette, a curious choice given that his past work included albums by David Lee Roth, Marilyn Manson, and grunge-metal bands like Saliva and Seether. If the aim was to give Skynyrd an outlaw edge again, the band—now composed of Rossington, Powell, Johnny Van Zant, Rickey Medlocke, bassist Ean Evans, and drummer Michael Cartellone, with Dale Rossington née Krantz moving in as a Honkette with singer Carol Bristow—was defiant only in its dive into half-witted redneck parody. The songs, mainly written years before by Hughie Thomasson, who had returned to the Outlaws before his untimely death in 2007, were odes to vapid right-wing paranoia blended with now tiresome grudges about the industry, even if it kept bending over backward to accommodate them. Sniffed Robert Christgau upon hearing it, "Really, [Johnny] ought to have some inkling that nobody worthy of his trepidation wants to ban hunting, burn the Bible, or slam old Uncle Sam."

⋆ ⋆ ⋆

Billy Powell had already laid down tracks for the album when, on January 28, 2009, he awakened in his Orange Park condo just after midnight, having trouble breathing. Powell, who lived with his wife Ellen Vera and their four children, had heart problems but had passed up a doctor's appointment the day before. He called 911, but by the time a rescue crew arrived, phone still in his hand, the fifty-six-year-old had lapsed into unconsciousness and was pronounced dead. No autopsy was done because his cardiologist signed the death certificate identifying the cause as a heart attack. The band and a horde of industry VIPs came to his funeral, but no Skynyrd music was played, only the religious rock he had recorded with the band Vision, sung by Kid Rock.

Only three months later, Ean Evans died of cancer at forty-eight. Braving what was now being called the "Skynyrd death curse," the band kept moving ahead, battered but unbowed. They hired Peter Keys of the 420 Funk Mob to play keyboards and Robert Kearns of the Bottle Rockets to play bass. Crowds were still generally big and full of verve, their fervor, as Faulkner wrote in "A Rose for Emily," "a sort of hereditary obligation"—not that Skynyrd had any obligation to political correctness. In 2010 they appeared at a thinly veiled political front billed as the Freedom Concert series, hosted by Sean Hannity, the right-wing radio and TV host who used their song "That Ain't My America" as a propaganda tool.

However, being an American "treasure," the band had been feted two years earlier by the US Congress and visited the White House, to be greeted by the president—a black president. It was quite a tightrope to walk, and they did. Though obviously pandering to a more hard-core Dixie crowd now, they were also something no one had believed Lynyrd Skynyrd could ever be—safe.

⋆ ⋆ ⋆

The sad rhetorical question Ronnie Van Zant had asked so long ago was answered: He certainly *was* remembered after he left here, sometimes in weird and mysterious ways. In the 1997 movie *Con Air*, "Free Bird" plays as escaped prisoners are partying on an airplane, prompting Steve Buscemi's character to muse, "Define irony: a bunch of idiots dancing around on a plane to a song made famous by a band that died in a plane crash." Like the mysterious Poe Toaster, who visits Edgar Allen Poe's grave on his birthdays, leaving a partially filled bottle of cognac and three roses, Skynyrd fans habitually visit Van Zant's grave with Jack Daniel's and old Skynyrd albums and raise a bottle to him. In 1981 a stone-carved bench beside his grave was stolen. In 2000, committed "fans," who should be committed, actually tried to dig up his body, necessitating that his remains be moved, to a fenced-in family plot at Riverside Memorial Park, where his firstborn daughter Tammy's plot still awaits beside his. Just to be sure, a cement slab was implanted under the surface of the grave, to prevent other ghoulish body-snatching attempts.

Judy Jenness, who turned sixty-five in 2013, retained the stringy-haired, hippie look of the twenty-one-year-old who fell for Ronnie Van Zant. Being remarried certainly did not crimp her commitment to preserving his memory and good name. After opening Made in the Shade Studios, she began a charity, the Freebird Foundation, though it soon suffered the same fate as the studio when it ran out of money and closed up in 2000. She also financed a Ronnie Van Zant Memorial Park down the road from the old Hell House grounds. The book and movie she envisioned never happened; Larkin Collins died in 2013 at age ninety-one, not having to fight anymore about it.

Judy still oversees the licensing empire. Ronnie's daughter Melody lives in the house on Brickyard Road where her parents lived at the time of the crash. In 2012 she married a man like her old man, guitarist Jasin Todd of the Jacksonville hard-rock band Shinedown, which has sold six million albums. The "Father of Southern Rock," Lacy Van Zant, toothless, with a white beard down to his belt buckle, died on August 3, 2004, four years after Sis Van Zant's heart gave out. Both of them had known the end was near—Sis had bought a new dress days before she died, giving instructions to bury her in it. Their home was opened to Skynyrd fans so they could see the couple's massive collection of the band's gold and platinum records.

Leonard Skinner, who was able to cash in on his name and enjoy a few minutes of being almost famous, had for many years posed for pictures with the ever-changing band and appeared in Skynyrd documentaries. Just how oversized that name had become was proven after the crash when a law firm for the band's corporation sent a letter to Skinner threatening legal action if he did not stop using *his own name*, a threat that was soon rescinded. In 2009, with Skinner near the end and suffering from Alzheimer's disease, a "Tribute to Coach Leonard Skinner & Southern Rock" was held at the old National Guard Armory on the west side, a satisfying moment a year before he died at age seventy-seven. Artimus Pyle, alone among the Skynyrd clan, made it a point to attend his funeral.

* * *

Pyle's constant verbal ragging of the band did not serve him well. His claim that the reborn Skynyrd had been doomed by "drugs, cocaine, alcohol, lying, cheating, thieving" that was "more important than the music" was something Rossington could neither forget or forgive. Gary blasted back, saying Pyle had been so drunk and high that he couldn't play drums anymore and that "everyone wanted to fire, get rid of him, so we did." More offensive to him was the role Pyle had taken as storyteller-in-chief of the plane-crash saga, especially the notion perpetuated by Pyle that he had saved lives after the accident.

"He didn't save our lives," Gary insisted. "He was so freaked out lookin' at us all sittin' there sufferin' and dyin' and burnin', and he ran away. People were comin' to get us, they saw us go down. He didn't run off and get the people to save us, that's *his* story."

After Wilkeson's death, Pyle believed the band should take him back at long last, as one of only two "originals" left, the final hurdle having been cleared when in 2009 he was acquitted on charges of failing to register as a sex offender when he renewed his Florida driver's license. Although his name and photograph are on the Florida Department of Law Enforcement sexual offender database website, the daughters he had been accused of molesting both came to court in his support, saying he had never in fact acted inappropriately. With his image thus rehabilitated, or so he thought, he offered his services to Skynyrd. "I would help them out if they needed me," he said, "and I think they need me."

However, Rossington said Pyle had never been anything but a replacement. Pyle then lashed out at Gary and Judy "for being so damn greedy. . . . All these lawyers and managers, fuck it, man. Judy wants all the money and Gary wants all the power. They fight with each other and everybody else loses. Dammit! . . . Why should they have a problem with me? They've got all the money, they've got the name. I'm just a little old drummer." He reiterated, "I left Skynyrd in '91 because of their massive, gluttonous consumption of cocaine and alcohol. I was a part of the real Skynyrd. I didn't want to be a part of something less." For rants like that, Pyle's 2012 album entitled *Artimus Venomous* could not have been more apt for *him*.

Pyle and Rossington, two old warhorses, had come through hell together and were indeed the last of a dyin' breed. They had long since left Jacksonville, Pyle to live in North Carolina, Rossington in Georgia. Time had healed their physical wounds. But with Skynyrd, personal grudges never seemed to heal.

* * *

Clearly not *Skynyrd* anymore, they weren't a rock-and-roll dynasty as much as a Duck Dynasty, full of gun erection and prideful simplemindedness. The soggy grits of their 2009 *God & Guns* were even soggier in 2012's *Last of a Dyin' Breed*, which Stephen Thomas Erlewine called "sturdy, old-time rock and roll for an audience that's likely peppered with Tea Partiers, the kind of Middle American worried that the world they knew is slipping away, and [for whom it] provides a bit of a rallying point." Ryan Reed, in the *Boston Phoenix*, was blunter: "The shit quality isn't much of a surprise: Skynyrd haven't released a listenable album since Ronnie Van Zant's plane-crash death. . . . [Now] the once-venerable flagship of genuine, heartfelt, inventive Southern Rock have plummeted with no remorse into the grimy waters of Redneck Rock. . . . Ronnie Van Zant rolls wildly in his grave. For God's sake, for America's sake, for Coon's sake, for Rock's sake—let's hope *Last of a Dying Breed* is an endangered species."

Still, whatever and whoever they were, they could position themselves between a South that had been new in the 1970s and a newer South that had begun to look a lot like the old South Van Zant had tried to navigate around. Late in 2013 another tour was announced with Skynyrd and Bad Company—Ronnie's favorite—coheadlining a fortieth anniversary summer tour, playing at venues such as Jiffy Lube Live in Barstow, Virginia. Then they would play on what they called the Simple

Man Cruise to Miami before jetting off to Australia for their first tour down under.

Once, Ronnie Van Zant had worried that the band he'd fought so hard for was becoming too mired in the mud of the South or crass provincialism. He craved the world. And while old Lucifer may have taken him down, those who perform under the name of Lynyrd Skynyrd do so on international stages and invoke his memory, even as they sell it short. That leaves Artimus Pyle with an even greater sense that the band not only sold him out but themselves out as well. He told Marley Brant, "If there would have been integrity and character within the band [they] would be able to raise money for cancer and AIDS and Eric Clapton would be jamming with us." For Charlie Brusco, the sense of loss was more personal, centering on their cursed front man. "Had Ronnie lived, he would have been the biggest rock star in America. He would have made solo albums—he was about to do one with Merle Haggard and Waylon Jennings when he died. Skynyrd would have been as big as the Rolling Stones. As big as they were, they never made a video, never won a Grammy, never had the artistic freedom to do exactly what they wanted to do, but they would have been given a king's ransom to do that—*if* Ronnie could have survived himself."

Nearly four decades after Van Zant ran out of time, the fighter surely remained, in spirit, punching through the lyrics of the old songs. It was the only thing left of Lynyrd Skynyrd that could pay for the whiskey bottles and the brand-new cars, and keep the smell of death and the clutches of the devil off them all. At least for one more day. God help them—please, just one more day.

POSTSCRIPT

★ ★ ★ ★ ★ ★ ★ ★ ★ ★ ★ ★ ★ ★

Literally one day before this book went to press, the author was contacted by someone who claimed he had been a member of the Skynyrd inner circle since the mid-1980s. He said he had "invaluable" information about the band and "[was] willing to help anyone who will try and tell the story of Skynyrd as it really was." But he would only share this insider information off the record for fear of retribution from the band, which he said would try and "shut down" the book if they discovered he was involved.

If one lives in or around the ongoing Skynyrd culture for many months, this is the sort of thing that often crops up. People who claim to know the "real story" of the band seem to exist far and wide, but especially in the beehive of Jacksonville and its environs, which is where the late-arriving source lived. Many of these people are flat-out crazy, drunk, or both—a byproduct of the band's legendary craziness and drunkenness—and these old-timers spend much of their time in the same honky-tonk bars as they did forty years ago. The difference was that this fellow was armed with a sheaf of documents and photos he said Artimus Pyle had given him years ago, and his name could be traced to some Skynyrd studio work.

And so the author interviewed him at length. While the results of this interview can hardly be called "the real story"—much of what he claimed seemed to be overwrought conspiracy theory, paranoid, and delusional (hey it's *Skynyrd* we're talkin' about here!)—he did add a counterpoint to several areas of discussion in the book. So though it goes against the author's grain to use unnamed sources, the saner claims are offered here in chronological order, mainly as a glimpse into the underbelly of the "this-is-the-real-truth" Skynyrd culture and with the caveat that, in the world of Skynyrd, reality can seem to appear at the bottom of a shot glass.

- Below the surface, Ed King was a more prominent member of the band than he let on. He purportedly "manipulated the band," and also ran up hotel tabs that at times reached $10,000. "Ed King used to tell people that Ronnie gave him permission to run the band. After a while, Ed was interfering in the band's business and Allen got real peeved about it. He'd say, 'Hiring Ed King was the worst thing we ever did.' And Ronnie agreed." A laugh. "I think Ed left before the band could kill him. He left without taking his guitars, just left 'em behind, blew out without telling anyone he was leaving."
- Ronnie came to so detest Gary Rossington that by 1977 he would call out, "yonder comes pretty boy" during Gary's solos. "In Ronnie's way of speaking, he was calling Gary a faggot, 'cause Ronnie thought that was what he was."
- Linda Blair may have served other purposes than as an underage conquest for Dean Kilpatrick. She was indicted for conspiracy to buy cocaine shortly after attending the Skynyrd funeral. After singing to the authorities, she was given three years' probation and a $5,000 fine. "Everyone in Skynyrd used Blair's dealer to buy their coke. But they were never charged, and I still can't believe they weren't. That's what big-time lawyers can do."
- "Allen Collins never had a thing with Dale Krantz. Dale first threw herself at Allen, who blew her off. Allen told me, 'Everyone bagged her but me.'" She then turned to Gary, in order to "gain power within the band," provoking the inevitable static between Allen and Gary.
- When Gary barred Allen from coming onto the stage any longer, "it killed Allen. That was Gary and Dale's payback to Allen. If you ask me, they murdered that man."

BIBLIOGRAPHY

★ ★ ★ ★ ★ ★ ★ ★ ★ ★ ★ ★ ★ ★

INTERVIEWS

Charlie Brusco, Bob Burns, Alex Hodges, Jimmy Johnson, Ed King, Rodney Mills, Barry Rudolph, Alan Walden.

BOOKS

Allman, Gregg with Alan Light. *My Cross to Bear*. New York: William Morrow, 2012.

Ballinger, Lee. *Lynyrd Skynyrd: An Oral History*. Los Angeles: XT377 Publishing, 1997.

Brant, Marley. *Freebirds: The Lynyrd Skynyrd Story*. New York: Billboard Books, 2002.

Brant, Marley. *Southern Rockers: The Roots and Legacy of Southern Rock*. New York: Billboard Books, 1999.

Goodwyn Jones, Anne and Susan Van D'Elden Donaldson. *Haunted Bodies: Gender and Southern Texts*. Charlottesville, VA: University of Virginia Press, 1998.

Kemp, Mark. *Dixie Lullaby: A Story of Music, Race, and New Beginnings in a New South*. New York: Free Press, 2004.

Kemp, Mark. "On Lynyrd Skynyrd's Ed King, and Trayvon Martin." *Rock's Backpages*, July 18, 2013. http://www.rocksbackpages.com/Library/Article/on-lynyrd-skynyrds-ed-king-and-trayvon-martin.

King, Richard H. and Helen Taylor. *Dixie Debates: Perspectives on Southern Cultures*. New York: New York University Press, 1996.

Kooper, Al. *Backstage Passes and Backstabbing Bastards: Memoirs of a Rock 'N' Roll Survivor*. New York: Hal Leonard Corporation, 2008.

Nuzum, Eric. *Parental Advisory: Music Censorship in America*. New York: HarperCollins, 2001.

Odom, Gene with Frank Dorman. *Lynyrd Skynyrd: Remembering the Free Birds of Rock*. New York: Broadway Books, 2002.

Watts, Trent. *White Masculinity in the Recent South*. Baton Rouge: Louisiana State University Press, 2008.

Young, Neil. *Waging Heavy Peace: A Hippie Dream*. London: Penguin Books, 2012.

ARTICLES

"1977—Ronnie Van Zant and Steve Gaines of Lynyrd . . ." This Day In Rock. www.thisdayinrock.com/index.php/general/1977-ronnie-van-zant-and-steve-gaines-of-lynyrd.

"Aircraft Accident Report, Convair 240, N55VM, Gillsburg, Mississippi, October 20, 1977, U.S. National Transportation Safety Board, Washington, D.C." www.airdisaster.com/reports/ntsb/AAR78-06.pdf.

Associated Press. "Billy Powell Obituary." Legacy.com, January 28, 2009. www.legacy.com/ns/obituary.aspx?n=billy-powell&pid=123423955.

Bell, June D. "Guitarist: Lynyrd Skynyrd Pushed Me Out." *Jacksonville Times-Union*, June 6, 1997. http://jacksonville.com/special/lynyrdskynyrd/guitaristtheypushedmeout.html.

"Billy Powell." *Wikipedia*. http://en.wikipedia.org/wiki/Billy_powell.

Boucher, Caroline, "Who the Hell Are Lynyrd Skynyrd?" *Disc and Music Echo*, February 1974.

Bull, Roger. "The Band Plays on—Lynyrd Skynyrd to Continue." *Florida Times-Union*, March 16, 2009. http://jacksonville.com/interact/blog/roger_bull/2009-03-16/the_band_plays_on_-_lynyrd_skynyrd_to_continue.

"Bryan Cole: Mose Jones." Sweethomemusic.fr. www.sweethomemusic.fr/Interviews/MoseJonesUS.php.

Campbell, Mary. "Lynyrd Skynyrd Works on Pride." *Hutchinson News*, May 30, 1975.

Carter, John. "Remembering Lynyrd Skynyrd," *Florida Times Union*, October 19, 1997. http://jacksonville.com/tu-online/stories/101997/1019Skyn.html.

Charlesworth, Chris. "Memories of Lynyrd Skynyrd and Peter Rudge." *Rock's Backpages*, 2001. www.rocksbackpages.com/Library/Article/memories-of-lynyrd-skynyrd-and-peter-rudge.

Charone, Barbara. "Lynyrd Skynyrd Interview." *Zoo World*, April 1974.

Clark, Rick. "American by Birth . . . (Southern by the Grace of God)." *Simple Man*, www.angelfire.com/tn/LSkynyrd/history.html.

Conroy, Pat, foreword to *Turn South at the Next Magnolia: Directions from a Lifelong Southerner*, by Nan Graham (Livingston, AL: Livingston Press, 2009).

Elwood, Phillip. "Rough, Rowdy, Ribald Rock." *San Francisco Examiner*, March 6, 1976.

Esposito, Jim. "Lynyrd Skynyrd: The 100 Proof Blues." *Creem*, October 1975.

Finotti, John. "Lynyrd Skynyrd: Unfynyshed Byzness." *Florida Trend*, September 1, 1999. www.floridatrend.com/article/13369/lynyrd-skynyrd-unfynyshed-byzness.

Flans, Robyn. "Artimus Pyle: Venomous After Lynyrd Skynyrd." *Modern Drummer*, July 25, 2007.

Glazer, Mitch. "One Mo' Brawl from the Road." *Crawdaddy!*, November 4, 1976.

Google groups: Talk, Politics, Guns, "Origins of 'Niggertown Saturday Night Special.'" https://groups.google.com/forum/#!topic/talk.politics.guns/TpJlSRCxO68.

"Gospel Singer Remembers Her Roots in Lynyrd Skynyrd," TriCities.com, December 27, 2012. www.tricities.com/archives/article_f8c56cc7-b4f8-5da0-9c75-14d2bb526247.html.

Hughes, Rob. "The Curse of Lynyrd Skynyrd." *Uncut*, May 2006. www.uncut.co.uk/lynyrd-skynyrd/the-curse-of-lynyrd-skynyrd-interview#HK73Qsokw0lyhhWz.99.

"Hughie Thomasson Obituary." *New York Times*, October 2, 2007.

Itzkoff, Dave. "Leonard Skinner, Namesake of Rock Band, Dies." *New York Times*, September 20, 2010.

"Lynyrd Skynyrd: A Blood Bath Every Night." *Super Rock Awards*, September 10, 1977.

"Lynyrd Skynyrd: The Early Days." Ed King Forum. http://edking.proboards.com/thread/31/early-days#ixzz2ify1vqW1.

"Lynyrd Skynyrd and Neil Young." Thrasher's Wheat—A Neil Young Archives. www.thrasherswheat.org/jammin/lynyrd.htm.

"The 'Lynyrd Skynyrd' Crash." Check-Six.com. www.check-six.com/Crash_Sites/LynyrdSkynyrd-N55VM.htm.

"Lynyrd Skynyrd Is Deceased." *Dallas Morning News*, October 22, 1977.

Maraghy, Mary. "Vandals Disturb Ronnie Van Zant's Grave." *Florida Times-Union*, June 29, 2000. http://jacksonville.com/tu-online/stories/062900/met_vanzant.html.

McConnell, Andy. "Ronnie Van Zant Kicked His Scotch Habit: It's Wine Now." *Sounds*, MAy 31, 1975.

Moore, Alex. "Lynyrd Skynyrd Just Realized the Confederate Flag Is Kinda Racist." *Death and Taxes*. www.deathandtaxesmag.com/188905/lynyrd-skynyrd-just-realized-the-confederate-flag-is-kinda-racist.

Morin, Alyssa. "The Legend of Artimus Pyle: Lynyrd Skynyrd's Drummer Lives to Tell the Tale." *Easy Reader News*, September 10, 2013. www.easyreadernews.com/74326/lynnyrd-skynyrd-artimus-pyle.

Murphy, Bridget. "Van Zant Arrested on Drug Charges. He Is Related to Former Lynyrd Skynyrd Leader, Ronnie Van Zant." *Florida Times-Union*, February 6, 2008.

"The Music Stopped and the Fight Started." *Jacksonville Journal*, July 7 1975.

"Mylon LeFevre." *Wikipedia*. http://en.wikipedia.org/wiki/Mylon_LeFevre.

Norman, Forrest. "Soundman God." *Miami New Times*, Jan 16, 2003.

Paul, Alan. "Prime Cuts: Lynyrd Skynyrd." *Guitar World*, March 4, 2009. http://wayback.archive.org/web/20130515175017/http://www.guitarworld.com/prime-cuts-lynyrd-skynyrd.

Peralta, Eyder. "Florida School Named After KKK Grand Wizard Will Get New Name." *The Two-Way* (blog). NPR. December 17, 2013. http://www.npr.org/blogs/thetwo-way/2013/12/17/251937557/florida-school-named-after-kkk-grand-wizard-will-get-new-name.

"Phil Walden." *Wikipedia*. http://en.wikipedia.org/wiki/Phil_Walden.

Reese, Willis, "Original Lynyrd Skynyrd Drummer Tells His Accounts of the Band's Early Days," *Examiner*, June 30, 2011. www.examiner.com/article/original-lynyrd-skynyrd-drummer-tells-his-accounts-of-the-band-s-early-days.

"Richard's." TheStripProject.com. www.thestripproject.com/TheStripProject/Richards.html.

Riegel, Richard. "Lynyrd Skynyrd: Does Their Conscience Bother Them?" *Creem*, December 1976.

"The Rotgut Life." *Time*, October 18, 1976.

Rudolph, Barry. "Lynyrd Skynyrd." Barry Rudolph Engineering /Production Services. www.barryrudolph.com/stories/skynyrd.html #top.

Smith, Michael Buffalo. "Skynyrd, The Allmans and Otis: Alan Walden's Career in Rock and Soul." Swampland.com, January 2002. http://swampland.com/articles/view/title:alan_walden.

Smith, Michela. "In Memory of America: A Conversation with the Allman Brothers Band's Butch Trucks." *Daily Free Press* (Boston), November 21, 2011.

"Stephan J Dike." Mugshots.com. http://mugshots.com/search.html ?q=van+zant%2C+ronnie.

Stewart, Tony. "Lynyrd Skynyrd: I See the Bloodbath That Was Hamburg." *New Musical Express*, October 25, 1975.

Sounds, May 31, 1975.

Sounds, October 25, 1975.

Sounds, November 16, 1976.

Tobler, John. "Sweetheart of the South." *Melody Maker*, March 1974.

Uhelszki, Jaan. "The Gibson Classic Interview: Lynyrd Skynyrd's Ed King." Gibson, September 13, 2010. www2.gibson.com/News -Lifestyle/Features/en-us/Lynyrd-Skynyrds-Ed-King-913.aspx.

Uhelszki, Jaan, "Lynyrd Skynyrd: Fifths and Fists for the Common Man." *Creem*, March 6, 1976.

REVIEWS

Altman, Billy. "Lynyrd Skynyrd 1991." *Rolling Stone*, August 8, 1991.

Christgau, Robert. "Lynyrd Skynyrd." Robert Christgau: Dean of American Rock Critics. www.robertchristgau.com/get_artist.php ?name=Lynyrd+Skynyrd.

Costa, Jean-Charles. "*Gimme Back My Bullets*." *Hit Parader*, August 1976.

Erlewine, Stephen Thomas. "Lynyrd Skynyrd: *Gimme Back My Bullets*." AllMusic.com. www.allmusic.com/album/gimme-back-my-bullets -mw0000196579.

———. "Lynyrd Skynyrd: *Last of a Dyin' Breed*." AllMusic.com. www .allmusic.com/album/last-of-a-dyin-breed-mw0002373661.

———. "Lynyrd Skynyrd: *One More From the Road*." AllMusic.com. www.allmusic.com/album/one-more-from-the-road -mw0000536195.

———. "Lynyrd Skynyrd: *Second Helping*." AllMusic.com www.allmusic.com/album/second-helping-mw0000273339.
———. "Lynyrd Skynyrd: *Skynyrd's First and . . . Last*." AllMusic.com. www.allmusic.com/album/skynyrds-first-andlast-mw0000190840.
"*Gimme Back My Bullets* Review." *Rolling Stone*, March 25, 1976.
Milward, John. "Lynyrd Skynyrd: *One More from the Road*." *Rolling Stone*, November 4, 1976.
Reed, Ryan. "Lynyrd Skynyrd: *Last of a Dyin' Breed*." *Phoenix* (Boston). http://thephoenix.com/boston/music/143345-lynyrd-skynyrd-last-of-a-dyin-breed.
Scoppa, Bud. "Lynyrd Skynyrd: *Nuthin' Fancy*." *Rolling Stone*, June 19, 1975.
———. "Lynyrd Skynyrd: *Second Helping*." *Crawdaddy!*, September 1974.
"*Second Helping* Review." *Rolling Stone*, November 7, 1974.
Walker, Billy. "Review: *Nuthin' Fancy*." *Sounds*, April 12, 1975.
Erlewine, Stephen Thomas. "Review: *One More from the Road*." AllMusic Guide, February 14, 2009. http://www.answers.com/topic/one-more-from-the-road.

VIDEOS

Freebird . . . The Movie. Cabin Fever Entertainment, 1996.
"Highs and Lows with Lynyrd Skynyrd." YouTube video. Posted by "The Year of Alabama Arts." April 30, 2007. www.youtube.com/watch?v=JRuAxmhRXS8.
"Lynyrd Skynyrd." *Behind the Music*, season 1, episode 7. VH1. Aired October 19, 1997.
"Lynyrd Skynyrd—Free Bird (1987)." YouTube video. Posted by "beeteep60." January 23, 2013. www.youtube.com/watch?v=JBwqtmdxqzI.
"Lynyrd Skynyrd bandmates talk about Ronnie Van Zant and life on the road as the real Lynyrd Skynyrd." YouTube video. Posted by "Tony Beazley." November 13, 2009. www.youtube.com/watch?v=MBftFjxWbN0.
"Lynyrd Skynyrd perform at the Rock and Roll Hall of Fame inductions 2006." YouTube video. Posted by "Rock and Roll Hall of Fame + Museum." June 23, 2010. www.youtube.com/watch?%20annotation_id=annotation_753542&feature=iv&src_vid=1S_UagucO0A&v=LFbnhzFMjkM.

"Lynyrd Skynyrd plane crash survivor Paul Welch talks with NFBC News." YouTube video. Posted by "NashvilleOnFacebook." February 27, 2011. www.youtube.com/watch?v=DTrf9greVqg.

"Ronnie Van Zant–Lynyrd Skynyrd–The story of Lynyrd Skynyrd." YouTube video. Posted by "RandallTSkynyrd." October 19, 2012. www.youtube.com/watch?v=AePnPCSFCfI.

"Skynyrd Uncivil War." YouTube video. Posted by "RandallTSkynyrd." November 30, 2012. www.youtube.com/watch?v=wFIkQjDtwOw.

LINER NOTES

Lynyrd Skynyrd. *One More from the Road Twenty-fifth Anniversary Deluxe Edition*, 2001, compact disc (reissue), liner notes. www.angelfire.com/tn/LSkynyrd/reissue.html.

INDEX

★ ★ ★ ★ ★ ★ ★ ★ ★ ★ ★ ★ ★ ★